GENERAL EDITOR'S INTRODUCTION TO THE SERIES   (iv)

AUTHORS' INTRODUCTION TO THE FIVE KINGDOMS AND BEHAVIOUR   (iv)

1   THE NEED FOR CLASSIFICATION   1

2   KINGDOM PROKARYOTAE - THE BACTERIA   8

3   KINGDOM PROTOCTISTA   15

4   KINGDOM FUNGI   29

5   THE PLANT KINGDOM   38

6   THE ANIMALS : INVERTEBRATES   57

7   THE ANIMALS : VERTEBRATES   81

8   VIRUSES   102

9   BEHAVIOUR   106

APPENDIX - MAKING AND USING KEYS   138

INDEX   139

General Editor's Introduction to the Series

Biology - Advanced Studies is a series of modular textbooks which are intended for students following advanced courses in biological subjects. The series offers the flexibility essential for working on modern syllabuses which often have core material and option topics. In particular, the books should be very useful for the new modular science courses which are emerging at A Level.

In most of the titles in the series, one of the authors is a very experienced teacher (often also an examiner) and is sympathetic to the problems of learning at this level. The second author usually has research experience and is familiar with the subject at a higher level. In addition, several members of the writing team have been closely involved in the development of the latest syllabuses.

As with all textbooks, the reader may expect not to read from cover to cover but to study one topic at a time, or dip in for information as needed. Where questions are asked, an attempt should be made at an answer because this type of active reading is the best way to develop an understanding of what is read.

We have referred throughout to *Biological nomenclature - Recommendations on terms, units and symbols,* Institute of Biology, London, 1989. We are delighted to be able to thank the many friends and colleagues who have helped with original ideas, the reading of drafts and the supply of illustrations.

Alan Cadogan
General Editor

Authors' Introduction to The Five Kingdoms and Behaviour

This book aims to survey the range of living organisms (biodiversity) and to link with some aspects of behaviour. Classification and Behaviour are two exciting aspects of biology; yet some people assume that classification is rooted in Victorian biology and behaviour is 'mere natural history'. They couldn't be more wrong.

It was Linnaeus who first brought some order to the general confusion of grouping organisms. Modern systems of classification use his ideas of common features as well as the skills of gene technology, embryology and biochemistry. In this book we use the Five Kingdom system of classification devised by Whittaker and modified by Margulis and Schwarz. The basis of this classification is explained, each kingdom is introduced and representative phyla are described. Care has been taken to include groups and species specified by the various examination boards.

Behaviour is central to any broad study of biology because every one of an organism's systems contributes to its behaviour; and it is through behaviour that it interacts with its environment.

Obviously the most studied aspects of behaviour relate to animals and the ethologist (the student of behaviour) is concerned for the welfare of wild and domesticated animals. Most students demand that the animals they study are alive and well treated. Every biology syllabus should have a place for studies of behaviour.

We hope that you will be attracted to the ideas presented in our book. We believe that the issues described are important for ecological studies and have become even more prominent since the signing in June 1992 by over 150 countries of the Convention on Biodiversity at Rio de Janeiro. If their recommendations for sustainable development and conservation are to be achieved, we must have enthusiastic biologists expert in biodiversity - 'the whole range of mammals, birds, reptiles, amphibians and fish, insects and other invertebrates, plants, fungi and microorganisms such as protists, bacteria and viruses' (UK Action Plan - Biodiversity 1994).

Roger Avery, Innes Cuthill, Ruth Miller and Gary Rowland

THE NEED FOR CLASSIFICATION

Can you imagine that about one and a half million types of living organisms have so far been described and named, and it is estimated that there may be as many as another ten million that have not yet been discovered? It is important to have a sensible system for naming them. If possible this system should be international in order to avoid confusion. Several attempts have been made to solve this problem, but the most famous scheme was devised in the 18th Century by a Swedish naturalist, Carl von Linné (otherwise known as Linnaeus).

Carl Linnaeus (1707-78) from an oil painting at the Linnean Society of London

Most people are aware that the 'scientific name' for humans is *Homo sapiens*. This type of *binomial* name is the result of the work of Linnaeus. He gave all organisms two-part names, in which the first part, common to all closely related members, is the *genus*, and the second is the *species*. Thus each two-part name is unique. In Linnaeus' binomial system, Latin names were given because this was a language which most educated people could understand at that time. We still use it now and any new species which are discovered must be given two-part names and have

detailed descriptions written (formerly in Latin). It is also the convention to use italics when printing the names. (However in handwritten accounts the names should be underlined.) The generic name always begins with a capital letter and the specific name with a lower case letter. A good example of how this works can be seen in the genus *Ranunculus*, the buttercups. There are several different species commonly found in the British Isles (Fig.1.1): *Ranunculus repens* (the creeping buttercup), *Ranunculus bulbosus* (the bulbous buttercup) and *Ranunculus acris* (the meadow buttercup).

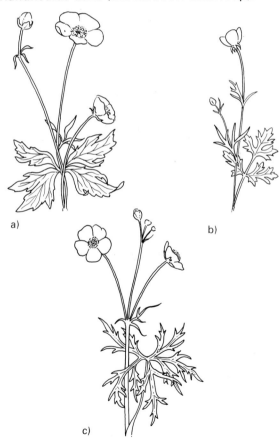

Figure 1.1 Three species of *Ranunculus* (a) *Ranunculus repens* (the creeping buttercup) (b) *Ranunculus bulbosus* (the bulbous buttercup) (c) *Ranunculus acris* (the meadow buttercup)

A generic name is only used for one particular group of organisms, but specific names can be descriptive: vulgaris ('common' as in *Primula vulgaris* - the common primrose), *terrestris* ('terrestrial' or 'of the earth' as in *Lumbricus terrestris* - the earthworm) and *repens* ('creeping' as in *Ranunculus repens* - the creeping buttercup) are examples. One particularly attractive example is *Capsella bursa-pastoris* (Fig.1.2), the Shepherd's Purse, where the specific name is a translation into Latin of the common name, which is descriptive of the shape of the fruits.

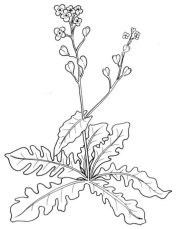

Figure 1.2 *Capsella bursa-pastoris* (Shepherd's Purse)

The use of Latin in these scientific names enables precise identification and accurate communication throughout the world. Common names are frequently used where this accuracy is not required, but these may lead to confusion as many organisms have different common names in different parts of a country. Examples of this are the alternative names for *Alliaria petiolata* of hedge garlic, garlic mustard and Jack-by-the-hedge, and the term 'eft' for newt in many parts of the UK.

Linnaeus put living organisms into groups, based on visible external structures, but this led to some associations which present-day taxonomists find strange: bats and birds in the same group because they had wings, and all long, thin animals with no legs placed in a group called 'Vermes', thus classifying worms and snakes together.

Since Linnaeus' time, studies of fossils and regard for Darwin's theories have contributed to a search for the perfect classification, one that would reflect the evolutionary history of groups of organisms - a 'family tree' or *phylogenetic* relationship. There are difficulties because the fossil record is incomplete and for no group has an uninterrupted sequence of fossils been found, linking a living species with all its ancestors. Modern attempts at classification use evidence from cell biology, embryology and biochemistry, as well as the more traditional structural features, to establish relationships between groups of organisms. Electron microscopy of plant and animal tissues has given us a great deal of valuable information about cell structures, and also contributed to a better understanding of the position of groups of organisms such as the Cyanobacteria. This group, formerly known as the Cyanophyta or blue-green algae, were classified as members of the algae, until electron microscopy revealed the nature of their cells and indicated that there was a closer relationship with the bacteria.

The basic unit of any system of classification is the *species*, generally defined as a group of individuals with a large number of features in common, which can interbreed and produce fertile offspring. The members of one species would not normally breed with members of another species. This definition is difficult to apply to all groups which are referred to as species, as it has not always been possible to observe breeding behaviour (especially in the case of fossils), so some species are only defined in terms of morphological or structural differences. Many widely distributed species have developed local or regional characteristics, justifying a split into a number of sub-species, varieties or races. The differences in structure will be small but significant, although not enough to prevent interbreeding.

Closely-related species are grouped into a *genus*, genera (plural of genus) into a *family*, families into an *order*, orders into a *class*, classes into a *phylum* and phyla into a *kingdom*. Each named group, for example a genus or an order, is known as a *taxon*, and the study of classification is known as *taxonomy*. As one proceeds in a classification from kingdom to species, the number of organisms in each category decreases, but the number of features shared increases, so that members of a phylum would share a few characteristics but members of a genus would share a large number (Table 1.1).

Kingdom	Animalia	Plantae	Protoctista	Animalia
Phylum	Chordata	Angiospermophyta	Phaeophyta	Chordata
Class	Mammalia	Monocotyledonae	Phaeophyceae	Mammalia
Order	Perissodactyla	Liliales	Fucales	Primate
Family	Rhinocerotidae	Liliaceae	Fucaceae	Hominidae
Genus	*Rhinoceros*	*Allium*	*Fucus*	*Homo*
Species	*R. unicornis*	*A. sativum*	*F. vesiculosus*	*H. sapiens*
Common name	Indian rhinoceros	Garlic	Bladder wrack	Human

Table 1.1 Classification of some organisms to show use of taxa

From this table we can see that a rhinoceros is a member of several recognisable groups or subsets; it is an animal, a mammal and a perissodactyl. Similarly, garlic is a plant, an angiosperm and a lily, and a human is an animal, a mammal and a primate. We might find it more convenient to place an organism in a larger or smaller group depending on the context, so all of these taxa are useful. In a scientific context, the most generally used taxa are kingdom, phylum, class and genus.

We have seen that the first attempts at classification grouped organisms together on the basis of similar characteristics, and if a system is going to show evolutionary relationships then the features chosen should be *homologous* not *analogous*. In other words, we should be careful not to group together organisms because they appear to have similar structures. Analogous structures have different origins and if they do have anatomical features in common, it is due to the fact that structures performing the same function are bound to resemble each other in some ways. Good examples of analogous structures are legs of arthropods and vertebrates. They perform the same function, but their structural organisation is quite different. Homologous structures such as vertebrate limbs can be used in the classification. The basic plan of the limb is essentially the same in all four groups of vertebrates - amphibians, reptiles, birds and mammals - and its origins can be traced back to the group of fossil fishes from which the amphibians evolved. During the course of evolution, modifications and adaptations have arisen, but it is still possible to recognise the main components of what is known as the pentadactyl limb (Fig.1.3).

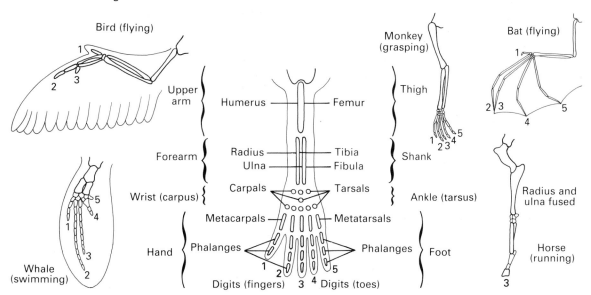

Figure 1.3 Pentadactyl limb plan and modifications

■ HOW MANY KINGDOMS?

Until the middle of this century, all living organisms were classified into two kingdoms, plant or animal, and this simple classification is still useful today. The distinction was based mainly on a difference in nutrition: animals need to be supplied with complex organic molecules (they are *heterotrophic*). Plants are able to synthesise complex organic molecules from simple inorganic ones using light as an energy source (they are *autotrophic* and carry out photosynthesis). Unicellular organisms were classified as plants if they possessed chlorophyll, the photosynthetic pigment, and as animals if they did not. The bacteria were placed in the plant kingdom, because they possessed cell walls, along with the fungi, which were considered to be plants that had lost their chlorophyll. Some genera of unicells caused a great deal of confusion. The genus *Euglena* (Fig.3.9) appears to straddle both kingdoms in that some species contain chlorophyll and some species do not. Those with chlorophyll can photosynthesise, but those without feed heterotrophically. In the species that do possess chlorophyll, prolonged absence of light causes the pigment to break down. The organism can then feed heterotrophically (like animals), but when exposed to light again it is capable of regenerating the pigment and photosynthetic ability is restored.

For this and many other reasons the two kingdom system was found to be unsatisfactory, particularly when the fine structure of bacterial cells was revealed by electron microscopy. However, many taxonomists then appeared to be content just to separate the bacteria from the plants and grant them kingdom status in their own right. This did not solve the problem of what to do about the fungi and the unicells.

In an attempt to achieve a more satisfactory classification, a number of alternative schemes were put forward. The one which has gained a great deal of support was proposed by an American biologist, R.H. Whittaker. He suggested that there should be five kingdoms:
• the animal kingdom for motile, multicellular, heterotrophic organisms
• the plant kingdom for multicellular, photosynthetic organisms
• the fungus kingdom

• the protist kingdom for protozoa and unicellular algae (see p.15)
• the monera kingdom for bacteria and blue-green algae which are *prokaryotic* (see p.8).

This system solved some of the problems caused by the two kingdom system, but it created others. It seemed artificial to separate the unicellular algae from the multicellular forms, so it was suggested that all the algae should be placed together in the protist kingdom, which was then renamed the Protoctista (Chapter 3). This kingdom now contains the green algae (Chlorophyta), the brown algae (Phaeophyta), the red algae (Rhodophyta), all the unicellular organisms (Protozoa), together with the slime moulds and some fungi. It is a strange kingdom, showing an enormous range of form and different types of nutrition, and because of this range of types it is the least satisfactory aspect of the five kingdom system. Many biologists do not like the Protoctista and feel that there is a good case for keeping the protist kingdom as a discrete group for the unicellular organisms. It is likely that this controversy will form the basis of discussions amongst taxonomists for some time to come. However, all the other kingdoms have quite clear-cut characteristics and the modified five kingdom system is now used quite widely (Fig.1.4). The name *Prokaryotae* has replaced *Monera* for the bacteria kingdom.

Some taxonomists would argue that the five kingdom scheme and others like it are not correct, and that there are very good grounds for regarding both the Fungi and the Protoctista as artificial groups. Some microbiologists maintain that there is a case for defining taxa at the molecular level (i.e. in terms of their chemistry) and would create a new taxon, the domain, above the level of kingdom. Life would then be seen as made up of three domains: the Bacteria, the Archeae (other bacterial forms) and the Eucarya (containing Animalia, Plantae, Fungi and others to be defined). The differences between the three domains are based on differences in cell membrane lipids and ribosomal RNA. For our purposes, the five kingdom system provides a scheme whereby we can recognise some relationships between organisms and appreciate a little of the evolutionary sequence that must have taken place.

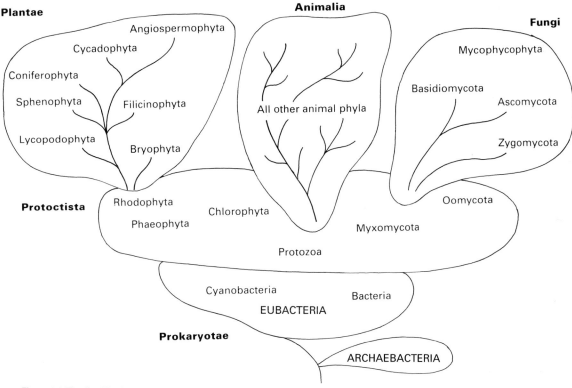

Figure 1.4 The five kingdom system

Viruses are not usually included in any system of classification as they are not cellular. They consist of DNA (or RNA) surrounded by a coat of protein and are much smaller than cells. They can only grow and reproduce inside a host organism, although some of them can survive for long periods of time in a crystalline state outside their host.

The five kingdoms classification is an example of an orthodox classification, where organisms are grouped together on the basis of features that appear to indicate their common ancestry. A group is defined by the features that all its members share, and it is possible to construct a family tree as shown in Fig.1.5.

There are other systems of classification in use which do not necessarily take account of the evolutionary history of a group. If the purpose of a classification is simply to provide a filing system or a convenient way of identifying organisms, then the evolutionary significance is not important. Both *phenetics* and *cladistics* involve looking for similarities between organisms and may use morphological, physiological, biochemical and behavioural features.

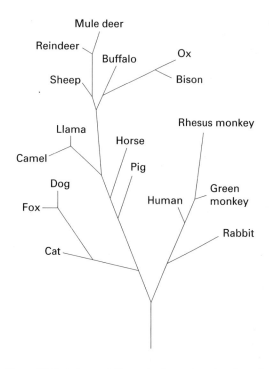

Figure 1.5 Part of an evolutionary family tree based on the amino acid sequence in the protein fibrinogen

5

A phenetic classification is particularly useful for dealing with large groups of organisms possessing relatively similar features. First of all, the organisms need to be described fully and then a list of suitable features is drawn up. Pairs of organisms are compared in turn, recording the number of matching features. The similarity is calculated by expressing the number of common characteristics as a percentage of the total number being considered. The organisms are then rearranged so that the most similar are grouped together in order that a branching diagram called a dendrogram can be drawn up. It is important to remember that this dendrogram does not necessarily reflect any evolutionary relationships.

In cladistics, each group, or clade, is defined by the unique structural or biochemical features, known as homologues, that are shared by all its members. As with phenetics, a list of features is drawn up, and those which are shared by two or more organisms are used to sort them into groups. Features common to all organisms are not used, as these can be used to define the group as a whole, nor are features which apply to only one organism. In the example shown in Table 1.2 we would discount jaws, as being common to all the organisms, and feathers, as only the birds have them.

In our example, birds form a clade because they have feathers, the bat and the mole form a clade because they have mammary glands and fur, but the bat, the crow and the magpie could also form a clade because they all have wings. All the animals belong to a larger clade through the possession of jaws.

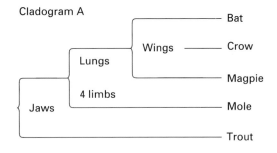

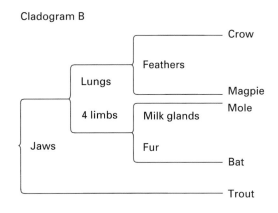

Figure 1.6 Cladograms A and B

The next step is to construct a cladogram, which will show the relationships of the clades to each other (Fig.1.6). There will often be more than one way in which this can be done. In our example, there are two reasonable possibilities, A and B.

B is preferable to A because it has more shared features. Some biologists do think of the cladogram as representing an evolutionary sequence, so the use of wings in A would not be very satisfactory, because it is not a homologue for this group, and so is not due to common ancestry. Careful choice of features will need to be made if the cladogram is to reflect evolutionary relationships.

The five kingdom classification is now used in most textbooks and students need only be familiar with orthodox classifications of this type, but it is interesting to note that other forms of classification do exist and, although they use the same methods, they do sometimes produce different results.

Animal / Feature	Bat	Crow	Magpie	Mole	Trout
Jaws	✓	✓	✓	✓	✓
Lungs	✓	✓	✓	✓	✗
Four limbs	✓	✓	✓	✓	✗
Fur/hair	✓	✗	✗	✓	✗
Milk glands in ♀	✓	✗	✗	✓	✗
Wings	✓	✓	✓	✗	✗
Feathers	✗	✓	✓	✗	✗

Table 1.2 Features of bat, crow, magpie, mole and trout

For this question, you may find it helpful to refer to the Appendix on p.138.

𝑄 Diagrams A, B and C show the structure of a typical woodlouse. The remaining diagrams below show six named woodlouse species. Construct a simple dichotomous key which could be used to identify the six named woodlouse species, using features labelled in diagrams A, B and C.

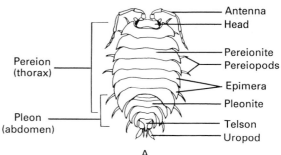

Antenna
Head
Pereion (thorax)
Pereionite
Pereiopods
Epimera
Pleonite
Pleon (abdomen)
Telson
Uropod

A

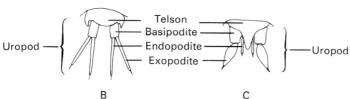

Uropod
Telson
Basipodite
Endopodite
Exopodite
Uropod

B   C

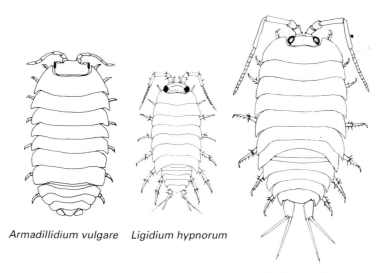

Armadillidium vulgare   *Ligidium hypnorum*

Ligia oceanica

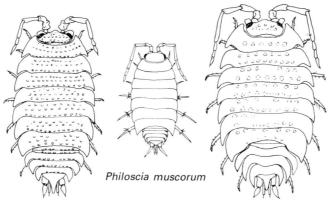

Philoscia muscorum

Porcellio scaber   *Oniscus asellus*

Question reproduced from the June 1993 Advanced Level Biology examination paper by permission of the University of London Examinations and Assessment Council.

KINGDOM PROKARYOTAE - THE BACTERIA

Bacteria are everywhere - in the air, in the soil, in water, on our skin, in our guts - but they are not evident because we cannot see them with the naked eye unless their numbers are enormous. Bacteria are very hardy; most can survive freezing, and some can actually thrive in hot springs and highly acidic conditions. Bacteria are very important in many aspects of our lives (in health, agriculture and forestry), and a number of techniques have been developed to prevent the bacterial contamination of our food. Some 10 000 species have been named.

The distinguishing features of the members of this kingdom are that they are:
• unicellular or filamentous
• prokaryotic
• heterotrophic or autotrophic.
The cells have a very similar, simple structure and, as the members of this kingdom are the only living organisms to show prokaryotic features, it is appropriate to point out the major differences between prokaryotic and eukaryotic cells (Table 2.1).

All bacteria can reproduce asexually by a process known as binary fission, which involves division of the DNA followed by the formation of a septum (or wall) across the cell to form two daughter cells. Under favourable growth conditions, this type of division can take place every twenty minutes in some species. Bacteria do not undergo sexual reproduction which involves gamete formation and the exchange of genetic material, but sometimes DNA is transferred from one bacterium to another. In *conjugation*, two cells come into contact and the 'donor' cell passes a copy of its DNA or a plasmid to the 'recipient', which then acquires new characteristics. Two alternatives to this have been observed: *transformation* where a bacterium absorbs DNA which has been

Prokaryotic	Eukaryotic
Smaller in size	Larger in size
Cell wall rigid; no cellulose or chitin (may contain peptidoglycan)	Cell wall, if present, rigid; contains chitin (Fungi), or cellulose (Plantae); no cell wall in Animalia
No membrane-bound organelles; cell surface membrane can invaginate to form mesosomes and photosynthetic membranes	Membrane-bound organelles present, including nucleus, chloroplasts (Plantae), mitochondria all surrounded by double membranes; Golgi bodies, vacuoles, lysosomes and ER have single membranes
Circular DNA present in the cytoplasm	DNA linear, associated with histones to form chromosomes enclosed in nucleus
Flagella or cilia, if present, consist of single microtubules of flagellin	Flagella or cilia, if present, have 9+2 arrangement of microtubules
Store glycogen and volutin	Store glycogen (Animalia), starch (Plantae), lipids

Table 2.1 The major differences between prokaryotic and eukaryotic cells

Transformation

Strand of
DNA enters host

Foreign DNA integrates itself into bacterial chromosome

After replication, one daughter cell has 'foreign' DNA

Transduction

Host

DNA from bacterial virus
(phage) enters host

Some phage incorporate
fragments of host DNA

Bacterial DNA carried
to new host

New bacterial DNA
integrates into host DNA

Figure 2.1 DNA transfer by transformation and transduction

released by another bacterium, and *transduction* in which DNA is transferred from one bacterium to another via a bacterial virus or bacteriophage (Fig.2.1). Bacterial DNA is joined into a circle.

The classification of bacteria is based more upon their metabolic activities than on their morphology or their external appearance. They can be divided into groups by their shape (Fig.2.2): cocci (spherical), bacilli (rod-shaped), spirilla (spiral) and vibrio (comma-shaped). They can also be divided into two distinct

groups by their reaction to a staining technique developed by Christian Gram in 1884. Gram positive bacteria, which with this technique stain deep purple, have a much thicker layer of peptidoglycan in their cell walls than Gram negative bacteria, which stain light pink. The Gram negative bacteria have, in addition, an outer membrane thought to form an extra physical barrier around the cells. (See *Biology Advanced Studies - Microbiology and Biotechnology* for details of the Gram staining technique.)

a) Cocci

  Capsule

Diplococcus pneumoniae
causes pneumonia

Staphylococcus aureus
causes boils and food
poisoning

Streptococcus pyogenes
causes sore throats

S. thermophilus
used in yoghurt making

b) (i)   Rods (bacilli)

Salmonella typhimurium
causes severe food poisoning

Escherichia coli
common symbiont of gut

(ii) Chains of rods

Azotobacter a free-living
soil nitrogen-fixing bacterium

 Endospore

Bacillus anthracis
causes anthrax

c)   Spirilla

Spirillum rubrum
saprophyte of fresh water

Treponema pallidum
causes the venereal disease
syphilis

d)   Vibrio

Vibrio cholerae
causes cholera

Figure 2.2 Classification of bacteria - rods, cocci and spirilla

Another major difference between groups of bacteria is their mode of nutrition. The majority of species are heterotrophic, dependent on their environment for their supplies of organic nutrients, but some are autotrophic and are able to synthesise their organic requirements from inorganic materials. Some autotrophs are *chemosynthetic*, deriving the energy needed for synthesis from chemical reactions, whilst others are photosynthetic and obtain the necessary energy from light. Both types of nutrition are important in the recycling processes in the biosphere.

Bacteria were probably the first living organisms and, although there is very little evidence, it has been suggested that there were bacteria around some 3400 million years ago. About 2000 million years ago, the cyanobacteria were probably responsible for a major change in the Earth's atmosphere. Until that time, the amount of oxygen in the atmosphere was probably less than 1%, but rose gradually to about 20% due to the photosynthetic activities of this group of bacteria.

As there is not much in the fossil record, there is little chance of detecting evolutionary relationships amongst the bacteria, but techniques involving the analysis of ribosomal RNA have provided us with some insight into this problem. Ribosomes are essential organelles for the assembly of proteins and they are common to both prokaryotes and eukaryotes, so changes in them through the course of evolution are likely to have been slow. Studies of the different types of ribosomal RNA have enabled the bacteria to be divided into two major groups:
• the *Archaebacteria* including **methanogenic**, **halophilic** and **thermoacidophilic** forms
• the *Eubacteria*.

If, however, they are classified according to the nature of their cell walls, then four groups are recognised:
• Division Mendosicutes (equivalent to the Archaebacteria) whose walls lack the chemical peptidoglycans (murein)
• Division Tenericutes (e.g. mycoplasmas) lacking rigid cell walls
• Division Firmicutes (e.g. *Clostridium*, *Diplococcus*) - Gram positive bacteria with thick peptidoglycan walls, no outer lipo-protein layer, can be cocci, bacilli, filamentous, many capable of forming complex spores, none photosynthetic
• Division Gracilicutes (e.g. *Anabaena*, *Azotobacter*, *Escherichia*) - Gram negative bacteria with thinner peptidoglycan layer.

All the prokaryotes, except the mycoplasmas, have a cell wall. It does not contain cellulose or chitin, but in the Eubacteria it consists mainly of murein, a chemical known as a peptidoglycan, and varies from 10 nm to 100 nm in thickness. In Gram positive bacteria (Fig.2.3a), the murein network, making up 40% of the cell wall, contains additional proteins and polysaccharides, forming a rigid structure. There is very little lipid present. Gram positive bacteria are sensitive to the antibiotic penicillin. It causes the cell walls of newly formed cells to burst because it interferes with the synthesis of the murein, preventing cross-linkages from forming. The walls of the Gram negative bacteria are different (Fig.2.3b). The layer of murein is much thinner and on the outside there is a layer of proteins, lipids and lipopolysaccharides forming a membrane. The cell walls of the Archaebacteria are thought to be made up of protein, but they do not have murein.

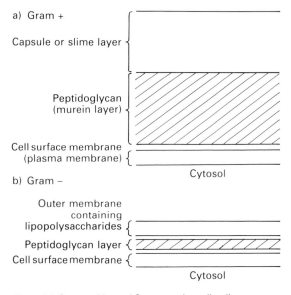

a) Gram +

Capsule or slime layer

Peptidoglycan (murein layer)

Cell surface membrane (plasma membrane)

Cytosol

b) Gram −

Outer membrane containing lipopolysaccharides

Peptidoglycan layer

Cell surface membrane

Cytosol

Figure 2.3 Gram positive and Gram negative cell walls

Methanogenic producing methane
Halophilic can live in salt solution
Thermoacidophilic can live in hot, acid soil

Fuel from Rubbish Tips?
Can Bacteria Solve our Energy Problems?

A rubbish tip near Coventry, accepting 3500 tonnes of domestic and industrial waste every day, produces 2 cubic metres of gas every minute. This gas, biogas, contains 60-70% methane and 30-40% carbon dioxide, together with small traces of hydrogen sulphide and other gases. At the Coventry tip, the gas is collected in pipes, the hydrogen sulphide removed and it is then compressed with air before being fed to a turbine to generate electricity.

Certain types of bacteria in the tip are producing the methane. Some other types of bacteria present in the rubbish tips can respire aerobically if oxygen is present and anaerobically in its absence. Under aerobic conditions, these bacteria produce carbon dioxide and water from the breakdown of glucose, but if there is little or no oxygen present then ethanoic acid accumulates as a waste product and must be got rid of. Methanogenic bacteria in the tip can use this ethanoic acid as a source of carbon for metabolic activities, releasing methane and carbon dioxide as their waste products. Methanogenic bacteria are also found in the anaerobic conditions which exist in marshes, sewage works and the digestive systems of cows.

The natural gas found under the North Sea was produced by methanogenic bacteria millions of years ago and we use this gas today to generate electricity. This natural gas provides us with about 15% of our total fuel in the UK at the present time, but it is a finite resource and will eventually run out. It has been estimated that if we could collect all the methane generated by rubbish tips and sewage works, together with that generated from farmyard waste, we could save 3% of the natural gas currently being used. This, in the long run, could mean that the supplies of North Sea gas would last longer. Is this feasible? The Coventry rubbish tip shows that it is, and that there are possibilities of even greater savings being made.

Small family-sized biogas generators have been in use for some time in China and parts of India. Dung from cows and humans, together with waste vegetable matter, is used and generates enough gas for cooking and lighting. The average family in India needs about 3 cubic metres of biogas each day. One cow produces about 7 kg of dung a day, which in turn yields 0.25 cubic metres of methane, so the average family would need to use the dung

The Puente Hills Landfill Gas Recovery Facility in California generates electrical power from methane gas released from a waste dump.

from about seven cows, together with their own excreta and household waste to generate sufficient methane for their needs. There are obvious advantages, such as disposing of human and animal excreta and avoiding the need to burn wood, but the digesters do have to be watertight and sealed to avoid the smell of hydrogen sulphide escaping.

It is obviously not feasible for every household in the UK to have its own biogas generator, but where animals are farmed intensively, it would solve the problem of getting rid of excreta without polluting the neighbourhood, at the same time saving the farmer money on heating. When you consider that the average pig produces 3 kg of manure each day, sufficient to generate biogas of the same energy value as 0.5 litre of oil, it is easy to see how considerable savings can be made after the initial costs involved in the installation of tanks and pipes.

In addition to the formation of biogas, the fermented dung and vegetable waste from the generators can be spread on agricultural land as a fertiliser, improving soil fertility without the need for artificially produced chemicals. We would be wise not to disregard the importance of the methanogenic bacteria in our quest for alternative sources of energy and a less polluted environment.

An outer, slimy layer of polysaccharide, called a capsule, is present in some bacteria. It is present in many parasitic species, where it acts as a protective barrier. It prevents desiccation and protects the bacterial cell from the digestive action of lysozyme, an anti-bacterial enzyme present in the body fluids of other organisms. The capsule also makes it difficult for white blood cells and antibodies to bind to the bacterial wall. Some soil bacteria, such as *Azotobacter*, possess slime layers, and these help to bind soil particles together, giving a good crumb structure.

The plasma membrane is very similar in structure to that of eukaryotic organisms, consisting of proteins and phospholipids. In many prokaryotes, there are infoldings of the plasma membrane to form structures called mesosomes, which are thought to be the site of respiration. These mesosomes are situated near the site of cell division and appear to be the location of metabolic activities such as ATP and enzyme synthesis. The folding of the membrane increases the surface area available for these reactions. Some bacteria have tubular or sac-like structures formed by the infolding of the plasma membrane on which are found photosynthetic pigments and associated enzymes. These are often referred to as chromatophores and are present in autotrophic purple and green sulphur bacteria. In the cyanobacteria, the membranes form lamellae, which are very similar to the thylakoids in the chloroplasts of green plants.

The cytoplasm contains ribosomes, of the 70 S type, which are sites of protein synthesis, together with granules of glycogen and other storage molecules. (Eukaryotes have the slightly larger ribosomes known as 80 S.)

The genetic material is in the form of a circular bacterial chromosome, consisting of DNA and able to encode about 3000 to 5000 genes. There are no histones and no nucleosomes, although it is suggested that there is some protein involved in holding the genetic material together. Prokaryotic DNA lacks introns (non-coding sequences of DNA), but functionally related genes appear to be situated quite close to each other, forming operons, which do not appear in eukaryotic DNA.

Three-quarters of all the bacteria possess, in addition to the main chromosome, plasmids.

These are small circles of double-stranded DNA, which can replicate independently of the main chromosome. The plasmids carry a few genes, which are not normally connected with growth, but may help the bacterium to survive under adverse conditions. Some plasmids carry genes for the formation of toxins which will kill other bacteria and others may confer resistance to antibiotics. Plasmids are useful tools for genetic engineers as they enable genes from other organisms to be introduced into bacterial cells. These new genes can become incorporated into the genome of the host bacterium and then used to make useful substances such as human growth hormone.

■ DIVISION MENDOSICUTES - ARCHAEBACTERIA

The Archaebacteria ('Greek' arkhaios = ancient + bacteria) differ from the other prokaryotes in that they do not have murein in their cell walls. They are strictly anaerobic and are chemoautotrophic, deriving their energy in the production of methane from carbon dioxide and hydrogen. They also have different sequences in their ribosomal RNA and are thought to have evolved more than 3 billion years ago, when the atmosphere contained more carbon dioxide and less oxygen. Some taxonomists consider that they should be placed on their own in a separate kingdom.

■ DIVISION GRACILICUTES - GRAM NEGATIVE BACTERIA

■ Phylum Cyanobacteria
Until fairly recently, the cyanobacteria were called the blue-green algae (Cyanophyta) and classified in the plant kingdom, together with their supposed relatives. Their exact structure was difficult to resolve with the light microscope, but the possession of photosynthetic pigments, particularly chlorophyll *a*, placed them in the plant kingdom. With the advent of the electron microscope, their prokaryotic nature became apparent, and they are now classified with the bacteria. They are different from most of the other photosynthetic bacteria in that they are aerobic and fix carbon dioxide in the same manner as the green plants, using light energy and producing oxygen as a waste product. In addition to being able to photosynthesise,

many cyanobacteria can also fix atmospheric nitrogen and build up organic nitrogen compounds. They are a widespread group, being found in many aquatic ecosystems, (where they are important producers) as well as in soil, on rocks and on the polar ice.

Anabaena is a genus of filamentous cyanobacteria (Fig.2.4), which grows profusely in warm, moist conditions. In the UK, it is found on the surface of ponds in summer, forming gelatinous colonies with trapped bubbles of gas. In the tropics, it is common in the flooded paddy fields of rice-growing areas, where it grows in such profusion that bluish-green mats are formed on the surface of the water. Each unbranched filament is made up of many identical photosynthetic cells, amongst which are interspersed, special, thick-walled colourless cells, called heterocysts. These cells are the sites of nitrogen fixation and contain the nitrogenase enzymes needed for the conversion of atmospheric nitrogen to organic compounds, a process which is anaerobic.

a)   Filament

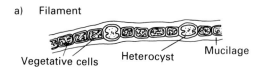

Vegetative cells   Heterocyst   Mucilage

b)   Vegetative cells and heterocyst

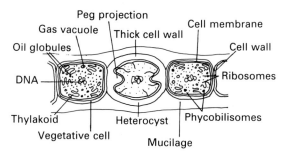

Figure 2.4 *Anabaena*

Included in this Division are the nitrogen-fixing aerobic bacteria *Azotobacter* and *Rhizobium*. These bacteria are aerobic, but can survive where oxygen is in lower concentrations. They are common in soil. *Azotobacter* consists of large oval or rod-shaped cells, with an outer covering of slime. The cells are able to grow rapidly, respiring carbohydrates, and can form thick-walled cysts which enable them to survive desiccation. *Rhizobium* does not form cysts or spores, but

penetrates the root hairs of members of the Papilionaceae (peas, beans, clover), inducing nodule formation in the tissues. Once situated inside the root nodule, the bacteria are able to fix nitrogen, obtaining the carbohydrates they require from the photosynthetic activities of the host plant.

Root nodules on bean plant

◼ Phylum Omnibacteria

This is a large, diverse group and includes many familiar Gram negative genera. The members of this phylum are able to respire aerobically if oxygen is present, but in its absence they respire anaerobically. The phylum is subdivided into the solitary, simple unicells, called enterobacteria, and the more complex stalked and budding types.

Probably the best-known bacterium belonging to this group is *Escherichia coli*, a rod-shaped organism common in the gut flora of humans. It can be cultivated easily and has been used in an enormous number of genetic experiments. It is used in gene technology and probably more is known about this one single organism than any other. It will grow in a temperature range of 5-40 °C, divide by binary fission every 21 minutes in good conditions and is used to grow vaccines.

Electron micrograph of the bacterium *Escherichia coli* in the early stages of binary fission

Another well-known member of the phylum is the genus *Salmonella*. There are about 2000 species in this genus and most are able to cause diseases of the human gut. *Salmonella typhi* causes typhoid fever, and *S. paratyphi* causes paratyphoid, both of which are serious diseases leading to septicaemia and sometimes death. *Salmonella typhimurium* and *S. enteritidis* cause salmonellosis food poisoning, with abdominal pain, vomiting and diarrhoea.

Salmonella spp. are motile, flagellated, rod-shaped bacteria, which adhere to the surface of the epithelial cells of the intestine and are then taken up by phagocytosis. The bacteria multiply, damaging the cells and releasing the toxins which produce high temperatures and inflammation.

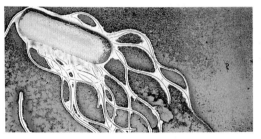

Electron micrograph of a single bacterium of the genus *Salmonella*

Chemoautotrophic bacteria associated with the nitrogen cycle, such as *Nitrobacter*, *Nitrosomonas* and *Nitrococcus*, are also members of this Division and are placed in a phylum of their own. *Nitrosomonas* oxidises ammonium compounds (NH_4^+) to nitrites (NO_2^-), and *Nitrobacter* and *Nitrococcus* oxidise nitrites (NO_2^-) to nitrates (NO_3^-). All these genera are strictly aerobic and derive their energy from the oxidation processes that they carry out. They are essential in the cycling of nitrogen compounds, because they convert compounds to a form in which they can be used by other organisms. *Thiobacillus* is a genus in the same phylum which can oxidise sulphur, and sulphur compounds such as sulphides (S^{2-}) and thiosulphates ($S_2O_3^{2-}$), to sulphates (SO_4^{2-}) which can be taken up by plants.

■ DIVISION FIRMICUTES

These are Gram positive bacteria and include several phyla containing familiar organisms.

All the Gram positive bacteria have thick walls mainly composed of murein, a peptidoglycan, and lacking a lipoprotein layer on the outside. The Gram positive fermenting bacteria include the lactic acid bacteria *Lactobacillus* and *Streptococcus*, which can ferment milk sugars to lactic acid, a property utilised by humans in the production of yoghurt and other dairy products. The genus *Clostridium* includes bacteria that can bring about fermentation of a wide variety of compounds. *Clostridium botulinum* produces powerful toxins; it can grow in animal tissue, causing diseases such as gas gangrene and botulism.

Some of the bacteria in this Division are able to form endospores (Fig.2.5), which are specialised reproductive structures resistant to high temperatures and desiccation. *Bacillus anthracis* is a good example of this group of bacteria. The bacterium causes the disease anthrax in cattle, and the spores are very resistant to toxic chemicals, as well as to drought and extremes of temperature. Anthrax spores are known to remain viable for more than 50 years. When conditions are favourable, the endospores can germinate and resume growth. (For further details of bacteria see *Biology Advanced Studies - Microbiology and Biotechnology*.)

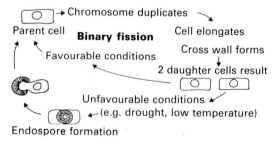

Figure 2.5 The life-cycle of *Bacillus subtilis* showing endospore formation

KINGDOM PROTOCTISTA

This is the 'awkward' taxon - a kingdom defined by exclusion. Its members are not animals, not plants, not fungi and not prokaryotes. However, we can say that all of the members of this kingdom are eukaryotic, with definite nuclei and membrane-bound organelles. Respiration is aerobic. All the genera included are either aquatic (some marine and many found in freshwater) or they are found in the body fluids or tissues of other organisms. Estimates vary as to the number of species in this kingdom, but there are believed to be up to 200 000.

Into this kingdom are gathered the so-called 'lower organisms', together with their close relatives. It seems quite natural that the single-celled, or unicellular, genera of the Protozoa should be grouped together, and to these have been added the slime moulds and water moulds (formerly included in the Fungi) and the algae. In some schemes of classification, all the unicellular organisms were placed in the Protista, but this divided the algae, where the range of form is from unicells to complex, multicellular structures. One way round the problem would have been to place the unicells in the kingdom of their nearest multicellular relatives, but this would have created even more difficulties. Some taxonomists have suggested that each of the major groups in the Protoctista deserves kingdom status, so that would involve the creation of yet more kingdoms, making the classification even more confusing than it is at present. As long as we can appreciate that no system of classification devised so far is perfect, it is possible to ignore the controversy and accept that the phyla included here are linked by their relatively simple structure, although their life cycles, cell organisation and patterns of cell division may vary.

In general, the phyla within the kingdom can be divided into two groups according to their mode of nutrition:
• photoautotrophs, which can build up complex organic compounds from simple inorganic molecules using light as an energy source

(Chlorophyta, Phaeophyta)
• heterotrophs, where organic food requirements have to be obtained from the environment or from other organisms (Rhizopoda, Oomycota).

When present, flagella and cilia (together known as *undulipodia* - because they undulate with waves of contraction) have a 9+2 arrangement of microtubules characteristic of the eukaryotes (see Fig.3.4).

As there are 27 different phyla in the generally accepted Margulis and Schwartz version of the Five Kingdoms scheme of classification, only a few have been selected for inclusion in this book. You will come across most of these in other parts of your course. They have been grouped together under the general headings of Protozoa, Oomycetes and Algae.

■ PROTOZOA

There are more than 50 000 known species included in the protozoan phyla of the Protoctista and they are all found in aquatic environments, whether they are free-living or parasitic. Each organism is an independent unit, able to carry out all the functions necessary to sustain life; some, like *Amoeba*, are relatively simple with few specialised organelles, while others, such as *Vorticella* or *Paramecium*, show a complex organisation with a high degree of specialisation of organelles. None have cell walls, though they all possess tough cell membranes, are heterotrophic and are able to move independently. The majority show sexual as well as asexual means of reproduction, the latter resulting in large numbers of offspring being produced if conditions for growth are favourable. (Some biologists maintain that the term 'unicellular' should not be used to describe the protozoans, and designate them as 'acellular' or 'non-cellular'.) It is a matter of little consequence, provided that it is understood that the cells of multicellular organisms are usually specialised to perform a particular function (muscle cells in animals, palisade cells in plants), whereas the protozoan cells are able to carry out many functions.

■ Phylum Rhizopoda

Amoeba (Fig.3.1) is probably the best-known genus of all the protozoans, as it has been used as an example of the simplest type of living organism, but it is not typical of the majority of protozoans as it does not have undulipodia, has no fixed shape and does not undergo meiosis. *Amoeba* is free living, found in the mud at the bottom of shallow fresh-water pools and streams. It is just about visible to the naked eye as a greyish-white speck, when viewed against a dark background, having a diameter of about 0.1 mm. Under the micro-scope it is seen to have an obvious, more or less centrally placed nucleus, usually one contractile vacuole and numerous food vacuoles in rather granular cytoplasm. The nucleus controls and coordinates the activities of the organism and contains 500-600 small chromosomes. The contractile vacuole is osmo-regulatory; this means that it gets rid of any excess water which enters the organism. It is usually spherical, and can be observed to fill up and then empty its contents to the outside. Concentrations of mitochondria have been seen around the contractile vacuole, suggesting that the process is energy-consuming as the water has to be moved into the vacuole against the concentration gradient. In the cytoplasm, it is possible to distinguish an outer, clear layer of plasmagel, referred to as the ectoplasm, from the inner, more granular plasmasol or endoplasm. Despite the lack of specific sensory organelles, *Amoeba* can respond to different stimuli. It will move away from bright light, irritant chemicals and sharp objects, and is able to distinguish food particles from inedible materials.

When observed under the microscope, *Amoeba* is continually changing its shape as it moves away from the bright light. It moves by producing pseudopodia, finger-like extensions of the cytoplasm, in the direction in which it is going. The formation of the pseudopodia, known as amoeboid movement, involves a colloidal change from the sol (more liquid) state of the cytoplasm to the gel (more jelly-like) type at the anterior end and from the gel to the sol state at the posterior end. There has been much speculation as to the mechanism of this change in state of the cytoplasm, but its exact nature has not been determined, although ATP is thought to be involved. Pseudopodia are also used to capture food particles, such as small algae, bacteria and other protozoans, prior to the formation of food vacuoles (Fig.3.2). The feeding method is called phagocytosis, and can be observed in other organisms (as well as in certain types of white blood corpuscles). Enzymes are secreted into the food vacuoles, the food particle is digested, the soluble products of digestion diffuse into the cytoplasm and the undigested residues are passed out when the vacuole moves to the cell membrane.

0.1 mm

Nucleus
Fat droplets
Pseudopodium
Contractile vacuole
Food vacuole
Plasmasol
Plasmagel
Cell surface membrane
Excretory crystals

Figure 3.1 The structure of *Amoeba*

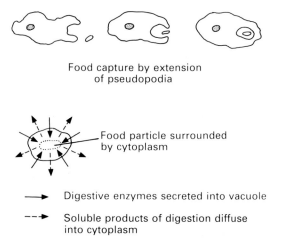

Food capture by extension of pseudopodia

Food particle surrounded by cytoplasm

→ Digestive enzymes secreted into vacuole

--→ Soluble products of digestion diffuse into cytoplasm

Figure 3.2 Food capture by extension of pseudopodia

Amoeba reproduces asexually (Fig.3.3) by means of binary fission, probably triggered by the increase in ratio of the volume of the cytoplasm to the volume of the nucleus. The two daughter *Amoebae* formed can feed and grow to the maximum size. This type of reproduction can result in a rapid increase in numbers when conditions are favourable and there is plenty of food available.

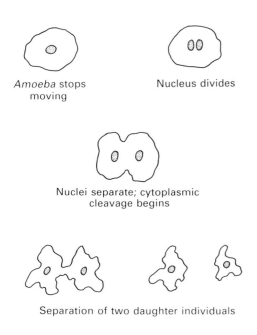

Amoeba stops moving

Nucleus divides

Nuclei separate; cytoplasmic cleavage begins

Separation of two daughter individuals

Figure 3.3 Asexual reproduction in *Amoeba*

Some species of Amoeba are hosts of the bacterium *Legionella pneumophila* which is responsible for Legionnaires' disease. The bacterium parasitises the *Amoeba spp.*, which can grow rapidly and reproduce in warm conditions, and if they get into water-cooled air-conditioning systems they can spread in droplets of water vapour which may be inhaled. The bacterium causes a severe form of pneumonia.

Entamoeba hystolitica, a close relative of *Amoeba*, is the organism which causes amoebic dysentry. It is able to form cysts, in which a layer of mucilage is secreted which affords the organism protection from unfavourable conditions. Cysts can pass out of infected people in the faeces and can contaminate drinking water.

■ Phylum Ciliophora

The members of this phylum (some 8000 species have been described) have a complex internal organisation. They are covered in large numbers of cilia, which are short, movable undulipodia, possessing the typical 9+2 arrangement of microtubules. The cilia are arranged diagonally in longitudinal rows, emerging in pairs from six-sided pits in the pellicle. Each cilium arises from a kinetosome, or basal body, situated in the plasmagel, the clear layer of ectoplasm beneath the pellicle. The kinetosomes of adjacent cilia are linked by fibrils, forming a complex network, the kinetodesmata (Fig.3.4a), which are responsible for coordinating the beating of the cilia. Also in the ectoplasm are the trichocysts (Fig.3.4b), which can discharge a fine thread when touched, and help to anchor the organism when it is feeding or may act as a defence mechanism. Cilia are used in locomotion and in setting up feeding currents (see Fig.3.6).

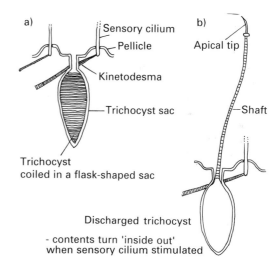

a)

Sensory cilium

Pellicle

Kinetodesma

Trichocyst sac

Trichocyst coiled in a flask-shaped sac

b)

Apical tip

Shaft

Discharged trichocyst

- contents turn 'inside out' when sensory cilium stimulated

Figure 3.4 The action of the trichocyst in *Paramecium*

In addition to the cilia, two types of nuclei are present: micronuclei, which are small and contain normal chromosomes; and macronuclei, which are much larger, lack typical chromosomes, but contain DNA broken up into a large number of chromatin bodies containing many copies of a few genes. The micronuclei are essential for the sexual process shown by the ciliates, but the macronuclei control the normal processes of growth and asexual reproduction.

Asexual reproduction occurs by means of transverse binary fission in the free-swimming ciliates, or by 'budding' in the fixed or sessile types. The sexual process, known as conjugation, involves the pairing of compatible mating types, followed by exchange of micronuclei, fusion and several divisions.

Paramecium (Fig.3.5) is probably the best-known of the ciliates. It is found in fresh water, which has decaying vegetation in it, and it feeds on bacteria. It has a fixed shape, maintained by the semi-rigid pellicle, being blunt at the anterior and tapering towards the posterior. It possesses a small micronucleus, a large macronucleus, two contractile vacuoles, and a ciliated oral groove leading to the gullet and cytostome, where food particles are ingested.

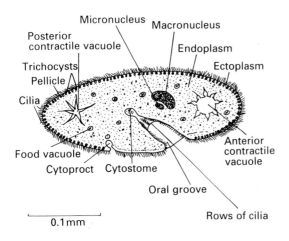

Figure 3.5 The structure of *Paramecium*

It moves by the rhythmic beating of its cilia, each one beating a little in advance of the one behind, creating waves of activity (metachronal rhythm). Each cilium has a downward power stroke, in which the cilium is held straight, followed by a recovery stroke. Because of the arrangement of the cilia and the nature of the beating mechanism, the organism swims in a spiral, rotating about its axis. *Paramecium* is able to detect external stimuli, such as touch, changes in light intensity and concentrations of different chemicals, probably by means of special, stiff cilia at the posterior end. In unfavourable conditions, the cilia can reverse their action, and the organism can change its direction.

Ciliary action sets up feeding currents and particles of food are wafted into the oral groove, and from there to the gullet. At the end of the gullet is the cytostome, where the food particles, together with a drop of water, are ingested and form food vacuoles by phagocytosis. The food vacuoles move around the body in a definite pathway (Fig.3.6), during which time their contents are digested. Any undigested material is voided at a fixed point towards the posterior end, the cytoproct.

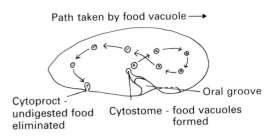

Figure 3.6 The path taken by food vacuoles through the cytoplasm of *Paramecium*

Osmoregulation is carried out by means of two contractile vacuoles, one at the anterior and the other at the posterior. Micrographs show that these contractile vacuoles are surrounded by a number of radial canals, or collecting ducts, which empty into them.

When *Paramecium* reproduces asexually, the micronucleus divides by mitosis (see *Biology Advanced Studies - Genetics and Evolution*), forming two daughter nuclei, which move to opposite ends of the organism. The macronucleus also divides by constricting in the middle, but there is no spindle. Following division of the two nuclei, the cytoplasm constricts in the middle.

Sexual reproduction, or conjugation (Fig.3.7), is a much more complex procedure and involves the reduction division, meiosis. Two compatible organisms pair up, becoming attached at their oral grooves. The pellicle in this region breaks down so that the cytoplasm of the conjugants is in contact. The micronuclei undergo meiosis, after which three of the four haploid daughter nuclei formed will disintegrate. The remaining nucleus divides by mitosis to form two 'gametes', one of which remains and the other migrates through the cytoplasmic connection into the other conjugant and fuses with the stationary nucleus.

1. Macronucleus breaks down. Meiosis of micronucleus   2. Nuclei are exchanged   3. Zygotic nuclei form after fusion

4. Zygotic nuclei divide again.   5. Binary fission now takes place

Three nuclei disappear.
Four become macronuclei,
one becomes a micronucleus

Figure 3.7 Sexual reproduction in *Paramecium*

The macronuclei break down. The exchange of genetic material having been achieved and the zygote formed, the conjugants separate and the nucleus divides to form eight daughter nuclei, four of which form macronuclei and one becomes a micronucleus. The rest of the nuclei disintegrate. Finally binary fission takes place twice, so that each conjugant gives rise to four new organisms.

The process of autogamy (Fig.3.8), observed in cultures of *Paramecium* kept for some time without undergoing sexual reproduction, involves similar behaviour of the nuclei as in conjugation, except that there is no pairing, so no exchange of genetic material occurs between individuals.

1. Micronucleus divides   2. Macronucleus breaks down. Micronucleus divides again   3. Zygotic nucleus forms

4. Zygotic nucleus divides   5. Two nuclei become micronuclei, two become macronuclei

6. Binary fission takes place

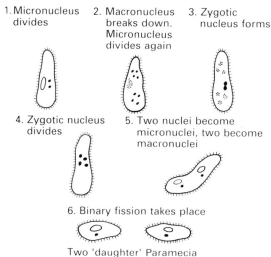

Two 'daughter' Paramecia

Figure 3.8 Autogamy in *Paramecium*

■ Phylum Euglenophyta

It is appropriate to mention this phylum briefly, as reference has already been made to *Euglena* in both this chapter and in Chapter 1, in connection with the difficulties of producing a truly natural classification.

The genus *Euglena* (Fig.3.9) was originally placed in the green algae on the basis that some of the species possessed chloroplasts and were able to photosynthesise, despite the fact that the cells lacked cellulose cell walls, having instead a flexible pellicle made of protein. The chloroplasts contained the photosynthetic pigments chlorophyll *a* and *b*, together with β-carotene and some xanthophylls, pigments which are identical with those found in green plants.

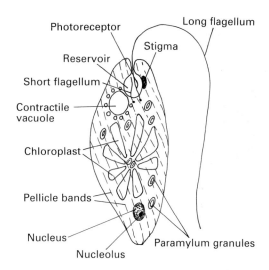

Photoreceptor   Long flagellum
Stigma
Reservoir
Short flagellum
Contractile vacuole
Chloroplast
Pellicle bands
Nucleus   Paramylum granules
Nucleolus

Figure 3.9 The structure of *Euglena viridis*

The species *Euglena gracilis* has been studied intensively and used to investigate the effects of light, temperature and other agents on the development of chloroplasts. If kept in the dark, the cells lose their chloroplasts and can no longer feed autotrophically; they become heterotrophic. If they are then exposed to light again, chloroplasts reappear and the organism can become photosynthetic. Exposure of *Euglena gracilis* to ultra-violet light destroys the mechanism responsible for the production of chloroplasts, without destroying the rest of the cell. Under these conditions, the cells lose their plant characteristics and remain heterotrophic, even when exposed to light.

Other studies on the growth requirements of the species have shown that very small quantities of vitamin B$_{12}$ are required. *Euglena gracilis* is so sensitive to the amount of the vitamin in its environment that it has been used in commercial assays, as it is more accurate than chemical tests.

Euglena is able to respond to light and will move towards the source unless it is very bright. This is a *positively phototactic* response. A tactic movement is where the whole organism moves in response to the stimulus and in a direction related to the stimulus. (Earthworms are negatively phototactic - see Chapter 9.)

Q How could you set up an experiment to investigate this, given a culture of *Euglena*? How could you find out to which particular intensity or wavelength of light the organism responds?

■ Phylum Zoomastigina

Most of the members of this phylum are unicellular and possess at least one undulipodium. They are all heterotrophic and they may be free-living or parasitic. Our example is the parasitic genus, *Trypanosoma* (Fig.3.10), some species of which cause sleeping sickness in humans and related diseases in domestic cattle. The single undulipodium extends forwards along the length of the body of the organism, projecting beyond the body at the front. It is attached by a fine membrane, the undulating membrane, and as the undulipodium moves it moves the membrane and the organism is propelled through the blood plasma of its host.

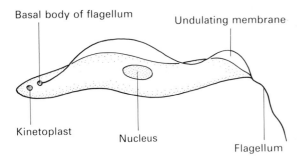

Basal body of flagellum
Undulating membrane
Kinetoplast
Nucleus
Flagellum

Figure 3.10 The parasitic genus, *Trypanosoma*

The organisms feed by absorbing the soluble products of the host's digestion from its blood, so there is no need for a gullet. Gaseous exchange is carried out through the pellicle and there are no specialised sensory organelles or contractile vacuoles. Osmoregulation is not necessary as the body contents of the parasite are at the same concentration as the body fluids of the host. The trypanosomes reproduce asexually by longitudinal binary fission, and there seems to be no evidence for the existence of a sexual process.

Trypanosoma gambiense occurs mainly in West and Central Africa, and *T. rhodesiense* in East Africa. Both have very similar life cycles (Fig.3.11) involving a human primary host and a secondary host, which is also the vector, the tsetse fly, *Glossina spp.* Adult trypanosomes are taken in by the tsetse flies when they take a blood meal from an infected person. The trypanosomes are retained in the gut of the fly and those that are not digested by the action of the insect's enzymes undergo binary fission, resulting in an increase in numbers. They migrate through the tissues to the salivary glands where they become attached and undergo another phase of binary fission. When the fly bites another person, infective trypanosomes are passed into the blood with the saliva of the fly.

The infected person suffers headaches, fever and gradually becomes lethargic due to the toxins released into the blood by the metabolic activities of the trypanosomes. The trypanosomes move into the lymph glands and cause swelling in the neck, armpits and groin, and when they get into the cerebro-spinal fluid, the infected person becomes even more lethargic, lacking even the energy to eat.

If the infection is detected in its early stages, it can be treated with drugs, but prevention is better than cure, so control measures have been investigated. It should be possible to eradicate the tsetse flies, but their numbers appear to be increasing and their range spreading. They need trees for shelter and for pupation, so a policy of tree and shrub clearance was carried out around settlements. Obviously, this has to be limited, otherwise severe deforestation would occur. Biological control by parasitic insects and insect-eating birds does not seem to make much impression on the tsetse fly population, and there is also the problem that trypanosomes are present in

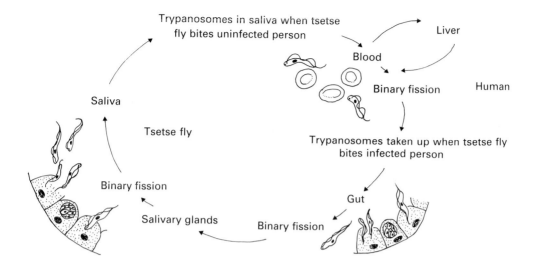

Figure 3.11 The life cycle of *Trypanosoma*

the blood of wild game, where they do not seem to produce the symptoms of disease. This means that there will always be a reservoir of infective organisms, even if domestic cattle are treated. Trypanosomes are considered to be fairly recent parasites of humans and domestic cattle, because they have such severe effects on their hosts. Well-established parasites do not do so much harm, managing to obtain the food they require without killing off their hosts which would obviously be a fatal disadvantage to the parasite.

▊ Phylum Apicomplexa

These are all spore-forming animal parasites, reproducing sexually with an alternation of haploid and diploid generations. One of the most famous genera is *Plasmodium*, which causes malaria.

Plasmodium (Fig.3.12) is transmitted to its human host by the female *Anopheles* mosquito, which is also the secondary host of the parasite. The mosquito feeds from an infected human and takes in gametocytes with the ingested blood. The gametocytes are

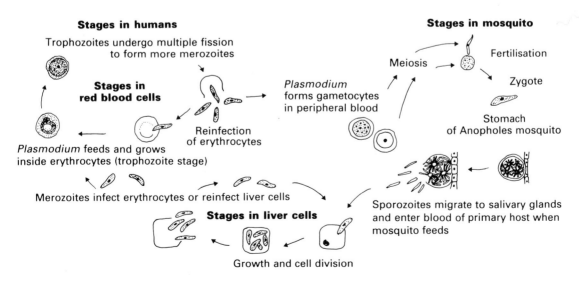

Figure 3.12 The life cycle of *Plasmodium vivax*

resistant to the digestive enzymes of the mosquito and develop into male and female gametes. The male gametocyte nucleus divides up and each part moves into a long cytoplasmic extension, which breaks off and is capable of fusing with a female gametocyte to form a zygote, known as an ookinete. This moves to the gut wall and forms a cyst, inside which meiosis occurs, followed by multiple fission. The result is the formation of large numbers of sporozoites which, when released, migrate to the salivary glands of the mosquito. When the female mosquito takes her next meal, some sporozoites are injected into the bloodstream of the human victim, along with the saliva containing anticoagulant. Once in the human bloodstream, the sporozoites are carried to the liver. They enter the liver cells and undergo a period of growth, developing into schizonts, which can undergo multiple fission, forming large numbers of merozoites. The merozoites are released into the blood from the liver cells and enter red blood cells, where they grow, feeding on the cell contents. Once they reach a certain size, they undergo another phase of multiple fission, resulting in the release of more merozoites into the blood. This cycle can continue until enormous numbers of merozoites are present. Some will develop into gametocytes and remain in the blood, without developing further, until taken up by another female mosquito.

Malaria is a common disease in the tropics, particularly in tropical Africa. The symptoms of very high fever are caused when the red blood cells release the merozoites, together with cell debris and toxic waste products, into the plasma. It is a debilitating disease and causes millions of deaths every year. Control measures involve the eradication of the breeding grounds of the mosquitoes by draining land, killing the larvae by oiling the surface waters or using insecticides to kill the adult females. Most of these measures have been successful, but the problem is a huge one. Prevention of infection can be helped by the use of mosquito nets, insect repellants and drugs. Drugs can also be used to treat the disease, but are usually only effective whilst the organism is in the blood. The drugs do not have much effect on the stages in the liver, where schizonts can remain dormant for long periods of time. There is increasing evidence to suggest that some strains of the organism are becoming tolerant to the drugs used and that the insects are developing resistance to the insecticides. Biological control methods, involving the use of carnivorous fish, which eat the larvae and pupae, have proved quite successful, but will not eliminate the problem as the mosquitoes breed in areas which are inaccessible to humans. With rapid intercontinental flights so easily available there is concern about the spread of insect vectors in aircraft. Some countries have a policy of spraying insecticide on all arriving flights. It should be noted by travellers to malaria areas that 12 returning Britons in 1991 died of malaria.

■ OOMYCETES

■ Phylum Oomycota

The oomycotes, or oomycetes, include the water moulds, white rusts and downy mildews, and were all previously classified with the fungi. They are heterotrophic, being either parasitic or saprotrophic (feeding by extending hyphae into the tissues of their host, secreting digestive enzymes and then absorbing the soluble products of digestion). The hyphae have cellulose walls and lack septa, or cross walls, except when formed in connection with the reproductive structures. They all form zoospores with two unequal undulipodia, one directed forwards and the other backwards. The zoospores are asexual spores and are formed in sporangia, borne at the apex of sporangiophores. Sexual reproduction involves the production of antheridia and oogonia at the tips of vegetative hyphae. The antheridium, when it comes into contact with an oogoniun, produces a fertilisation tube, which penetrates the oogonium, providing a passage through which the nuclei migrate. Fertilisation of the oospheres results in the formation of oóspores, the zygotes. These may develop thick walls and become resistant to unfavourable conditions such as cold temperatures and desiccation.

Phytophthora infestans, belonging to the class Peronospora, is the organism which causes late blight of potatoes, and it is found wherever potatoes are grown. In the middle of the 19th century it was responsible for the failure of potato crops in Ireland, causing deprivation and famine, as a result of which hundreds of thousands died and thousands more emigrated to the United States of America.

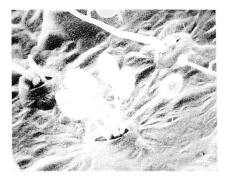

Electron micrograph of potato blight sporangia emerging from a potato leaf

The first signs of infection of a potato crop are small brown patches appearing on the leaves. These patches spread rapidly in wet conditions until the whole plant may become brown and rotten, by which time the photosynthetic activities of the plant have ceased and no more food is being sent to the tubers for storage. The disease overwinters in infected potato tubers and a mycelium develops, producing enormous numbers of asexual sporangia, which are easily detached and spread by means of air currents to healthy plants. The sporangia land on the leaves and, if conditions are wet, release motile zoospores, which germinate and produce a fine germ tube able to penetrate the host. Once inside the host tissue, the hyphae grow between the cells, sending haustoria into the cells to absorb nutrients. Growth is rapid and after a few days

sporangiophores are produced which emerge through the stomata on the underside of the leaves. Sporangia develop at the tips, become detached and are carried away by air currents to uninfected leaves. This cycle is favoured by cool, humid conditions, when the sporangia will release their motile zoospores which can spread the infection more rapidly. If conditions are hot or dry, then the sporangia do not release zoospores, but behave as single spores and produce a germ tube which can penetrate the host. The sexual reproductive phase is not seen in the UK. (See Fig.3.13.)

In order to control the disease, strict measures need to be taken to ensure that all infected material is burnt, and that only disease-free tubers are planted. The foliage of the plants can be destroyed before the tubers are harvested, thus minimising the risk of spores landing on the crop. 'Earthing-up' the potatoes also makes it difficult for spores to reach the tubers before they are harvested. If the disease is seen, then the crop must be sprayed with a fungicide regularly. Bordeaux mixture, consisting of copper sulphate and lime, used to be used but nowadays organic fungicides such as dithiocarbamates (maneb, zineb) are used. They are protectant fungicides which coat the leaves. When taken up by the fungus, they result in loss of enzyme function, killing the mycelium. The planting of different varieties of potatoes can help: Majestic is not as susceptible to the blight as King Edwards.

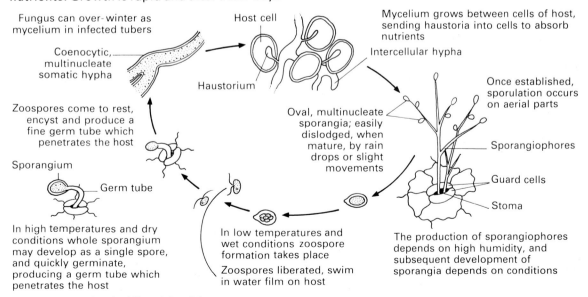

Fungus can over-winter as mycelium in infected tubers

Coenocytic, multinucleate somatic hypha

Host cell

Mycelium grows between cells of host, sending haustoria into cells to absorb nutrients

Intercellular hypha

Haustorium

Once established, sporulation occurs on aerial parts

Zoospores come to rest, encyst and produce a fine germ tube which penetrates the host

Oval, multinucleate sporangia; easily dislodged, when mature, by rain drops or slight movements

Sporangiophores

Sporangium

Guard cells

Germ tube

Stoma

In high temperatures and dry conditions whole sporangium may develop as a single spore, and quickly germinate, producing a germ tube which penetrates the host

In low temperatures and wet conditions zoospore formation takes place

Zoospores liberated, swim in water film on host

The production of sporangiophores depends on high humidity, and subsequent development of sporangia depends on conditions

Figure 3.13 Asexual cycle of *Phytophthora infestans*

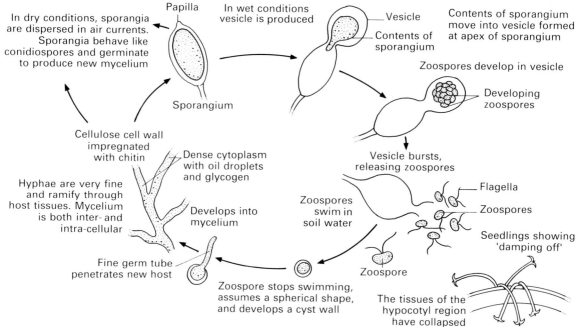

In dry conditions, sporangia are dispersed in air currents. Sporangia behave like conidiospores and germinate to produce new mycelium

Papilla

In wet conditions vesicle is produced

Vesicle

Contents of sporangium

Contents of sporangium move into vesicle formed at apex of sporangium

Zoospores develop in vesicle

Developing zoospores

Sporangium

Cellulose cell wall impregnated with chitin

Dense cytoplasm with oil droplets and glycogen

Vesicle bursts, releasing zoospores

Flagella

Hyphae are very fine and ramify through host tissues. Mycelium is both inter- and intra-cellular

Develops into mycelium

Zoospores swim in soil water

Zoospores

Seedlings showing 'damping off'

Fine germ tube penetrates new host

Zoospore stops swimming, assumes a spherical shape, and develops a cyst wall

Zoospore

The tissues of the hypocotyl region have collapsed

Figure 3.14 Asexual cycle of *Pythium debaryanum*

Pythium sp. (Fig.3.14) is another plant pathogen, which belongs to the class Peronospora. It grows saprotrophically in the soil, but causes the damping-off disease of seedlings, and can be a problem in glasshouses where the humid conditions enable it to spread rapidly. It can be controlled by steam-sterilising the soil of glasshouses and by avoiding growing seedlings in overcrowded conditions.

■ ALGAE

It is still convenient to use the term 'alga' for the seaweeds and their relatives, despite the fact that they are classified with the Protoctista. All the algae possess chlorophyll *a*, together with a variety of other photosynthetic pigments, characteristic of the different groups to which they belong. There is an enormous range of structure, from tiny unicells to large multicellular organisms, but little internal cell differentiation or organisation. The sex organs are usually unicellular.

■ Phylum Chlorophyta
These are the green algae that form zoospores with two equal undulipodia, have cup-shaped chloroplasts and photosynthetic pigments

similar to those found in the plant kingdom. They make up a large part of the freshwater phytoplankton and are responsible for fixing about 1000 million tonnes of carbon every year. Most of the green algae store starch as their food reserve. Asexual reproduction does occur, usually taking the form of simple division into 2, 4 or 8 daughter cells, and sexual reproduction ranges from isogamy, where two identical gametes fuse, to oogamy, in which a small, motile male gamete fuses with a large, stationary female gamete.

Within the class Chlorococcales (a diverse group) eight families are recognised. Common members of this class are *Chlorococcum* (*Pleurococcus*), the powdery green covering on tree trunks and park benches, *Chorella*, famous as a laboratory and research organism, and *Chlamydomonas*, all of which are unicellular. There are colonial forms such as *Volvox*, and *thalloid* (flattened, leaf-like) examples, such as *Ulva* (the sea lettuce) and *Enteromorpha*, which is common in estuaries and where sewage outflow occurs round our coasts.

Chlamydomonas (Fig.3.15) is perhaps the most typical of the unicells. It possesses a cup-shaped chloroplast surrounding a centrally placed nucleus. Two equal undulipodia are inserted in the anterior end and there are two contractile vacuoles for osmoregulation, a pyrenoid concerned with starch formation and an eyespot, or stigma, which is a photoreceptive organelle. The undulipodia beat, enabling the organism to swim, and it rotates about its longitudinal axis as it moves forward.

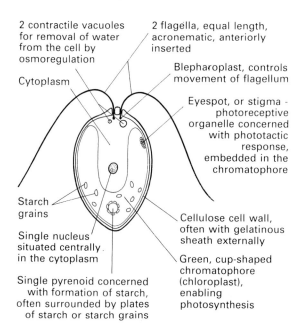

2 contractile vacuoles for removal of water from the cell by osmoregulation

Cytoplasm

2 flagella, equal length, acronematic, anteriorly inserted

Blepharoplast, controls movement of flagellum

Eyespot, or stigma - photoreceptive organelle concerned with phototactic response, embedded in the chromatophore

Starch grains

Single nucleus situated centrally in the cytoplasm

Single pyrenoid concerned with formation of starch, often surrounded by plates of starch or starch grains

Cellulose cell wall, often with gelatinous sheath externally

Green, cup-shaped chromatophore (chloroplast), enabling photosynthesis

Figure 3.15 Vegetative cell of *Chlamydomonas*

Asexual reproduction (Fig.3.16) involves division of the cell contents into 2, 4, 8 or 16 daughter cells. In sexual reproduction (Fig.3.17) the vegetative cells function as gametes, pair up and swim around together until fusion occurs.

Chlamydomonas spp. are found in freshwater, in soil, in mine wastes, on other organisms and in reservoirs. One species, *C. nivalis*, grows on snow and ice, which it colours red due to the accumulation of carotenoid pigments in the cytoplasm.

The genus *Chlorella* differs from *Chlamydomonas* in the lack of undulipodia, although it is found in similar situations. It can be grown easily in the laboratory in culture, and has been used to determine metabolic pathways. Calvin and his co-workers used *Chlorella* in their classic 'lollipop' apparatus, to determine the first products of photosynthesis, thus enabling them to work out the photosynthetic pathway referred to as the Calvin cycle (see *Biology Advanced Studies - Biochemistry*).

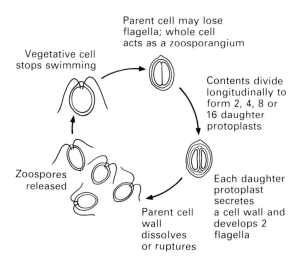

Parent cell may lose flagella; whole cell acts as a zoosporangium

Vegetative cell stops swimming

Contents divide longitudinally to form 2, 4, 8 or 16 daughter protoplasts

Zoospores released

Each daughter protoplast secretes a cell wall and develops 2 flagella

Parent cell wall dissolves or ruptures

Figure 3.16 Asexual cycle in *Chlamydomonas*

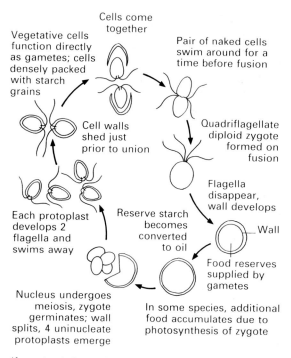

Cells come together

Vegetative cells function directly as gametes; cells densely packed with starch grains

Pair of naked cells swim around for a time before fusion

Cell walls shed just prior to union

Quadriflagellate diploid zygote formed on fusion

Flagella disappear, wall develops

Wall

Each protoplast develops 2 flagella and swims away

Reserve starch becomes converted to oil

Food reserves supplied by gametes

Nucleus undergoes meiosis, zygote germinates; wall splits, 4 uninucleate protoplasts emerge

In some species, additional food accumulates due to photosynthesis of zygote

If species is homothallic, gametes are formed from the same parent, but if species is heterothallic gametes are formed from different parents

Figure 3.17 Sexual cycle in *Chlamydomonas*

Investigations were made into its use as a food, as it can be grown quickly in large quantities. It is an efficient converter of light energy into chemical energy, and yields a large amount of protein, but it would be very expensive and it has obviously seemed more profitable to invest in the production of mycoprotein. *Chlorella* (Fig.3.18) is also used to purify sewage effluent. When grown in shallow tanks, it provides oxygen for bacterial action and can absorb the minerals released on the breakdown of the sewage.

a)

Thin cellulose cell wall

Cytoplasm

Oil globule

Green, plate-like chromatophore which is often extended in older cells

Pyrenoids, involved with starch formation

Starch grains - more numerous in older cells

b)

Parent cell wall

Contents divided up to form autospores (typically 2-16 are formed, depending on the species)

Autospores set free when parent cell wall breaks down

All nuclear divisions occur first, followed by cleavage of the cytoplasm

Figure 3.18 Chlorella (a) Vegetative cells of *Chlorella* (b) Asexual reproduction - no sexual stages have been observed in *Chlorella*

■ Phylum Phaeophyta

You are likely to encounter members of this phylum on visits to the seaside - either for holiday or on field trips.

The brown algae are all members of this phylum and they are mostly marine. They include some of the largest of the Protoctista, the giant kelps growing to lengths of more than 100 metres. Although many do grow quite large, they do not show much internal cell specialisation or tissue differentiation. They are all photosynthetic, containing the brown pigment, fucoxanthin, in addition to chlorophylls *a* and *c*. Lipids and a carbohydrate called laminarin are formed as storage products, and many can synthesise secondary metabolites, which are being investigated as

sources of drugs and food. Most of the brown algae are found growing along rocky seashores, although some like *Sargassum* grow in the middle of the ocean, where they provide an important habitat for a variety of other organisms. The seashore species prefer temperate climates and often show characteristic zonation.

Brown, green and red algae at low tide, Wembury, Devon

The genus *Fucus* (Fig.3.19) is common around the shores of the UK. *Fucus spiralis*, the spiral wrack, grows high up on the shore, enduring most exposure and only being submerged for a short time, apart from the spring tides. *Fucus vesiculosus*, the bladder wrack, is typical of the middle zone and *Fucus serratus*, the serrated wrack, grows lower down the shore near low tide level. Each is adapted to life at one level of the shore with a typical regime of different proportions of time under water and exposed in the air.

Fucus is seen to consist of a disc-like holdfast, which attaches the organism to the rocks, a tough, flexible stipe, which keeps it in position, and a leathery lamina. The whole structure is adapted to withstand wave action and maintain its position on the shore. The bladder wrack possesses air bladders along its lamina, on either side of the midrib, and these provide buoyancy, so that the lamina floats as the tide comes in and it is able to obtain sufficient light for efficient photosynthesis.

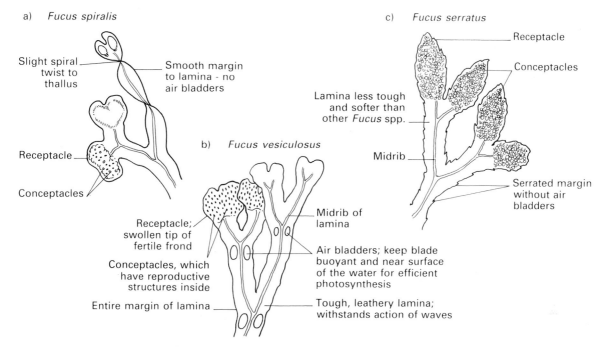

a) *Fucus spiralis*

Slight spiral twist to thallus

Smooth margin to lamina - no air bladders

Receptacle

Conceptacles

b) *Fucus vesiculosus*

Receptacle; swollen tip of fertile frond

Conceptacles, which have reproductive structures inside

Entire margin of lamina

Midrib of lamina

Air bladders; keep blade buoyant and near surface of the water for efficient photosynthesis

Tough, leathery lamina; withstands action of waves

c) *Fucus serratus*

Receptacle

Conceptacles

Lamina less tough and softer than other *Fucus* spp.

Midrib

Serrated margin without air bladders

Figure 3.19 Three types of *Fucus*

Many of the brown algae show a definite alternation of generations, with a diploid sporophyte generation. Typically, two types of zoosporangia occur on the sporophyte: unilocular and plurilocular. The zoospores are formed by mitosis in the plurilocular sporangia, and are thus diploid. When released they germinate to form diploid sporophytes. Meiosis occurs during the formation of zoospores in the unilocular sporangia, so they are haploid and on germination give rise to haploid gametophytes. Gametangia, in which gametes are produced, develop on the gametophytes. Fusion of a male gamete with a female gamete results in the restoration of the diploid condition and a sporophyte is produced.

The Fucales do not show this type of life cycle (see Fig.3.20). The reproductive organs develop at the tips of the fronds in cavities called conceptacles. In some species, both antheridia and oogonia are found on the same organism, while in others they are separate. Antherozoids with two undulipodia are formed and the oospheres are larger, with food reserves. At low tide, the thallus dries out and the mature gametangia are extruded. When the tide comes in the gametes are liberated

and fertilisation occurs. The zygote develops into a young thallus which soon attaches itself to a rock.

The Fucales do not have a great economic importance although some are used as a source of iodine and others are used in foods.

■ **Phylum Bacillariophyta and Phylum Rhodophyta**

Two other phyla of algae are noteworthy: the Bacillariophyta, or diatoms, and the Rhodophyta, or red algae. The diatoms are widespread and found in freshwater as well as marine and terrestrial habitats. They are abundant in the phytoplankton. Their cell walls are impregnated with silica and occur in two halves, often having distinctive patterns and markings. They can be elongated, resembling date boxes, or round like petri dishes. There is an extensive fossil record, because the silica walls persist long after the contents have decayed. Over millions of years, the silica cases have accumulated at the bottom of lakes and seas, forming diatomaceous earth, which has been quarried and used as an abrasive. It has been included in toothpastes, polishes and as an inert mineral filler in paints and plastics. Because of the uniformity of the markings on the walls, the cases have been used to check the resolving power of microscope lenses.

Oogamous and showing no alternation of generations

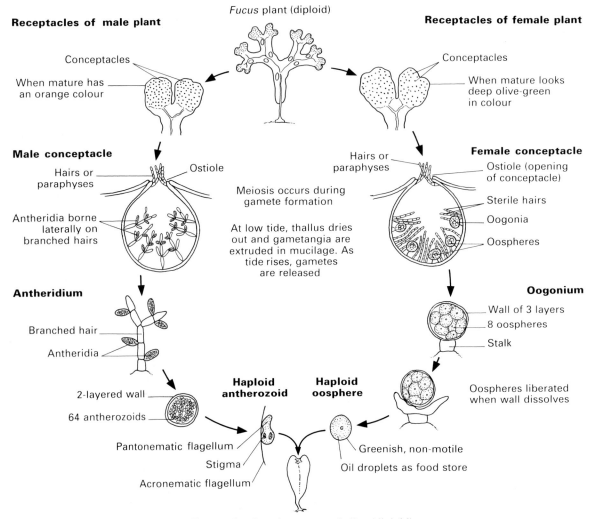

Fucus plant (diploid)

Receptacles of male plant

Conceptacles

When mature has an orange colour

Receptacles of female plant

Conceptacles

When mature looks deep olive-green in colour

Male conceptacle

Hairs or paraphyses

Ostiole

Antheridia borne laterally on branched hairs

Meiosis occurs during gamete formation

At low tide, thallus dries out and gametangia are extruded in mucilage. As tide rises, gametes are released

Hairs or paraphyses

Female conceptacle

Ostiole (opening of conceptacle)

Sterile hairs

Oogonia

Oospheres

Antheridium

Branched hair

Antheridia

2-layered wall

64 antherozoids

Oogonium

Wall of 3 layers

8 oospheres

Stalk

Oospheres liberated when wall dissolves

Haploid antherozoid

Haploid oosphere

Pantonematic flagellum

Stigma

Acronematic flagellum

Greenish, non-motile

Oil droplets as food store

Zygote develops into young thallus (diploid)

Figure 3.20 The life cycle of *Fucus vesiculosus*

Micrograph of an array of marine diatoms

The red algae, the Phylum Rhodophyta, are mostly marine and consist of both filamentous and thalloid forms. Some grow attached to rocks, but many grow as *epiphytes* on other algae. Their most characteristic feature is the possession of a red photosynthetic pigment, phycoerythrin, which masks the other pigments present and gives these algae their colour. Many of the red algae are found in deep water, where blue light predominates and it is thought that this pigment enables a more efficient use of the available light for photosynthesis. There are other important differences in the life cycle and in their reproductive structures.

CHAPTER 4

KINGDOM FUNGI

The term 'fungus' has been used in systems of classification for a long time to describe plant-like organisms lacking chlorophyll. In the Margulis and Schwartz system of classification, the fungi are given kingdom status, and are defined as spore-forming eukaryotic organisms, without cellulose in their walls and lacking undulipodia (flagella) at any stage in their life cycle. The kingdom is divided into five phyla, which differ from each other in the complexity of the structure of the hyphae and in the nature of the spore-producing structures.

Fungi are unicellular, as in the yeasts, or more usually filamentous. Individual filaments are called hyphae and develop directly from the germination of single spores. There is no embryo stage. The hyphae grow together to form a mycelium (Fig.4.1), which may remain as a loose network of threads, or which may become compacted to form a more solid structure such as the familiar edible mushroom, *Agaricus*. The hyphae have chitinous walls which may be divided by cross partitions, called septa, into 'cells', and each cell may be uninucleate, binucleate or multinucleate, depending on the species. In one phylum, the Zygomycota, the hyphae are multinucleate with no cross walls and are referred to as coenocytic. In the Ascomycota and Basidiomycota, the septa have pores so that the cytoplasm is continuous and cell-to-cell communication is possible. These pores can be quite large, allowing nuclei to pass through.

Fungi are eukaryotic organisms and their cytoplasm contains membrane-bound organelles, such as mitochondria, Golgi bodies, endoplasmic reticula and ribosomes. The nuclei are bounded by a nuclear envelope with pores. Vacuoles develop in the cytoplasm, and in the older parts of a mycelium, the hyphae have only peripheral cytoplasm surrounding a large central vacuole. Most of the growth of a mycelium takes place at the tips of the hyphae, where soluble organic molecules, inorganic ions and water are absorbed. Under favourable conditions, this growth can be rapid. Most fungi require organic sources of carbon (glucose), nitrogen (amino acids), together with inorganic ions and one or more vitamins.

Most fungi grow best at temperatures around 25-35 °C when kept in culture in laboratory conditions. They are aerobic and can be kept on agar or in liquid culture at pH values between 4.5 and 6.5. This acidic pH has the effect of reducing bacterial contamination of the cultures.

The great majority of fungi are terrestrial and saprotrophic, feeding on the dead and decaying remains of plants and animals. The fungus secretes enzymes on to its food substrate and absorbs the soluble products of this extra-cellular digestion. Some species are parasitic, obtaining food from a host organism. Two sorts of parasites are distinguished: obligate, where the fungus can only survive while the host remains alive, and facultative, where the fungus parasitises a living host, but can live on the dead, organic remains when the host has been killed. Parasitic fungi may have special absorptive hyphae, called haustoria, which penetrate the cells of the host and absorb soluble food substances.

Some fungi form symbiotic associations with other living organisms. Fungi which live in or on the roots of green plants are called mycorrhizae, and this association benefits both members of the partnership. The green plant benefits from the larger surface area available for the absorption of the mineral ions,

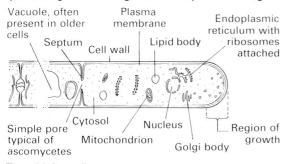

Vacuole, often present in older cells
Plasma membrane
Endoplasmic reticulum with ribosomes attached
Septum
Cell wall
Lipid body
Simple pore typical of ascomycetes
Cytosol
Mitochondrion
Nucleus
Golgi body
Region of growth

Figure 4.1 A mycelium

especially nitrates and phosphates, from the soil, and the fungus obtains its carbon source from the photosynthetic activities of the green plant. There are two types of mycorrhizae:

- Ectotrophic mycorrhizae are usually members of the Basidiomycota. The fungal mycelium is external, often surrounding the smaller roots, and hyphae penetrate between the cell walls of the outer part of the root of the host.
- Endotrophic mycorrhizae are usually Zygomycota, where the mycelium is internal and the hyphae produce haustoria which enter the root cells.

Most trees and shrubs have ectotrophic mycorrhizae and there is much evidence to suggest that the growth of these plants on poorer soils is more rapid due to the presence of the fungus. Endotrophic mycorrhizae are characteristic of orchids, where the germinating seeds and young plants depend on the fungus for organic compounds.

A lichen is a very close association between a fungus and an alga, and does not resemble either partner. In the Five Kingdom classification, the lichens are given phylum status within the Fungi (the Mycophycophyta, to which they belong will be discussed later in this chapter).

The fungi reproduce both sexually and asexually. Sexual reproduction involves the fusion or conjugation of hyphae of different mating types, or strains, to form a dikaryotic mycelium. Pairs of haploid nuclei do not fuse immediately, but grow and divide within the hyphae. Eventually, often at a much later stage, fusion of the haploid nuclei occurs to form diploid zygotes. At some stage, the zygotes undergo meiosis to form haploid spores, which can develop directly into hyphae to form a new mycelium. Many members of this kingdom produce quite complex and distinctive fruiting structures, called sporophores, after sexual fusion.

Asexual reproduction is usually by means of spores: sporangiospores, if produced in a sporangium, and conidiospores formed at the apex of a specialised hypha called a conidiophore. The asexual methods of reproduction result in the formation of vast numbers of tiny, light spores, each surrounded by a resistant wall. This method of reproduction usually occurs in all groups when conditions for growth are favourable, but it is the only type of reproduction in the Phylum Deuteromycota, where no organs

of sexual reproduction have been observed.

Fungi are of great economic importance. On the one hand, parasitic fungi are responsible for diseases of crop plants and forest trees, and saprotrophs can cause spoilage of stored food and products made of paper and leather. On the other hand, saprotrophs are important in ecosystems as decomposers of the remains of plants and animals, releasing and recycling valuable mineral nutrients into the soil. These mineral nutrients are essential for the growth of green plants. Fungi are also important in the production of alcoholic beverages such as beer, wine and spirits, for giving characteristic flavours to Roquefort and Camembert cheeses, for providing the raising agent in the baking industry and directly as food (cultivated mushrooms and truffles) and as sources of vitamins. In addition, fungi are sources of antibiotics (*Penicillium*) and have been used in research into biochemical pathways and genetics (*Neurospora* and *Sordaria*).

It is difficult to trace the ancestry of the fungi, because they differ so much from plants and animals, although the oldest fossils have been found in the Devonian period in association with plant tissue. It seems most likely that they evolved from protoctistan ancestors. It is estimated that there are about 100 000 species of fungi in existence at the present time, with the probability that many more exist and are as yet undiscovered.

Five phyla are recognised in the Five Kingdom system of classification:

- Phylum Zygomycota (*Mucor, Rhizopus*)
- Phylum Ascomycota (*Saccharomyces, Neurospora*)
- Phylum Basidiomycota (*Agaricus, Puccinia*)
- Phylum Deuteromycota (*Penicillium*)
- Phylum Mycophycophyta (*Cladonia, Xanthoria*).

■ PHYLUM ZYGOMYCOTA

The members of this phylum lack cross walls, or septa, except where they are formed in connection with the reproductive structures. There are about 600 species, mostly terrestrial and found growing on decaying vegetation, although some are parasitic on animals.

Zygomycetes reproduce asexually (Fig.4.2) by the production of sporangiospores, which develop inside sporangia borne on special hyphae, the sporangiophores. Sporangiospores are haploid (*n*) and give rise to a haploid mycelium on germination. Sexual reproduction (Fig.4.3) involves the formation of gametangia, of opposite mating types, which grow towards each other and fuse. The fused gametangia develop a thick wall, forming a zygospore, inside which the nuclei fuse in pairs (2*n*), followed by meiosis to form haploid (*n*) spores. Both types of reproduction, the asexual cycle and the sexual, are well shown in the Mucorales.

The Mucorales, to which both *Mucor* and *Rhizopus* belong, includes saprotrophs which feed on a wide variety of organic substrates. They are very common in soil and in the air, and can be found on dung, bread and cooked food as well as decaying plant and animal matter, so it is not difficult to obtain examples by exposing a piece of moistened brown bread to the atmosphere for 24 hours. If this is then covered and kept in a warm place, cottony white threads appear on the surface

after a few days, followed by the appearance of masses of tiny black sporangia. There are a few parasitic genera, which cause soft rots.

Electron micrograph of a sporangium of the common bread mould *Mucor mucedo*

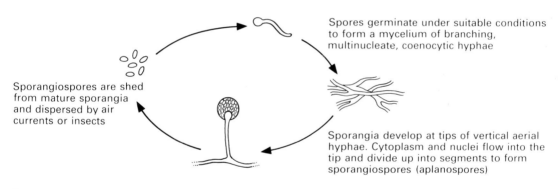

Spores germinate under suitable conditions to form a mycelium of branching, multinucleate, coenocytic hyphae

Sporangia develop at tips of vertical aerial hyphae. Cytoplasm and nuclei flow into the tip and divide up into segments to form sporangiospores (aplanospores)

Sporangiospores are shed from mature sporangia and dispersed by air currents or insects

Figure 4.2 Asexual cycle of *Mucor*

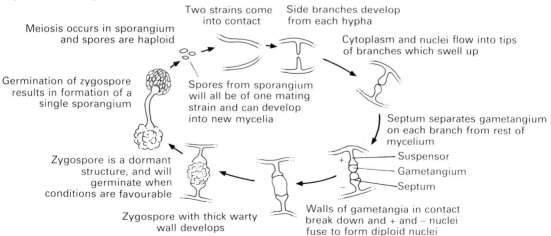

Two strains come into contact

Side branches develop from each hypha

Cytoplasm and nuclei flow into tips of branches which swell up

Meiosis occurs in sporangium and spores are haploid

Septum separates gametangium on each branch from rest of mycelium

Suspensor

Gametangium

Septum

Germination of zygospore results in formation of a single sporangium

Spores from sporangium will all be of one mating strain and can develop into new mycelia

Walls of gametangia in contact break down and + and – nuclei fuse to form diploid nuclei

Zygospore is a dormant structure, and will germinate when conditions are favourable

Zygospore with thick warty wall develops

Figure 4.3 Sexual cycle of *Mucor*

The zygomycete *Pilobolus kleinii* is found on the fresh dung of herbivores such as sheep, horses and rabbits. After growing for four or five days the spore mass is carried on a sporangiophore about 1 cm high. It is explosively squirted a distance of a metre or more away from the dung and on to the grass. A new herbivore injests spores with the grass and the spores survive the intestinal journey to be deposited with the animal's dung and to germinate. The fascinating point is that the sporangiophore grows towards the incident light. As can be seen in Fig.4.4 there is a type of 'simple eye' where the clear rounded part acts as a lens and focuses light on to an orange coloured 'retina'. If there is uneven illumination, a rapid growth on one side of the sporangiophore causes the sticky spore mass to be pointed to the light before the turgid cell explodes.

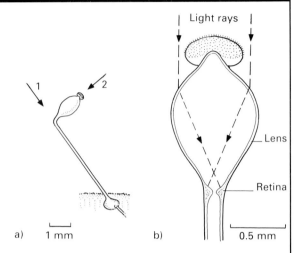

Figure 4.4 *Pilobolus kleinii* (a) growing from dung towards light 1 and bending when direction of illumination was changed to 2. (b) showing how sporangiophore acts as simple eye so that spore mass is projected towards light source.

■ PHYLUM ASCOMYCOTA

Ascomycetes, which include the yeasts and bread moulds, are distinguished from the other groups of fungi by possessing hyphae with cross-walls and forming ascospores in an ascus. The cells of the hyphae are usually uninucleate and the walls contain large amounts of chitin (see p. 67). Asexual reproduction is achieved by means of conidiospores, which are formed in succession at the tip of a conidiophore. These spores are easily detached and light, so are readily dispersed in air currents. Sexual reproduction involves the fusion of two compatible nuclei within an ascus to produce a diploid zygote nucleus. This will undergo a meiotic division immediately, producing four haploid nuclei, each of which divides by mitosis. Eight haploid nuclei result and develop into ascospores. The formation of the asci occurs in a number of different ways, characteristic of the groups within the phylum. In most genera, the asci are produced in some kind of fruiting structure called an ascocarp, and release of the ascospores is brought about by their forcible ejection through a pore in the apex of the ascus.

Saccharomyces (Fig.4.5) is a genus of unicellular ascomycetes which do not form hyphae. Several related species have economic significance in the baking and brewing industries:
- *S. cerevisiae* (bakers' or brewers' yeast) used in the brewing of beer and baking
- *S. carlsbergensis* used in the brewing of lager
- *S. ellipsoideus* used in wine-making.

The cells are ellipsoidal to spherical, surrounded by a cell wall composed of polymers of glucose and mannose. The cytoplasm contains typical eukaryotic organelles, glycogen granules, oil globules and a large, usually centrally situated vacuole. The nucleus is situated to one side of the vacuole.

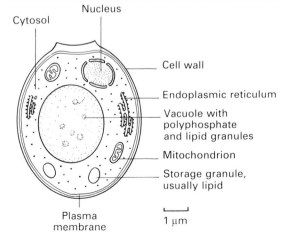

Figure 4.5 *Saccharomyces* structure as revealed by electron microscopy

In the life cycle (Fig.4.6), there is an alternation of a haploid (*n*) generation with a diploid (*2n*) one. The vegetative cells are diploid and grow, reproducing by a process called budding. They can undergo meiosis to form an ascus containing four ascospores, two of the plus (+) mating type, or strain, and two of the minus (–) type. Each ascospore can behave as a gamete and fuses with a gamete of the opposite mating strain, restoring the diploid condition. The diploid zygote resumes growth and budding.

Saccharomyces will respire aerobically in the presence of oxygen, forming carbon dioxide and water as waste products. In the absence of oxygen, or if it is in low concentration, anaerobic respiration, or fermentation, takes place, resulting in the formation of carbon dioxide and ethanol. In baking, yeast, together with some sugar, is mixed with the dough and it respires both aerobically and anaerobically, as no attempt is made to exclude oxygen. Bubbles of carbon dioxide are produced, which are trapped in the elastic dough, making it spongy. When the dough is cooked at a high temperature, any water and ethanol formed evaporate.

In beer brewing (Fig.4.7), yeast is added to the cooled wort, a sugary liquid obtained from the malting barley which has been allowed to germinate and is then crushed. The yeast converts the sugars in the wort, mostly maltose, to ethanol and carbon dioxide in about 2-5 days. The yeast is then separated from the liquid; some is kept to inoculate the next batch of wort and the rest is sold to make products such as yeast extract and vitamin preparations.

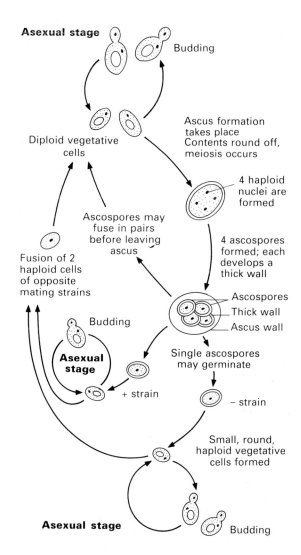

Figure 4.6 The life cycle of *Saccharomyces cerevisiae*

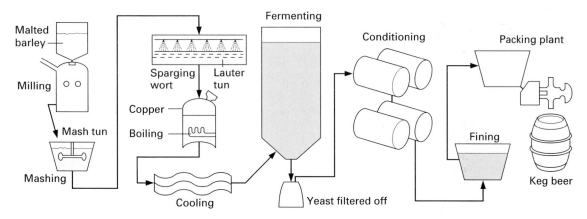

Figure 4.7 Summary diagram of beer manufacture

In wine-making, the grapes are crushed, releasing the sugary juices. Traditionally, the grapes would be left untreated, but in some areas, sulphur dioxide is used to kill off organisms on the outside of the skins. If the grapes are untreated, then the naturally occurring yeasts would bring about the fermentation of the sugars, but if treated, the juices have to be inoculated with the wine yeast, *Saccharomyces ellipsoideus*. The fermentation takes several days. The juice from both black, or red, and white grapes yields a white wine, but in order to get red wine, the skins of the grapes are left in so the the alcohol dissolves the red pigment which gives the wine its colour. For the production of white wine, the skins of the grapes are removed before fermentation starts. Some wines undergo a secondary fermentation, in which extra sugar is added. The carbon dioxide which is produced makes the wines carbonated, giving them the 'fizz' associated with sparkling wines of the champagne type.

Neurospora crassa (Fig.4.8), the red bread mould, is more typical of the ascomycetes, in that a mycelium is formed and eight ascospores are produced in each ascus. *Neurospora* has been used widely in genetic research. Meiosis occurs in each ascus and the four cells produced undergo a mitotic division, eventually resulting in the formation of eight ascospores. The ascospores stay in a row in the order in which they were formed. Each of them can be removed and grown separately, so that the genetic constitution can be determined. Such information can enable the behaviour of the chromosomes during meiosis to be worked out, and hence the location on the chromosome of certain genes.

■ PHYLUM BASIDIOMYCOTA

This phylum includes the smuts, rusts, mushrooms and stinkhorns, and is distinguished from the other phyla by the production of basidiospores on the outside of basidia. In addition, many basidiomycetes form compact fruiting bodies and possess clamp connections between adjacent cells of the mycelium.

Basidiospores germinate to produce a primary mycelium, which develops septa, dividing the hyphae up into uninucleate 'cells' or segments. Adjacent uninucleate cells may fuse and give rise to a secondary mycelium of binucleate cells. This mycelium can grow by

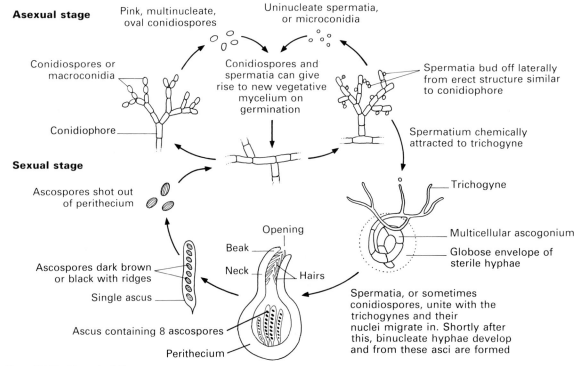

Asexual stage

Pink, multinucleate, oval conidiospores

Uninucleate spermatia, or microconidia

Conidiospores or macroconidia

Conidiospores and spermatia can give rise to new vegetative mycelium on germination

Spermatia bud off laterally from erect structure similar to conidiophore

Conidiophore

Sexual stage

Spermatium chemically attracted to trichogyne

Ascospores shot out of perithecium

Trichogyne

Multicellular ascogonium

Opening

Beak

Globose envelope of sterile hyphae

Ascospores dark brown or black with ridges

Neck

Hairs

Single ascus

Spermatia, or sometimes conidiospores, unite with the trichogynes and their nuclei migrate in. Shortly after this, binucleate hyphae develop and from these asci are formed

Ascus containing 8 ascospores

Perithecium

Figure 4.8 The life cycle of *Neurospora crassa*

producing daughter cells, the two nuclei in the parent cells dividing simultaneously. During this process, clamp connections are often formed (Fig.4.9) as a result of a mechanism which ensures that sister nuclei are separated during daughter cell formation.

Clamp connections are formed during the growth of the secondary mycelium

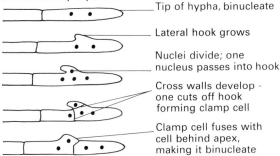

- Tip of hypha, binucleate
- Lateral hook grows
- Nuclei divide; one nucleus passes into hook
- Cross walls develop - one cuts off hook forming clamp cell
- Clamp cell fuses with cell behind apex, making it binucleate

Figure 4.9 Clamp connection formation

Basidia only develop on the secondary mycelium. Each basidium contains two haploid nuclei, which fuse to give rise to a diploid zygote nucleus. This undergoes meiosis, forming four haploid nuclei, which migrate into swellings, called sterigmata, at the apex of the basidium. Each developing basidiospore is then separated from the basidium by a cross wall. In *Agaricus* (Fig.4.10), the field mushroom, the nucleus of each basidiospore divides mitotically, so that the basidiospores are binucleate when they are discharged.

Some of the Basidiomycota are of economic importance as they can cause serious diseases to crops and timber. The smuts and the rusts can affect crops such as coffee, beans and cereals, and have been known as pathogens (disease-producing) since Roman times. Some species can infect forest trees and destroy timber. *Serpula lacrymans*, the dry rot fungus, can cause extensive damage to houses, infecting damp timber and spreading rapidly in the right conditions. Many form mycorrhizal associations with forest trees, and this is the reason for certain species of agarics (mushroom-like basidiomycetes) growing in specific types of woodland. One good example of this is the occurrence of the fly agaric, with its red cap dotted with white spots, amongst birch trees. Many of the agarics are edible, sought after for their flavour rather than for their nutritional value, but amateurs should beware of eating unknown species, as there are some which are definitely poisonous and many which have a disagreeable taste.

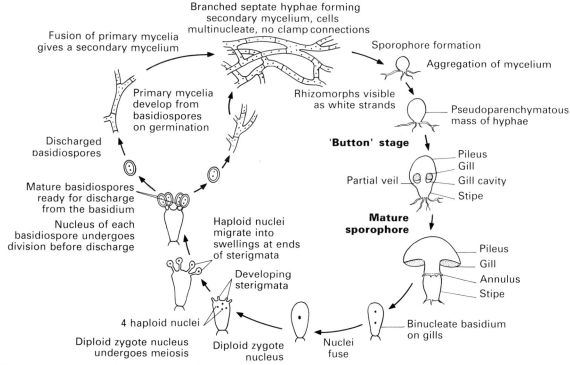

Figure 4.10 The life cycle of *Agaricus campestris*

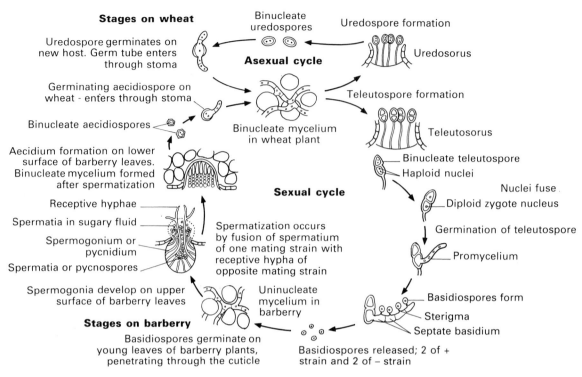

Stages on wheat

Uredospore germinates on new host. Germ tube enters through stoma

Germinating aecidiospore on wheat - enters through stoma

Binucleate aecidiospores

Aecidium formation on lower surface of barberry leaves. Binucleate mycelium formed after spermatization

Receptive hyphae

Spermatia in sugary fluid

Spermogonium or pycnidium

Spermatia or pycnospores

Spermogonia develop on upper surface of barberry leaves

Stages on barberry

Basidiospores germinate on young leaves of barberry plants, penetrating through the cuticle

Binucleate uredospores

Uredospore formation

Asexual cycle

Uredosorus

Teleutospore formation

Binucleate mycelium in wheat plant

Teleutosorus

Binucleate teleutospore

Haploid nuclei

Nuclei fuse

Diploid zygote nucleus

Germination of teleutospore

Promycelium

Basidiospores form

Sterigma

Septate basidium

Sexual cycle

Spermatization occurs by fusion of spermatium of one mating strain with receptive hypha of opposite mating strain

Uninucleate mycelium in barberry

Basidiospores released; 2 of + strain and 2 of − strain

Figure 4.11 The life cycle of *Puccinia graminis*

Puccinia graminis causes black stem rust of cereals. It does not kill its host, but it causes serious losses in yield because its main effect is to reduce the size of the grains. It has a complicated life cycle (Fig.4.11), with two hosts, wheat plants and the barberry, *Berberis vulgaris*. Control of the disease can be achieved by using disease-resistant varieties of wheat, eradication of the secondary host, the barberry, and the use of fungicides.

■ PHYLUM DEUTEROMYCOTA

This phylum does not represent such a natural grouping of species and genera as do the Zygomycota, Ascomycota and Basidiomycota. The main characteristic which links the organisms, apart from the fact that they all have septate hyphae and produce spores, is that they lack sexual reproductive structures. In evolutionary terms, this group consists of members of the Ascomycota and Basidiomycota which have lost the ability to form asci or basidia. In some cases, organisms classified in this phylum have later been shown to reproduce sexually, often leading to their reclassification, a new name and a certain amount of subsequent confusion as to their identity.

Penicillium spp. are used in the ripening of some cheeses. Camembert gets its distinctive properties by being sprayed with the spores of *Penicillium camembertii*, and spores of *Penicillium roqueforti* are injected into the curd which will eventually form Roquefort cheese. *Penicillium notatum* (Fig.4.12) is well-known as the source of the antibiotic penicillin, discovered by accident by Alexander Fleming. He found that colonies of the bacterium *Streptococcus* were killed by a substance which had been produced by a fungal colony contaminating one of his cultures. The mould was identified as *Penicillium notatum* and the substance extracted, purified and eventually produced commercially. This took many years as the penicillin was difficult to produce in large quantities. Other *Penicillium* species were investigated and another species, *P. chrysogenum* was found to produce penicillin in greater quantities than *P. notatum*. *P. chrysogenum* was also easier to use in the large-scale fermenters which had been developed to cope with the increased demand for the antibiotic. Nowadays, genetically engineered strains of the fungus are used, yielding much more antibiotic than the naturally occurring species.

A condiophore with the terminal chains of conidia is known as a penicillus, because of its brush-like appearance

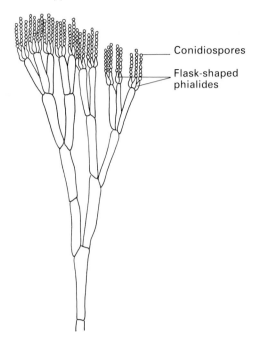

Conidiospores

Flask-shaped phialides

Figure 4.12 Imperfect (asexual) stages of *Penicillium* spp.

Antibiotics, such as penicillin, are secondary metabolites, produced at later stages of growth and not usually while the organism is in the beginning of the exponential phase.

■ PHYLUM MYCOPHYCOPHYTA

Lichens are partnerships between a fungus and an alga or a bacterium. The two partners grow in very close association with each other, so that neither is distinguishable and they form organisms with quite distinct features. The fungal component, or mycobiont, is usually a member of the Ascomycota, and the other partner, referred to as the phycobiont, usually belongs to the Chlorophyta or the Cyanobacteria. There are about 25 000 species, and in the majority the phycobiont is either *Trebouxia*, a chlorophyte, or *Nostoc*, a cyanobacterium.

The phycobiont is able to photosynthesise and supplies carbohydrates for the mycobiont, which in its turn probably supplies minerals to the phycobiont. Fungal hyphae form the vegetative thallus and the fruiting structures. The phycobiont structures are confined to a thin layer just below the surface (Fig. 4.13).

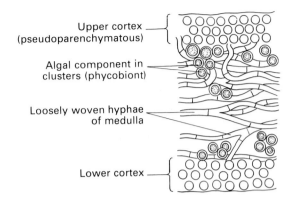

Upper cortex (pseudoparenchymatous)

Algal component in clusters (phycobiont)

Loosely woven hyphae of medulla

Lower cortex

Figure 4.13 Section through thallus of *Xanthoria*

There are three types of growth form:
• crustose, e.g. *Xanthoria*, found as encrustations on rocks and gravestones
• fruticose, e.g. *Cladonia*, shrubby, upright types
• foliose, e.g. *Parmelia*, leaflike, on twigs and branches, amongst vegetation.

Lichens are found growing in a variety of situations, and many species are able to survive where other organisms could not. Lichens are important colonisers of bare rock, able to survive for long periods of time in very dry conditions. They are extremely sensitive to atmospheric pollutants such as sulphur dioxide, as this penetrates to the phycobiont and destroys the chlorophyll, causing irreversible damage. Indicator species, varying in their tolerance to specific pollutants, are recognised and used to monitor pollution levels quantitatively. Lack of lichens on the trees and buildings in towns and cities has been attributed to the lower humidity and higher temperatures of these areas, as well as to the higher levels of pollution.

Xanthoria parientina on limestone rock

THE PLANT KINGDOM

■ GENERAL CHARACTERISTICS

Until now you were probably quite sure about what is a plant. It is easy to forget about the smaller ones and to be unaware of Cycads, horsetails and Club mosses. So what is a plant?

The distinguishing features of the members of the plant kingdom are that they:
• are multicellular
• are eukaryotic
• are photosynthetic
• possess cellulose cell walls
• all develop from embryos.
An embryo is the result of the fusion of gametes during the sexual stage of the life cycle, so all plants will have a sexual stage or have evolved from ancestors that did.

In the life cycle, there is an alternation of haploid generation with diploid generation. The haploid generation produces gametes on a plant called a gametophyte, whereas the diploid generation is called the sporophyte and produces spores. (The terms haploid and diploid describe the chromosome number. Cells which are haploid (n) have half the number of chromosomes found in diploid ($2n$) cells. In meiosis the chromosome number is halved; in fertilisation the diploid number is restored (see Fig.5.1).

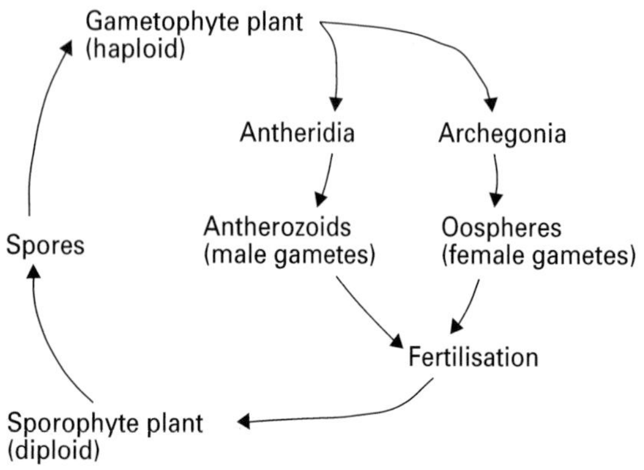

The kingdom can be subdivided into the bryophytes and the tracheophytes, on the presence or absence of specialised conducting tissue, the vascular tissue. This and the further subdivision into phyla is shown in Fig.5.2. The phyla shown are the most abundant, but there are four other tracheophyte phyla containing fewer present-day species:
• Phylum Psilophyta
• Phylum Cycadophyta (cycads)
• Phylum Ginkgophyta (Maidenhair tree)
• Phylum Gnetophyta.

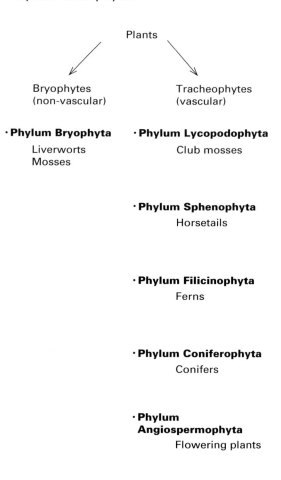

Figure 5.2 The major phyla of the plant kingdom

Figure 5.1 Alternation of generations

FOOD FROM LUPINS!

Relatives of the humble garden lupin may soon be grown for food on a large scale, possibly replacing soya beans in importance. The cultivation of certain species of the genus *Lupinus* dates from pre-history and they have been identified as food plants as far back as 4000 BC.

Now there is renewed interest in them because of their ability to produce high yields when grown on relatively infertile soils. Lupins can tolerate acidic soils, low in nutrients and organic matter. They will thrive on free-draining soils, but are not adapted to alkaline soils.

Until fairly recently, lupins were grown mainly as soil improvers and with cereals for grazing or silage. Narrow-leaved lupin, *Lupinus angustifolius*, is a dual-purpose crop in parts of Australia, South Africa, Spain and Portugal. It is grazed by sheep during the middle period of its growth and then left to flower and set seed before being harvested for its grain. Recently the growth of this lupin in Western Australia as a grain legume in arable rotations has expanded with remarkable success, and international surveys have indicated that large areas of the Soviet Union, Europe, South America and South Africa would be suitable for cultivation, providing high yields in cool, temperate climates.

With world food shortages always in our thoughts, any novel way of producing valuable edible protein, especially in less fertile regions, bears investigation and further research. Crops such as soya beans, peas and field beans are well established as supplying useful nutrients, but recent analysis of lupin grains compares very favourably with these

more widely grown legumes. *Lupinus albus* (white lupin), *L. angustifolius* (narrow-leafed lupin) and *L. luteus* (yellow lupin) are three European species which have been cultivated.

In addition to their nutritive content, all the grain legumes, including soya beans and lupins, contain chemicals, such as alkaloids, which are not nutritionally beneficial; some reduce growth and others can cause infertility and severe illnesses. The levels of these substances in lupins are generally low, and it is possible to breed so-called 'sweet' or low-alkaloid cultivars which are acceptable.

Research has shown that, although lupin grains have been incorporated into animal feed, their use for human food has not yet been fully exploited. There is great potential for the manufacture of lupin seed meal and hydrolysed lupin protein as a substitute for soya flour, and these products also appear to give satisfactory results when used in the preparation of fermented Asian foods as well as in the experimental preparation of biscuits and milk substitutes.

As with most things, the future of lupins as a cash crop will be decided by economic forces, but they offer an interesting alternative to other grain legumes.

Mean nutrient composition of whole seed (% dry matter)

Species	Protein	Lipid	Carbohydrate	Fibre
L. albus	40	12	40	7
L. angustifolius	33	6	41	15
Soya bean	38	19	34	5
Field bean	26	2	60	8

Table 5.1 Comparison of food content of some lupins with other legumes

(Adapted from 'Exploited Plants: Lupins' by Watkin Williams, *Biologist*, 36 (4), published by the Institute of Biology.)

The news item illustrates the importance of plants to all the other living organisms on the planet, as they are the producers, able to fix carbon dioxide and build up complex organic compounds using light energy. Very few other organisms have this ability and it is the basis of all food chains and food webs, so, without plants, life as we know it would be unsustainable.

All the members of the plant kingdom show adaptations to life on land, although many depend on water for reproduction or as their habitat at some stage in their life cycle. It is generally accepted that green land plants evolved from green algae, similar to the present-day Chlorophyta. The two groups possess many common features, such as similar photosynthetic pigments, cellulose cell walls and patterns of mitosis.

Tracheophyte land plants are thought to have evolved during the Devonian Period, about 400 million years ago (Fig.5.3). Evidence for this comes from dating the rocks in which fossils of the earliest plants have been found. The bryophytes do not have hard tissues such as xylem, so their fossil record is scanty and it is not easy to estimate more precisely when their evolution took place, but presumably it pre-dates the tracheophytes, which are considered to have more advanced features.

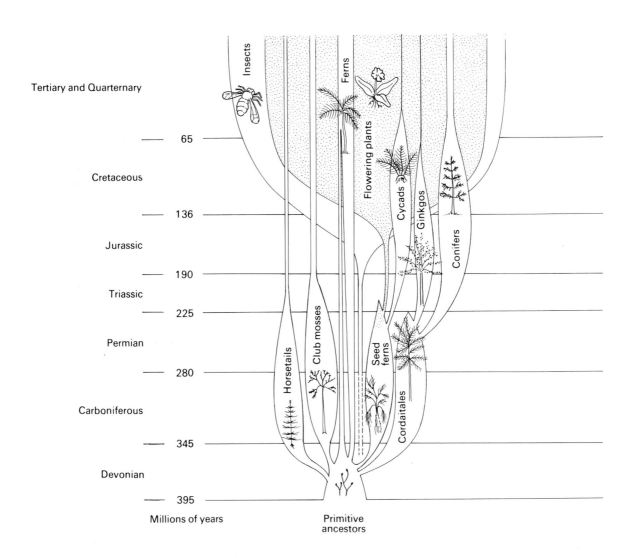

Figure 5.3 Geological time scale showing evolution of flowering plants and insects

Today the flowering plants dominate the land, with more than a quarter of a million known species. It is a remarkable fact that each survey of new areas, particularly the species-rich rain forests, discovers new species, some of which have been used as foods or medicines by the indigenous people. How many more remain to be discovered and named by botanists? Sadly many of these areas are being destroyed before the questions can be answered.

Flowering plants are of considerable economic importance, providing food crops for human beings and their domestic animals, as well as building materials, fuel and fibres. Together with the other phyla in the kingdom, their photosynthetic activities convert solar energy into chemical energy, whilst at the same time maintaining the balance of gases in the atmosphere. Green plants are producers and are fundamental to the food chains in the biosphere.

Phylum	Features
Bryophyta	Dominant gametophyte generation; sporophyte dependent on gametophyte; no true roots, but rhizoids for anchorage; no waterproof cuticle; male gametes with a pair of undulipodia; environmental water needed for fertilisation.
Lycopodophyta	Dominant sporophyte generation; small leaves spirally arranged; sporangia in cones; some with one type of spore, some with microspores and megaspores; gametophyte small, short-lived, may be underground; male gametes with a pair of undulipodia; environmental water needed for fertilisation.
Sphenophyta	Dominant sporophyte generation; small leaves in whorls (rings) around stem; sporangia in cones; spores of one type only; two types of gametophyte produced, male and female; male gametes with several undulipodia; environmental water needed for fertilisation.
Filicinophyta	Dominant sporophyte generation; large leaves; sporangia in sori (groups) on backs of leaves; spores of one type only; gametophyte small (prothallus), short-lived; male gametes with numerous undulipodia; environmental water needed for fertilisation.
Coniferophyta	Dominant sporophyte generation; gametophyte generation much reduced, dependent on sporophyte; cone-bearing; microspores and megaspores produced; no true flowers or fruits; produce naked seeds, no undulipodia; no environmental water needed for fertilisation; mostly trees, very few shrubs.
Angiospermophyta	Dominant sporophyte generation; gametophyte reduced to a few cells enclosed within sporophyte; produce true flowers; microspores (pollen grains) and megaspores; seeds enclosed within fruit; no environmental water needed for fertilisation; no undulipodia; herbs, trees and shrubs.

Table 5.2 Some characteristic features of the major phyla

PHYLUM BRYOPHYTA

The members of this phylum can be regarded as the amphibians of the plant world! They, like frogs and toads, show adaptations to life on land whilst retaining features associated with life in water. Most bryophytes will not show any growth unless they are in a damp habitat, but they can remain dry for long periods, reviving spectacularly when water is available again. Their distribution is therefore limited by their dependence on water.

The phylum consists of three classes:
- Hepaticae (the liverworts) with about 9000 species
- Anthocerotae (the hornworts) with about 100 species
- Musci (the mosses) with about 16 000 species.

They are all small plants, lacking xylem and phloem, although some of the larger species of mosses do have conducting tissue. They have some features in common with the green algae, posessing male gametes with two forwardly directed undulipodia, or flagella, and identical photosynthetic pigments. The most conspicuous feature of the bryophytes is their clear-cut alternation of generations (Fig.5.4), where the gametophyte is dominant.

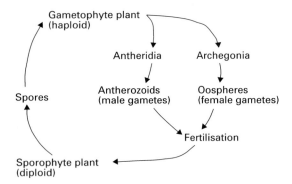

Figure 5.4 Alternation of generations in bryophytes

The gametophyte is a leafy (thalloid) structure, anchored to its substrate (soil, tree trunk, etc.) by tiny root-like rhizoids. When leaves are present, they are small, one cell thick and do not have a cuticle, so they dry up very easily. The sporophyte develops from the fertilised oosphere and grows out of the female archegonium. It is dependent on the gametophyte for water and for food. In the liverworts, the sporophyte is totally dependent on the gametophyte until the spores are released, but in the mosses the capsule can become green and carry out photosynthesis. It is the sporophyte which shows adaptations to life on land in that it can have pores or stomata for the exchange of gases and there is a mechanism for spore dispersal which involves drying out of the capsule.

Vegetative reproduction (asexual) is very efficient: the production of tiny groups of cells called gemmae occurs in many species. These are formed on the surface of the gametophyte, often in cup-shaped structures, drop off the parent gametophyte plant and grow in suitably moist conditions. Small pieces of the gametophyte or sporophyte plants can also break off and grow into new plants in the right conditions.

Bryophytes are important colonisers of bare soil, growing rapidly on sand dunes, mountains and in areas where burning has occurred, and even in plant pots in glasshouses. Many species are found in tropical regions, where they grow as epiphytes on the trees in the rain forests. The genus *Sphagnum* is important in the formation of peat bogs worldwide. Peat is economically important as a domestic fuel: it is cut into blocks, dried and stored for later use, particularly in Ireland and Scotland. In Scandinavia and Ireland it is used as a fuel for power stations and is gathered in large quantities. Dry *Sphagnum* can absorb large quantities of water, and for this reason it has been used as an absorbent in surgical dressings and in babies' nappies. Peat moss is used by florists, gardeners and horticulturalists for its water-holding properties, and for packing live plants where moisture is required. The increasing use of peat by gardeners has resulted in a threat to peatland habitats and there is now a demand for an alternative growing medium such as coconut fibre.

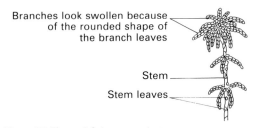

Branches look swollen because of the rounded shape of the branch leaves

Stem

Stem leaves

Figure 5.5 Plants of *Sphagnum palustre*

The liverworts and mosses have many similar features, but differ in certain details (Table 5.3).

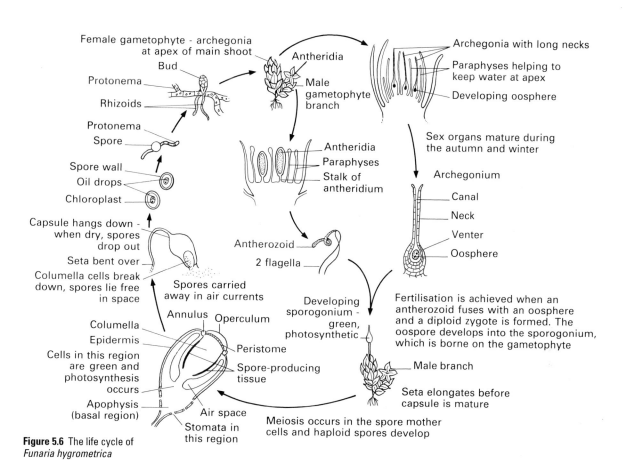

Figure 5.6 The life cycle of *Funaria hygrometrica*

Feature	Liverworts	Mosses
Form of gametophyte	A few (16%) thalloid Most (84%) leafy	All leafy
Leaves	No midrib Arranged in rows on stem Simple or lobed	Midrib often present Spirally arranged Simple, never lobed
Rhizoids	Unicellular	Multicellular
Sporophyte	Simple Dependent on gametophyte No stomata - photosynthetic	Complex Partially dependent on gametophyte Photosynthetic with stomata
Capsule	Splits into valves when mature	Has operculum (lid) which is forced off at maturity
Spore dispersal	Aided by elaters	Aided by peristome teeth
Spore germination	Gametophyte formed directly	Protonema formed which produces buds which give rise to gametophyte

Table 5.3 Differences between liverworts and mosses

■ PHYLUM LYCOPODOPHYTA

The modern representatives of this phylum, some five genera containing 1000 species, are inconspicuous plants, mostly found in tropical regions, where they grow on the trunks of trees as epiphytes. In colder regions, the plants are smaller, with erect or creeping stems, and are restricted to mountainous areas in the north and west of the British Isles. The lycopods were most numerous in the swamp forests of the Upper Carboniferous period, about 300 million years ago. Around 200 different species of tree lycopods have been described from fossil remains, so the members of this phylum would have contributed significantly to the vegetation during that period and subsequently to the coal produced. Competition from the gymnosperms and angiosperms, as they evolved, resulted in the majority of species of lycopods becoming extinct.

The sporophyte is the dominant, and persistent, stage of the life cycle. It consists of a stem, bearing small leaves (microphylls), which are arranged spirally, and true, dichotomously branched, adventitious roots. There are fertile leaves bearing sporangia on their upper surfaces, called sporophylls, and these are grouped together at the apex of the stem forming a cone or strobilus. Spores are formed within the sporangia and when released they germinate into gametophytes, which bear male antheridia and female archegonia. Fertilisation is achieved by the fusion of a male gamete, an antherozoid, which swims by means of its two undulipodia, with a female gamete, an oosphere, situated at the base of an archegonium. The fertilised egg will develop into a new sporophyte, thus completing the alternation of generations.

Two genera are particularly well known: *Lycopodium*, from which the phylum gets its name, containing about 200 species, and *Selaginella*, containing about 700 species. Together these two genera make up the bulk of the living lycopods. A comparison of their life cycles shows that they differ from one another in that *Lycopodium* is homosporous, producing only one type of spore, whereas *Selaginella* is heterosporous, producing microspores and megaspores. This feature of *Selaginella*, together with other aspects of the life cycle (Table 5.4; Fig.5.7), indicates an evolutionary trend towards the production of a 'seed', which would have been of significant survival value in a terrestrial environment. In some species of the genus, there is a food store associated with the female spores (megaspores), female gametophytes develop within the megaspores and are sometimes retained on the parent sporophyte plant, where fertilisation takes place before the megaspore is shed. We know from the fossil record that many tree lycopods had 'seeds', but it is unlikely that the angiosperms evolved directly from members of this phylum, although the genus does provide some insight into the increasing adaptations to the terrestrial environment and a great reduction in the size and importance of the gametophyte generation - trends which led to the evolution of true seed plants.

The modern lycopods have very little economic importance, but they are ecologically significant as members of the vegetation of peaty, upland moors about 600 m above sea level.

■ PHYLUM SPHENOPHYTA

Only one genus of this phylum survives today: the genus *Equisetum* (the horsetails) with some 25 species, all herbaceous. As with the lycopods, there is an extensive fossil record, indicating a great variety of different species, some tree-like and achieving heights of about 15 metres. In the Devonian and Carboniferous periods, the Sphenophyta were the dominant plants of swampy forests, but nowadays the survivors are found in damp places along river banks, in marshy areas and on railway embankments.

Field horsetails
(*Equisetum arvense*)

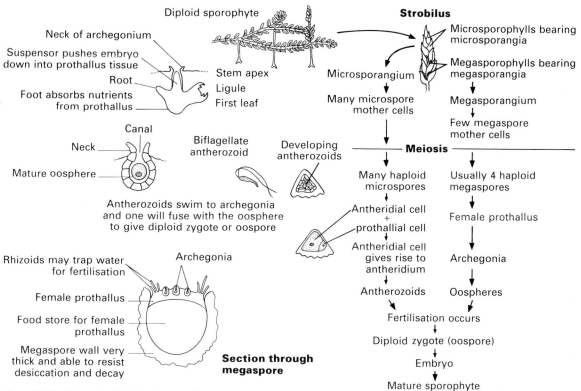

Figure 5.7 The life cycle of *Selaginella kraussiana*

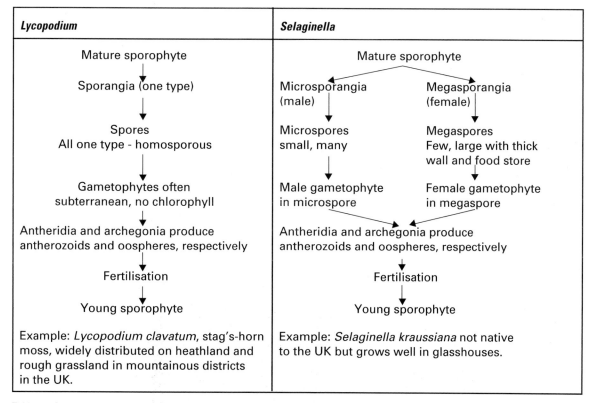

Lycopodium	Selaginella	
Mature sporophyte	Mature sporophyte	
↓	Microsporangia (male)	Megasporangia (female)
Sporangia (one type)	↓	↓
↓	Microspores small, many	Megaspores Few, large with thick wall and food store
Spores All one type - homosporous	↓	↓
↓	Male gametophyte in microspore	Female gametophyte in megaspore
Gametophytes often subterranean, no chlorophyll		
↓		
Antheridia and archegonia produce antherozoids and oospheres, respectively	Antheridia and archegonia produce antherozoids and oospheres, respectively	
↓	↓	
Fertilisation	Fertilisation	
↓	↓	
Young sporophyte	Young sporophyte	
Example: *Lycopodium clavatum*, stag's-horn moss, widely distributed on heathland and rough grassland in mountainous districts in the UK.	Example: *Selaginella kraussiana* not native to the UK but grows well in glasshouses.	

Table 5.4 Comparison of the life cycles of *Lycopodium* and *Selaginella*

The sporophyte of *Equisetum* is easily identified by its pale green, photosynthetic aerial shoots with whorls of branches arising from each node. Above the bases of the branches is a ring of small, colourless leaves. The stems are hollow and ribbed, and grow from an underground rhizome. In temperate regions, new shoots are produced each Spring, dying back at the end of the growing season. In some species, the sporangia are borne on specialised, unbranched shoots, terminating in a cone or strobilus. These shoots appear early in the growing season, before the vegetative shoots. In other species, the strobilus (Fig.5.8) occurs at the apex of the vegetative shoot.

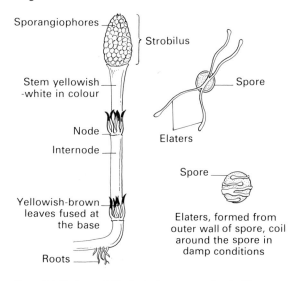

Figure 5.8 *Equisetum* (a) In *Equisetum arvense*, the strobilus develops on a specialized stem which lacks chlorophyll. (b) In dry conditions, the arms of the elaters unwind with jerky movements and help in the dispersal of the spores.

Each cone consists of some 50 sporangiophores bearing sporangia, inside which the spores develop. Each spore is wrapped around by long, coiled elaters which dry out in the air, with violent movements, thus aiding dispersal into any available wind currents. Only one type of spore is produced. The spores germinate to form tiny, photosynthetic gametophytes of two kinds: some are fairly short-lived and produce only male organs (antheridia), while others survive longer, producing first antheridia and then the female organs (the archegonia). Fertilisation requires a film of water in which the male gametes swim to the archegonia.

Equisetum spp. can be a nuisance to gardeners, because of the underground rhizome which is difficult to get rid of, and it is known to be poisonous to cattle and horses, due to the presence of an enzyme which breaks down thiamine. However, there are records of *Equisetum* being eaten by peasants in parts of Europe and by the American Indians. Because of its rough texture (due to the presence of silica in the epidermal cells) it has been used to clean cooking pots and pans, hence one of its common names, 'scouring rush'.

■ PHYLUM FILICINOPHYTA

The true ferns are a large group of plants containing about 12 000 living species, most of which are found in humid, tropical habitats. They show a great range of form, from very small water ferns such as *Salvinia* and *Azolla*, filmy ferns with leaves one cell thick and very little vascular tissue, to tree ferns with trunks 20 metres high, where support for the stem is achieved by means of persistent leaf bases. However diverse, all the members of the phylum have a dominant, diploid sporophyte generation alternating with a small, haploid free-living gametophyte, and require the presence of environmental water for fertilisation to occur.

As with the lycopods and the horsetails, there is an extensive fossil record for the true ferns. They appeared first in the Devonian period and were a major feature of the vegetation during the Carboniferous, eventually giving way to competition from the gymnosperms and then the angiosperms. The distinguishing feature which separates the true ferns from their allies is the presence of large leaves, called megaphylls, which are thought to have evolved from the fusion of lateral branches.

Fossilised leaves of *Alethopteris lonchitidis*, a plant from the Upper Carboniferous period

46

The leaves, or fronds, of the sporophytes of many ferns growing in temperate regions are pinnate, or deeply divided, and develop at the apex of a creeping underground rhizome bearing adventitious roots. Most of these ferns produce spores of one kind only (homosporous). The spores develop in sporangia which are found on the undersides of the fertile fronds. These fertile fronds can resemble the vegetative fronds (in *Dryopteris*, *Pteridium*), or they can be quite different (*Blechnum*). The sporangia either occur in clusters, called sori, or at the margins of the fronds. In both cases there is often a flap of protective tissue, the indusium, which shrivels as the sporangia ripen. The spores are catapulted out by the splitting open of the mature sporangium when it dries - an adaptation to life on land.

The gametophytes are small, green structures called prothalli, which are anchored to the soil by rhizoids. Usually each prothallus will bear both male and female reproductive organs (antheridia and archegonia, respectively). Though photosynthetic and totally independent of the sporophyte generation, the prothalli are delicate structures, liable to desiccation because they have no cuticle, and so they are relatively short-lived.

In temperate regions, such as the British Isles, the ferns are herbaceous plants confined to habitats which are moist at some time. *Dryopteris filix-mas* (Fig.5.9), the male fern, is common in damp woods and in hedgerows, whereas bracken, *Pteridium aquilinum*, is found typically on heathland, preferring acid soils. One of the smallest water ferns, *Azolla filiculoides*, has formed an association with a nitrogen-fixing cyanobacterium, *Anabaena*, and provides nitrogen in rice paddies, where the fern grows.

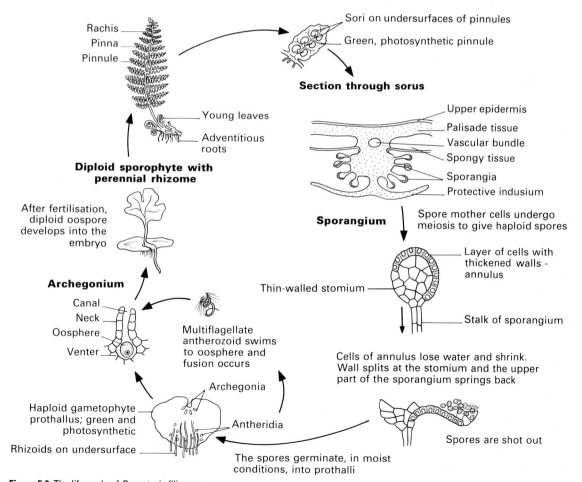

Figure 5.9 The life cycle of *Dryopteris filix-mas*

Dryopteris carthusiana

Cycad cones

The ferns are of little economic importance, except as sources of drugs and occasionally food. An oil extracted from *Dryopteris spp.* has been used to treat people infected with tapeworms (see p.63). The drug is supposed to dislodge the tapeworm, but unfortunately the scolex often remains attached to the gut wall and continues to produce segments. The young leaves of certain species may be used as food, but there is no evidence that ferns have any great nutritional value. In parts of the Andes, the Indians use the trunks of tree ferns as building material in preference to timber, because they do not shatter during earthquakes. Bracken is a nuisance to farmers as it is poisonous to grazing animals if eaten in large quantities. In hilly areas, the farmers will cut the bracken to prevent the sheep eating it; it is then often dried and used as bedding for the animals in winter.

■ PHYLUM CONIFEROPHYTA

This phylum, together with the Cycadophyta, Ginkgophyta and Gnetophyta, make up the group of plants formerly known as the gymnosperms (from Greek *gymnos* = naked and *sperma* = seed). These plants had naked seeds and dominated the land vegetation during the Jurassic and Cretaceous periods. Gymnosperms evolved during the late Carboniferous period, probably from seed ferns, all now extinct. During the Permian period they evolved rapidly, competing successfully with the tree lycopods and horsetails.

The Cycadophyta, shrubs with large, fern-like leaves, are confined to tropical and sub-tropical regions and there are about 100 living species. Their reproductive structures are borne in cones or strobili, on separate male and female plants. They are cultivated as ornamental plants and need to be grown in glasshouses in temperate regions. Some cycads are used for food in the tropics.

The Ginkgophyta is represented by one living species, *Ginkgo biloba* (Fig.5.10), the maidenhair tree, with its characteristic deciduous, bi-lobed leaves. It is now a cultivated tree; it is resistant to pollution and to insects, so is popular in gardens and ornamental parks.

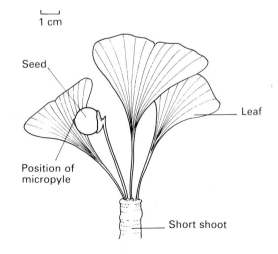

Figure 5.10 *Ginkgo biloba*. Tip of short shoot bearing ripe seed

Members of the Gnetophyta are restricted to tropical regions. They are of interest because they combine both conifer and angiosperm features. They have naked seeds and no undulipodia, like the conifers, but have water-conducting vessels in the xylem like the angiosperms. One genus, *Ephedra*, was the source of the drug ephedrine, used in the treatment of hay fever and asthma.

There are about 550 living species of conifers, most of which are tall trees, with needle-like leaves, dominating forests in temperate regions in both the northern and the southern hemispheres. Conifers are also quite common in the tropics. The phylum includes some familiar genera such as *Pinus* (pine), *Larix* (larch), *Picea* (spruce), *Taxus* (yew) and the largest of living plants, the giant sequoia (*Sequoiadendron gigantea*) found in California and achieving heights of 100 metres with a width of 8 metres.

Giant sequoia, Yosemite, California

In conifers, the apical bud continues to grow each year (monopodial growth), resulting in a characteristically cone-shaped or pyramidal tree. Their roots do not penetrate very deeply into the soil and often are associated with fungi, mycorrhizae). These associations are considered to be beneficial, if not essential, to the growth of trees, and enable them to thrive on poor soil.

In most conifers, male and female reproductive structures are borne in cones, produced on different parts of the same tree. Male cones consist of microsporophylls, each bearing two microsporangia, arranged

Pinus sylvestris
male flowers and
cone

spirally around a central axis. Inside the microsporangia, spore mother cells divide meiotically to produce haploid spores, called pollen grains. These pollen grains are often winged and easily dispersed by wind or air currents. Female cones vary in shape and size, according to the species, but conform to a basic pattern of woody ovuliferous scales spirally arranged, with two ovules on the surface of each scale.

Wind pollination occurs, the scales of the female cone opening up to allow the pollen grains in. The scales of the female cone then close tightly and remain closed during the time it takes for fertilisation to occur. Germination and the growth of the pollen grains inside the female cone is slow, and it is not until the second season that fertilisation takes place.

Pinus radiata, showing (top) first and second year cones, and (below) second and third year cones

The gametophyte generation is very much reduced, consisting of a few cells within the microspore in the male, and a prothallus bearing archegonia, situated in the ovule, in the female. In neither case are the gametophytes independent of the dominant sporophyte generation. The microspore germinates to produce a pollen tube which conveys the male gamete to the female archegonium, thus eliminating the need for environmental water for fertilisation (Fig.5.11). The male gametes do not have undulipodia.

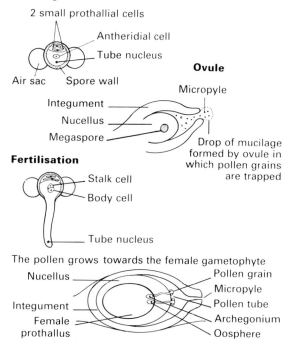

Pollen grain

2 small prothallial cells

Antheridial cell

Tube nucleus

Air sac   Spore wall

Ovule

Micropyle

Integument

Nucellus

Megaspore

Drop of mucilage formed by ovule in which pollen grains are trapped

Fertilisation

Stalk cell

Body cell

Tube nucleus

The pollen grows towards the female gametophyte

Nucellus

Pollen grain

Micropyle

Integument

Pollen tube

Female prothallus

Archegonium

Oosphere

Figure 5.11 The life cycle of *Pinus sylvestris*

Conifers are of great economic importance as they are a major source of timber for building and for the paper industry. The timber is called softwood, and it is widely used in the manufacture of chipboard and insulation board as well as for joinery and furniture. Many species of conifers produce large quantities of resin, which is a source of turpentine.

The female cones get bigger and eventually open up during the third season after pollination, to release the ripe seeds. Each seed has a papery wing attached to it, assisting dispersal in the air currents.

Conifers grow relatively quickly and can be grown successfully in less fertile areas, so they have been widely planted by the Forestry Commission throughout Great Britain and also by commercial growers. Initially, the Forestry Commission planted large areas of a single species, felling them all at the same time, but more recently these plantations have been replaced by mixed species, where the felling is staggered, thus preserving the habitats and preventing the possibility of soil erosion, as well as being aesthetically more pleasing to look at.

■ PHYLUM ANGIOSPERMOPHYTA

This phylum includes the plants known as the angiosperms or flowering plants, characterised by having enclosed seeds and reproductive organs in specialised structures called flowers. The members of this phylum form the dominant vegetation on the Earth today, able to colonise and survive in a wider range of terrestrial habitats than any other group of plants. The angiosperms evolved during the Cretaceous period and there are now more than 300 different flowering plant families with some 230 000 recognised species. The dominance of this group seems to be related to the simultaneous evolution of the insects and terrestrial chordates.

The angiosperms share many characteristics with the conifers, but there are significant differences which are summarised in Table 5.5. The angiosperms show a wide range of form, from large, woody trees such as oak (*Quercus* spp.) and beech (*Fagus* spp.) which form deciduous woodlands, to tiny herbaceous types such as groundsel (*Senecio* spp.) and shepherd's purse (*Capsella bursa-pastoris*), which are common garden weeds able to produce several generations during one growing season. The factor which links these extremes of form is the evolution of the seed, with its tough outer coat, its food store and its embryo. This group of plants is of considerable economic importance, providing food, drugs and medicines for humans, fibres for clothing and textiles, materials for furniture and housing, and food and pasture for domestic animals.

The phylum is sub-divided into two classes:
• Class Monocotyledones (mostly herbaceous plants)
• Class Dicotyledones (herbaceous and woody plants.

Coniferophyta	Angiospermophyta
Xylem tissue composed of tracheids only	Xylem tissue composed of vessels and tracheids
Reproductive structures in cones	Reproductive structures in flowers
Cones unisexual, containing either male or female spores	Flowers may be unisexual, but more usually hermaphrodite, containing both male and female structures
Wind pollination only	Wind and insect pollination
Female gametophyte multicellular	Female gametophyte much reduced; represented by embryo sac, a vacuolated cell containing eight nuclei
Archegonia formed in ovule	No archegonia formed
At fertilisation, one male nucleus fuses with the female oosphere nucleus; the second male nucleus breaks down	At fertilisation, one male nucleus fuses with the female nucleus; the second male nucleus fuses with two other nuclei (polar nuclei) in the embryo sac to give a 3N endosperm nucleus - process known as double fertilisation
Ovules develop on the surface of ovuliferous scales; not enclosed	Ovules develop within a closed structure, the carpel
Seeds have one integument	Seeds have two integuments
Worldwide distribution, limited range in form; mainly trees, with a few shrubs	Worldwide distribution, with great variety of different forms; trees, shrubs and herbaceous plants

Table 5.5 Summary of differences between Coniferophyta and Angiospermophyta

■ MONOCOTYLEDONES

■ Gramineae

The Gramineae is one of the largest families of the flowering plants, containing about 9000 species. In temperate regions, species form large areas of grassland which are important for the grazing of both wild and domesticated animals. Members of this family are also of economic significance as crop plants and have been cultivated for many centuries, providing cereal grains for the production of flour. (For further details of Gramineae used as food see *Biology Advanced Studies - Food Production*.) A few species are annuals (oats, wheat and meadow grass), but many are perennials, possessing runners or rhizomes. One common weed of gardens and farm crops is the common couch grass, which has persistent underground rhizomes which are very difficult to eradicate. Even the smallest portion left in the ground is able to regenerate the plant. The flowers of the Gramineae are unusual in that they do not have coloured petals and sepals (Fig.5.12). They are hermaphrodite, borne in spikelets and enclosed in structures called glumes or bracts. There are usually three stamens, with long filaments bearing large anthers, which hang out of the flower when mature. The female part of the flower consists of a single carpel, bearing two long feathery stigmas. These also hang out of the flower when the carpel is mature, so that available pollen can be trapped. Wind pollination is usual, although many of the cereals, such as wheat and barley, are self-pollinated.

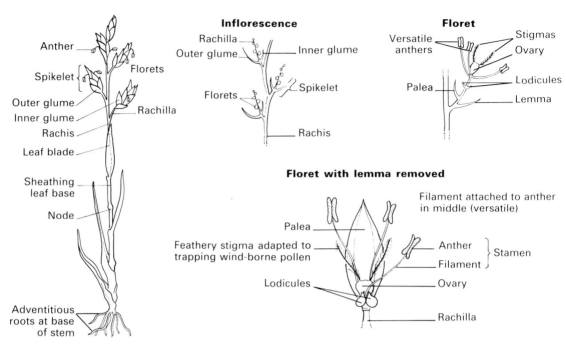

Figure 5.12 Grass inflorescence and flower structure

Monocotyledones	Dicotyledones
One cotyledon, or seed leaf, in the embryo	Two cotyledons, or seed leaves, in the embryo
Foliage leaves usually parallel-veined with smooth margins	Foliage leaves narrow at base, may be stalked or sessile, net veined (reticulate venation), frequently serrated, lobed or compound
Stems and roots very rarely become secondarily thickened (cambium tissue rare)	Stems and roots may become secondarily thickened (cambium tissue present)
Flower parts in 3s and multiples of 3; often no distinction between petals and sepals, called perianth	Flower parts in 4s or 5s, or multiples of these numbers; petals, forming the corolla, and sepals, forming the calyx, usually distinguishable
Mostly herbaceous, only a few species showing palm-like growth; no true trees; herbaceous plants may be annual or perennial	Herbaceous and woody; herbaceous plants may be annual, biennial, ephemeral or perennial
Examples of families: Gramineae (grasses) Liliaceae (bluebells) Iridaceae (crocus) Amaryllidaceae (daffodil)	Examples of families: Cruciferae (cabbage family) Papilionaceae (peas, beans) Rosaceae (apples, pears)

Table 5.6 Comparison of the Monocotyledones and Dicotyledones

The ovary contains one ovule and, after fertilisation, this develops into a one-seeded fruit called a caryopsis, where the ovary wall and the testa of the seed are fused.

The Gramineae include a wide range of important food plants.

Cereals:
Triticum vulgare (wheat)
Hordeum vulgare (barley)
Secale cereale (rye)
Avena sativa (oat)
Zea mais (maize)
Oryza sativa (rice).

Sugar:
Saccharum officinarum (sugar cane).

Bamboo (*Bambusa spp.*) is used for building and construction, and the rice grass (*Spartina townsendii*), has been planted in estuaries to reclaim land from the sea. The latter can become something of a problem if it is allowed to grow unchecked, as it is a hybrid and competes very successfully with other plants. In some parts of the world, species of grass have been used for paper-making.

■ DICOTYLEDONES

■ Cruciferae

The Cruciferae (Fig.5.13) are found mainly in the temperate regions of the world, and include a variety of edible food plants as well as others which have ornamental value. The family gets its name from the cross-shaped, or cruciform, appearance of the petals. The flowers possess four sepals, in addition to the four petals already mentioned, surrounding six stamens, two of which are short and four long, and two carpels. The ovary begins as a one-chambered structure, but is divided later by the growth of a partition down the middle called a false septum. At the base of two of the sepals, there are often pouch-like structures which hold the nectar from the nectaries at the base of the filaments of the lateral stamens. Long-tongued insects visit the flowers for the nectar and consequently bring about pollination.

Many of the Cruciferae are cultivated in flower gardens, including familiar examples such as wallflowers (*Cheiranthus cheiri*), honesty (*Lunaria annua*), *Aubretia* and *Alyssum*. Those cultivated for food include:
Brassica oleracea - cabbages, Brussels sprout,

cauliflower, kale and kohl-rabi
Brassica rapa - turnip
Brassica napus - swede and rape
Nasturtium officinale - watercress
Raphanus sativus - radish.

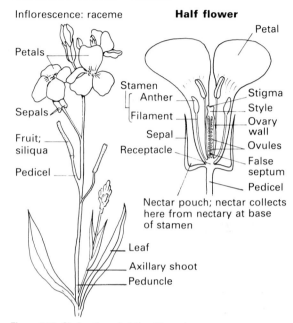

Figure 5.13 *Cheiranthus cheiri* (wallflower)

■ Papilionaceae

This is actually a sub-family of one of the largest of the flowering plant families, the Leguminosae, and is of considerable economic importance in a number of ways. As well as providing ornamental species (sweet peas, lupins) and many of our common wild flowers (gorse, broom, vetches, restharrow, trefoils), the family contains a number of important food plants such as peas, beans and pulses, together with fodder plants. Most of the members of this family also form root nodules containing the nitrogen-fixing bacterium *Rhizobium*, which can use atmospheric nitrogen and build it up into ammonium compounds and amino acids. Some of the products of the bacterial activity are able to be used by the plant, which benefits, while the bacterium obtains its organic carbon requirements from the photosynthetic activities of the plant. The plants are able to grow well on nitrogen-deficient soils and can increase the nitrogen content of soils when their remains decay or are ploughed in. For these reasons, leguminous plants are often used in crop rotations.

The flowers are irregular, or zygomorphic. The calyx is formed either by two united sepals (gorse) or by five sepals joined at the base as in the garden pea. The corolla consists of five petals: one large standard at the back, two laterals forming wings at the sides and two smaller joined at their lower margins forming a keel. There are ten stamens, either all are joined by their filaments forming a tube (broom) or nine are joined and one, the upper, is free (pea, broad bean). There is one carpel consisting of an ovary containing several ovules, a single style and stigma. In the species which have the filaments of all ten stamens joined, no nectar is produced (Fig.5.14); it is thought that visiting insects are attracted by the large amounts of pollen available. In the other species, nectar is produced in nectaries situated at the base of the filaments.

Half flower

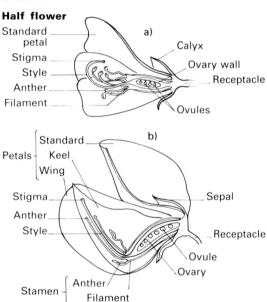

Figure 5.14 Pea flower structure (a) Broom (b) Lupin. These flowers do not produce nectar but attract insects for their extra pollen. Some pollen is deposited on the back of the insect and some is deposited on the underside

Pollination is usually carried out by bees and there are several interesting examples of pollination mechanisms which ensure that cross-pollination occurs. In flowers such as clover, the floral parts are usually enclosed within the petals, so only the heavier insects alighting on the wings will press the keel downwards, exposing the stamens and stigma. Pollen is brushed on to the underside of the bee as it probes the flower for the nectar.

When it visits another flower, some of this pollen could become attached to the stigma. In the pea, the stamens shed their pollen on the inside of the keel, and as the stigma is forced out when the bee lands, pollen is brushed on to the body of the bee by hairs on the style (Fig.5.15). In broom, the stamens and style are released suddenly when the bee lands, sending a shower of pollen over the insect. In this case, the stamens and style do not return to their original positions but remain exposed.

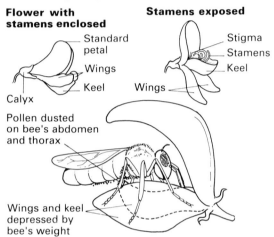

Figure 5.15 Bee pollination. The style and stamens are held in a relatively small keel. When an insect alights on the wings, the keel is depressed and the stamens and style are released suddenly, sending a shower of pollen over the insect. The stamens and style do not return to their original positions but remain exposed

The fruit is a legume, or pod. It is dry when ripe and splits along both margins, exposing the seeds and often expelling them violently if the pericarp twists as it dries.
Members of this family used for food are:
Pisum sativum - garden pea
Phaseolus multiflorus - runner and haricot beans
Phaseolus vulgaris - French, kidney and dwarf beans
Lens esculenta - lentils
Glycine max - soya bean
Arachis hypogaea - groundnut, peanut
Trifolium spp. - clover for animal fodder
Medicago sativa - lucerne, alfalfa for fodder.
Ornamental species include:
Lathyrus odoratus - sweet pea
Cytisus scoparius - broom
Wistaria spp.
(For more details of this important family see *Biology Advanced Studies - Plant Science*.)

■ Rosaceae

The family Rosaceae contains about 100 genera of both wild and cultivated plants, many of which are familiar in our gardens as either ornamental (roses) or producing food (apples, strawberries). There is a wide range of different forms of plants from herbaceous plants (*Geum*), shrubs (hawthorn) and trees (apple, almond, apricot, plum). Many examples of vegetative reproduction occur, such as runner formation in strawberries and suckers in raspberry, and many commercial varieties are maintained by artificial budding (roses) and grafting techniques (apples, pears).

The leaves are usually spirally arranged, often with stipules, and commonly compound. The flowers are mostly hermaphrodite, regular, or actinomorphic, and all the floral parts are free, not joined. The calyx consists of five sepals and there are five free petals alternating with the sepals, making up the corolla. There is a variable number of stamens present, and the number of carpels can range from one in cherry to a large number in strawberry. Each carpel consists of an ovary, with a style and a stigma. If nectaries are present, they are situated on the receptacle of the flower between the stamens and the carpels. The flowers are usually insect-pollinated. There are several different groups of genera within the family.

• In the apple and pear group (Fig.5.16) the receptacle of the flower grows around the carpels and joins with them. The wall of the carpel becomes tough, forming the 'core' of the apple and pear, while the receptacle tissue becomes succulent and sweet, so it is actually known as a 'false fruit'.

• In the strawberry group (Fig.5.17) the receptacle ranges from a flat disc to a cup-shaped structure. In strawberry, the receptacle becomes fleshy and sweet after fertilisation, but in the blackberries and raspberries, it is dry, but the carpels are fleshy.

• In the peach and cherry group (Fig.5.18) there is one carpel. The pericarp of the fruit becomes fleshy and succulent when ripe.

This group also contains the genus *Rosa*, the familiar garden rose, which was derived from the wild rose, or dog rose, *Rosa canina*. The name 'dog rose' is thought to have been given to the plant because, according to ancient tradition, the roots would cure the bite from a mad dog. This seems unlikely and other sources

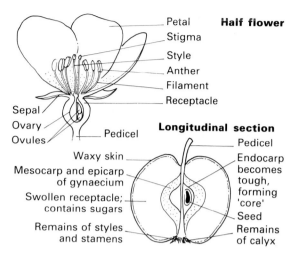

Half flower

Petal
Stigma
Style
Anther
Filament
Receptacle
Sepal
Ovary
Ovules
Pedicel

Longitudinal section

Pedicel
Waxy skin
Mesocarp and epicarp of gynaecium
Swollen receptacle; contains sugars
Remains of styles and stamens
Endocarp becomes tough, forming 'core'
Seed
Remains of calyx

Figure 5.16 Apple flower and fruit

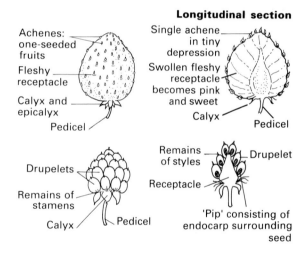

Longitudinal section

Achenes: one-seeded fruits
Fleshy receptacle
Calyx and epicalyx
Pedicel
Single achene in tiny depression
Swollen fleshy receptacle becomes pink and sweet
Calyx
Pedicel

Drupelets
Remains of stamens
Calyx
Pedicel
Remains of styles
Drupelet
Receptacle
'Pip' consisting of endocarp surrounding seed

Figure 5.17 Strawberry and blackberry structure

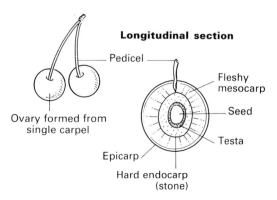

Longitudinal section

Pedicel
Ovary formed from single carpel
Fleshy mesocarp
Seed
Testa
Epicarp
Hard endocarp (stone)

Figure 5.18 Cherry structure

indicate that 'dog' might be a corruption of 'dag', referring to the dagger-like thorns. The hips (Fig.5.19), or fruits, of the wild rose have been eaten for centuries. The pulp was separated from the seeds and mixed with wine and sugar, to be eaten as a dessert. Rose hips are said to contain large amounts of Vitamin C: four times as much as blackcurrants and twenty times as much as oranges. The leaves can be used to make tea.

This is an important family, providing many varieties of fruit trees and bushes, and the propagation of successful varieties of these fruits has been extensively studied. Commercially acceptable varieties, which yield good-quality, disease-free crops, have been produced.

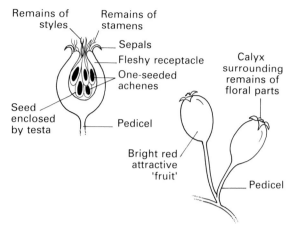

Figure 5.19 *Rosa* sp. (rose hip)

BEHAVIOUR FILE

PLANT KINGDOM

Do plants behave?

They certainly respond to external stimuli and in some cases very rapidly too. *Mimosa pudica* is a sensitive plant, the leaflets of which collapse speedily and fold along the midrib when touched. Perhaps to herbivores it no longer looks like a meal?

And what about the Venus fly-trap? The two parts of the leaf hinge together to prevent the escape of an insect crawling over the leaf. It makes a rapid response when sensitive hairs on the leaf surface are triggered by the insect. The leaf cells produce enzymes that break down the soft tissues of the insect, and the soluble molecules are absorbed by the plant. It seems to be a means of getting nitrogen in the form of amino acids - unusual for green plants! There is evidence that the response movements are brought about by the transmission of an impulse (rather like a nerve impulse, but slower) in the fly-traps and Mimosa.

Nastic movements are those made in response to external stimuli - but they are not related to a particular direction. The response to touch (as in the two examples above) is known as *thigmonasty* and the movement of opening and closing petals is either *thermonasty* or *photonasty*.

Tropic movements are the growth movements of parts of a plant in response to the direction of a particular external stimulus. The well known types are *hydrotropism*, *geotropism*, and *phototropism*, each a one-sided growth response to the one-sided stimulus of water, gravity or light.

Tactic movements occur as a response by the locomotion of the whole organism to an outside stimulus (see p.129).

6 THE ANIMALS: INVERTEBRATES

It probably seems obvious what animals are - although they are actually quite difficult to define. Technically, animals are metazoans (i.e. multicellular) and have a heterotrophic (see p.4) mode of feeding. The majority are able to move from place to place (powers of *locomotion*). Those few which cannot move about, like sponges or adult barnacles, are called *sessile*.

During the course of evolution, the biggest animals have become progressively larger and their organisation more complex. Nothing is known about the earliest metazoan animals. They evolved during the Precambrian Era, more than 600 million years ago. They must have been small and soft-bodied. Since it was usually only animals with hardened structures such as an external cuticle or a bony skeleton which became fossilised, there is no direct evidence of what they looked like.

■ PHYLUM PORIFERA

The simplest metazoan animals alive today are sponges. They are simple because they have no organs, and they are made up of only a few different kinds of cells. They are sessile, attaching to hard surfaces - usually rocks or stones - in the sea, or occasionally in freshwater. Some of the cells have flagella, and these create currents of water which are channeled into spaces between the cells. Particles of organic debris and bacteria in suspension in the water are removed at the surfaces of the cells lining the spaces, and digested. This is a kind of *filter feeding*.

Yellow Tube Sponge (*Aplysina fistularis*) and Gorgonians

How do sessile animals colonise new environments? The answer is that they have *larvae*, which can move around (*motile*). Sponge larvae are smaller and simpler than adult sponges. The external cells have flagella which face outwards and their beating propels the larva forwards. They are rather like *Paramecium* (p.18), except that they are multicellular.

There is one important respect in which sponges are quite specialised. They have skeletons, which are secreted by the cells (*extracellular*) and provide support. The natural bathsponge that you can buy in a chemist's shop is actually the skeleton of a sponge.

■ PHYLUM CNIDARIA (sometimes called Coelenterata, especially in older textbooks)

Animals belonging to this phylum have the body cells arranged in two layers. The outer cells (*epidermis*) are mainly for protection. The inner cells (*gastrodermis*) surround a *gastric cavity*, and are concerned mainly with digestion. The outer layer of all metazoan animals is called *ectoderm*, the inner layer *endoderm*.

The body plan of cnidarians shows *radial symmetry*: they are symmetrical about their longitudinal axis. This is actually quite unusual amongst animals; most are *bilaterally symmetrical*. (The difference can be illustrated by comparing a circular cake and a loaf of bread. The cake can be cut into many radial wedges which are all identical to one another. A loaf of bread cannot, but if it is sliced by a downward cut along the longitudinal axis, the result is two halves which are mirror-images of one another. The loaf is bilaterally symmetrical.)

Sea anemones and jellyfish are probably the most familiar cnidarians. The basic structure of cnidarians is more easily understood, however, by examining simpler forms such as *Hydra* (which lives in fresh water) and *Obelia* (which is marine).

Sea anemone (*Anthopleura artemisia*)

Moon jellyfish (*Aurelia aurita*)

Hydra look superficially like little pieces of thread; they are usually less than 1 cm in length. Detailed examination shows that they have a ring of *tentacles* at one end. These surround the mouth. Hydras can be found in ponds, attached to plants (the undersides of water-lily leaves are good places to look for them). Each individual is called a *polyp*.

The cells in the outer layer are mostly unspecialised (although they often contain muscle fibres), but sensory cells, nerve cells, and some very specialised cells called *nematocysts* (Fig.6.1) are also found there. Nematocysts are 'stinging' cells: they contain a small pointed structure called a *stylet* which has backwardly-pointing hooks. This is attached to the inside of the cell by a coiled thread. The stylet functions like a harpoon. The nematocyst also has a small hairlike extension pointing outwards into the surrounding water. This acts as a trigger; if it is touched, or stimulated by movement in the water nearby, it causes the stylet to be extruded from the cell. If the stylet touches a small animal which might act as food for the hydra (such as a water-flea, see p.73) it injects a paralysing poison. It is also sticky, so that the prey becomes attached to the epidermis.

Nematocysts are found only on the tentacles; once a piece of food has become attached, it can easily be transferred to the mouth.

Hydra is able to reproduce in two different ways. In the simplest form, a small outgrowth on the surface of the animal begins to elongate, differentiates into epidermis and gastrodermis, develops tentacles, and eventually drops off to form a new *Hydra*. This is a kind of asexual reproduction. The other sort of reproduction in *Hydra* is sexual; and it usually occurs only in the late summer or autumn. In this process, cells in the epidermis develop as gonads. These may be male (producing spermatozoa) or female (producing ova). The fertilisation of ova by spermatozoa produces zygotes which develop to form embryos. Each embryo secretes a horny envelope around itself for protection, and at this stage drops off the parent *Hydra*. It does not develop further until the following spring, when it loses the envelope and enlarges to form a fully grown *Hydra*. Any individual *Hydra* polyp contains both male and female sex organs; such animals are called *hermaphrodites*.

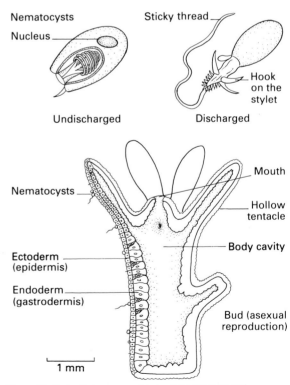

Figure 6.1 *Hydra*. Cut-away section to show structure and (above) nematocysts

The cells in the gastrodermis of hydra are mostly either gland cells (which produce enzymes which help to break the food into small particles) and digestive cells (which ingest the food particles and then digest them in a food vacuole, see p.16). Many of the cells of the gastrodermis contain algae (p.24). These are symbionts (see p.29), and supply the *Hydra* with some oxygen, protein and other materials as a result of their photosynthesis. In return they obtain protection by living within the cells of the *Hydra*. There are several different species of algae which may live symbiotically within *Hydra*, and they determine the colour of the polyp; some species of Hydras are green, some brown, some grey.

Obelia (Fig.6.2) is an example of a cnidarian which is colonial; a number of individuals are attached to one another, with no barrier between them. The colonies are usually found on seaweeds. *Obelia* has a more complicated life cycle than *Hydra*: the forms which are produced by asexual reproduction are completely different from their parents. They are disc-shaped *medusae*, with a ring of short tentacles around the edges. They swim freely in the water by means of muscular contractions which cause the edges of the disc to flip backwards. This locomotion is important for dispersal. Medusae also bear the gonads, but this is not a true alternation of generations (such as that seen on p.38) because the gonad cells actually first develop in the original colony. In the jellyfishes, the medusa stage is the more important one; the other stage which is equivalent to the polyp lives for only a very short time.

The corals are cnidarians which secrete a hard skeleton of calcium carbonate. They are important because they can occur in vast numbers and form massive underwater structures called coral reefs. Corals occur only in shallow water, because like some *Hydra* they contain symbiotic algae, and these need light for photosynthesis. Coral reefs are found only in the tropics and sub-tropics where the sea water is permanently warm. Because they have a very diverse fauna associated with them, which often includes many species of colourful fishes, they have become popular places for snorkelling and scuba-diving. They are vulnerable to disturbance and pollution, however, and many now need careful conservation if they are to survive. Some important reef habitats are being destroyed by a population explosion of the Crown of Thorns starfish.

Coral reef with goldfish

■ PHYLUM PLATYHELMINTHES

Animals in the phylum Cnidaria have only two layers of cells, and are relatively simple. The next step during evolution was the development of a third layer of cells, the *mesoderm*, which lies between the ectoderm and the endoderm. This was one of the most

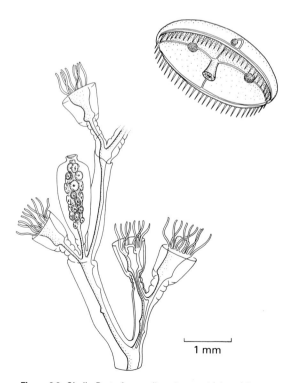

Figure 6.2 *Obelia*. Part of a sessile colony and (above) free-swimming medusa

1 mm

59

important advances in the whole of animal evolution. You may think that this is a strange claim and wonder why. The reason is that since the mesoderm does not have to fulfil the functions of protection or digestion, it can differentiate into organ systems which can perform a whole range of other specialised functions. As evolution progressed, the space occupied by mesoderm became bigger, and most larger animals also develop a fluid-filled space called the *body cavity* or *coelom* within the mesoderm.

Animals which have three layers of cells are called *triploblastic*. The earliest triploblastic animals were probably like very small worms, but we cannot be certain of this because such small soft animals did not produce fossils. Rather similar animals can be found today; some live in the spaces between grains of sand on muddy beaches and estuaries (these worms are not found in clean sand because there isn't enough food for them). They are called acoeles. They move by means of cilia, and have no gut. Simple triploblastic worms are placed in the phylum Platyhelminthes; they are sometimes called 'flatworms', but this is not an entirely appropriate name as not all of them are flat!

Platyhelminthes are particularly interesting because some of them are parasitic. Others, however, are free living like the acoeles. The best known examples are turbellarian worms (class Turbellaria). Most of these live in fresh water, in ponds, streams, lakes and rivers. They are sometimes called planarians (Fig.6.3) because one of the commonest genera in Europe is *Planaria*, although the species which are most abundant in the UK are *Polycelis nigra* (which is black in colour) and *Dendrocoelium lacteum* (which is milky-white in colour). Turbellarians are flattened dorsoventrally (so they are genuine 'flatworms'). They move by means of cilia, like acoeles, but they have a gut. This is relatively inefficient, however, since there is no anus; once the food has been digested, the remains must be eliminated back through the mouth. The front part of the gut, which is called the *pharynx*, can be everted (pushed out) to engulf the food, which consists of other small invertebrates. The worms have a fairly complicated reproductive system. Most of the remainder of the body cavity is filled with unspecialised cells called *parenchyma*, which is a kind of packaging.

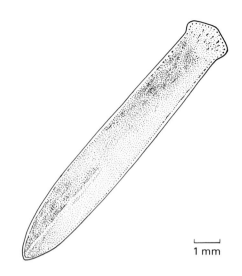

Figure 6.3 Dorsal view of a planarian worm (*Polycelis nigra*)

There are a number of species of turbellarian worms which are terrestrial, although they are mostly confined to the tropics and subtropics. They live in moist places such as leaf litter beneath trees or spaces underneath stones and logs, because they have no protection against desiccation (loss of water by evaporation).

Artiposthia triangulata, originally from New Zealand, has recently attracted concern in parts of the UK. Although introduced accidentally, it has proved capable of surviving and breeding, and decimates the populations of earthworms which are its principal food. The ecological balance has been upset in places where earthworm numbers have been reduced by introduced turbellarians, because earthworms are an essential part of the ecology of the soil (see p.66). The Ministry of Agriculture, Fisheries and Food is working hard to overcome the problem, but so far with little success. Several freshwater turbellarians have also been accidentally introduced into the UK, and there is concern that they too may upset the ecological balance where they occur. *Phagocata woodworthi*, from North America, has been found in Loch Ness. The first specimens were captured near the sewage outlet of a large hotel on the banks of the lake, and it is believed that they were transferred on equipment brought over by American biologists looking for the Loch Ness Monster.

There are two major groups of Platyhelminthes which are parasitic, the flukes and the tapeworms. Flukes are not segmented. They are placed within a class of the phylum Platyhelminthes called the Trematoda.

Fasciola hepatica, the liver fluke (Fig.6.4), is an example of a Trematode. These worms are leaf-like in appearance and are usually 2-3 cm in length. They live within the bile ducts in the livers of sheep and cattle, and occasionally other hosts including man, where they can do a great deal of harm. There are two muscular suckers, one around the mouth and one on the ventral surface, which help them to attach to the inner surfaces of the bile ducts. The flukes feed mainly on red blood corpuscles which are released from blood capillaries which get broken when the tissues are damaged by the suckers of the worms. Liver flukes are much more complex animals than planarians. In order to understand their detailed structure, it is necessary to consider the constituent parts, which are shown diagrammatically in Fig.6.4.

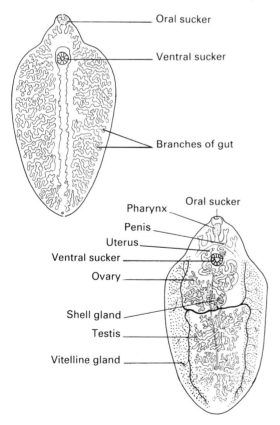

Figure 6.4 Liver fluke (*Fasciola hepatica*). Diagrams showing (above) the gut and (below) the reproductive system

Why do these two figures differ so dramatically? The answer is that most of the organs of *Fasciola* are diffuse, giving them a very complicated appearance which is simplified in the diagram. The reason the organs are diffuse stems from the requirement, common to all parasites, for a high reproductive rate. *Fasciola hepatica* need to produce a lot of eggs to stand a chance of reaching the next host. A single worm may produce 20 000 eggs each day. A *Fasciola* was once recorded as surviving for 22 years, so it may have produced more than one hundred million eggs during its lifetime! An individual needs to process an enormous amount of food to provide the raw materials and energy needed to sustain this production. The gut is highly branched, which increases the surface area available for digestion and absorption. All of the other organs have to be fitted into the spaces which remain. The most important of these organs are ovaries (which produce ova) and testes (which produce spermatozoa). Ovaries and testes in vertebrates are rather solid organs. This arrangement wouldn't work in *Fasciola* - there isn't room. So the cells which produce the ova and the spermatozoa are arranged in small clusters, a bit like bunches of grapes. Each cluster is called a follicle, and the arrangement of cells is called *follicular*.

The eggs of *Fasciola* are surrounded by a protective *shell*. Nourishment for the developing embryo is provided by *yolk*. This is produced by *vitelline glands*, which are also follicular. The eggs pass into the *uterus*, and they are moved along this tubular organ by muscular *peristalsis* in the same way that food is moved along the intestine of a vertebrate.

Each *Fasciola hepatica* contains both testes and ovaries. Such hermaphroditism is often found in parasitic worms because it enables the animals to reproduce even when only one is present in a host, or if individuals are so dispersed within a host that they can't find one another. This is yet another way in which parasites are adapted to maximise their total reproductive output.

Fasciola hepatica has a fairly complex anatomy - and a complex life cycle (Fig.6.5), too. The eggs, after they have been expelled from the uterus of a worm, are carried with the flow of bile to the intestine, and from there by peristalsis to the anus, where they pass out of

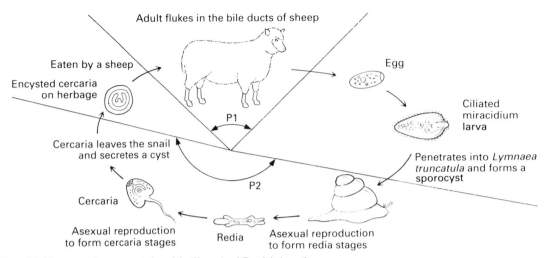

Figure 6.5 Diagrammatic representation of the life cycle of *Fasciola hepatica*.
P1 indicates the part of the life cycle in sheep, P2 indicates the parts of the life cycle in a snail

the host with the faeces. They continue their development while lying on the ground, the ovum dividing to form an embryo, which continues differentiating to become a ciliated larva called a *miracidium*. Miracidia (this is the plural form of miracidium) look rather like Ciliophora (p.17) but are multicellular. They hatch from the eggs, but will only survive if the egg is in a wet place; if it's dry, they die. This is one of the reasons why *Fasciola hepatica* need to produce so many eggs. A very small amount of water, such as a dewdrop or the surface film on a wet leaf, will do. The miracidia swim around in this water. They do not feed, and can only survive for about 24 hours. If a miracidium is to develop further, it must come into contact with a small amphibious snail during this period, and penetrate into it through the soft parts of the body. Miracidia cannot get through the shell. The snail must belong to a particular species; in the UK this is *Lymnaea truncatula*, but other species may be utilised elsewhere. Most miracidia don't find such a snail, and so die. This is yet another reason why *Fasciola hepatica* must produce so many eggs. The life of a parasite is full of hazards!

The miracidium becomes a parasite within the snail, which is called its *intermediate host* (the animal which harbours the adult worm within its liver is called the *definitive host*). It changes its form (metamorphoses) through a series of stages, reproducing asexually each time. Eventually, a stage called the *cercaria* is reached. Each cercaria breaks out of the snail (again through the epidermis, not the shell) and

secretes a covering of mucus around itself for protection. It is now called a *metacercaria*. A metacercaria can survive for many months. It will develop further only if it is swallowed by a suitable definitive host, usually a grazing animal such as a sheep or cow. When people become infected with *Fasciola hepatica*, it is usually as a result of eating unwashed watercress which is contaminated with metacercaria stages. These are surrounded by mucus which protects the parasites from gastric acid as they pass through the host's stomach. The mucus is then digested away in the intestines of the definitive host, exposing what is essentially a little fluke; it has oral and ventral suckers, but not yet a fully developed gut or reproductive structures. The little fluke bores through the wall of the intestine and gets into the body cavity. It migrates to the surface of the liver, penetrates it, and spends about six weeks feeding on the highly nutritious liver cells. A great deal of damage is caused to the liver if a lot of flukes at this stage of the life cycle are present, and this is one of the reasons why the disease caused by flukes can be a serious problem for farmers. The flukes grow rapidly while they are feeding on liver cells, but they cannot remain at this site because there is no way in which their eggs could reach the external world and so perpetuate the species. For this to occur, the flukes must make their way into the bile ducts. The life cycle has now been completed, and a new generation of eggs can reach the exterior via the bile ducts, intestine and anus.

Why does *Fasciola hepatica* have such a complicated life cycle? Part of the reason is that intermediate hosts provide protection and a rich source of nutrition, making further reproduction possible; one miracidium can give rise to thousands of cercaria stages. However, all of the many hundreds of species of flukes whose life cycles have been determined (there are many which have not) utilise molluscs as their intermediate hosts. There is no obvious reason why this should be the case; other parasites have larvae which are able to develop in other sorts of intermediate hosts (tapeworms, for example; see below). Although several theories have been put forward to try to explain why flukes only develop in molluscs, none of them is entirely convincing.

Tapeworms, although they are also parasites, are superficially very different from flukes. The body is divided into a large number of segments (which are more correctly called *proglottides*). There are many thousands in *Taenia solium*, the human pork tapeworm, which is taken as a representative of the group. Each individual proglottis (this is the singular of proglottides) has a structure rather like that of a fluke, although there are no suckers or gut. It's a bit like a piece of ravioli: the 'meat' is represented by reproductive organs, packed in unspecialised paranchyma cells. The 'pasta' consists of layers of muscle cells, and is bounded by a specialised layer called the *tegument*. Because tapeworms have no gut they must absorb food materials across the body wall, and so the tegument serves both as a protective layer and as a surface for absorption. Studies by electron microscopy have shown that the tegument has a complex structure: the nuclei are not separated by cell walls (such tissues are called *syncytia*, and the outer surface has numerous tiny projections called *microtriches* - see Fig.6.6).

About three thousand species of tapeworms have been described; they are mostly parasites within the intestine of vertebrates. Many species are quite large in relation to the size of their hosts; the human pork tapeworm, for example, may be as much as 10 m in length. Other species, however, may be very small; there is a tapeworm in dogs which is never more than 7 mm in length. Tapeworms are in great danger of being carried away by the movement of food in the intestine produced by peristalsis, and so they have an anchor called a

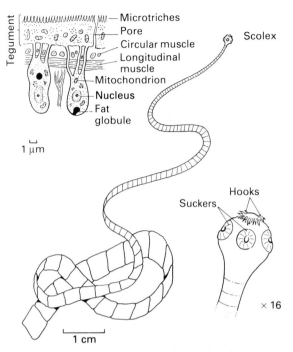

Figure 6.6 Drawing of a pork tapeworm, with enlargements showing the scolex and the histology of the tegument. The scolex is drawn from a specimen mounted on a microscope slide and the orientation of the suckers has been affected by pressure from the coverslip

scolex. Its structure varies from species to species. In the pork tapeworm and related species it has four muscular suckers facing outwards at right angles to one another (rather like the faces of the clock of Big Ben at the Houses of Parliament in London) and two rings of outwardly pointing *hooks* on a small knob of tissue called the *rostellum* at the front end (Fig.6.6). The hooks are made of a hard material called *chitin*, which also forms the exoskeleton of insects and other arthropods (see p.67). A tapeworm attaches to the inside surface of the intestine of its host by allowing some of the hooks to catch in the epithelial cells and by adhering to the surface using one or more of the suckers.

Tapeworms usually continue growing all their lives. The proliferation of cells immediately behind the scolex causes the tissues to move backwards. As a group of cells moves backwards they continue dividing; each segment gets older and eventually differentiates to form tissues and organs. The proglottides in the middle region of the worm are called 'mature', because it is here that the reproductive organs become fully developed.

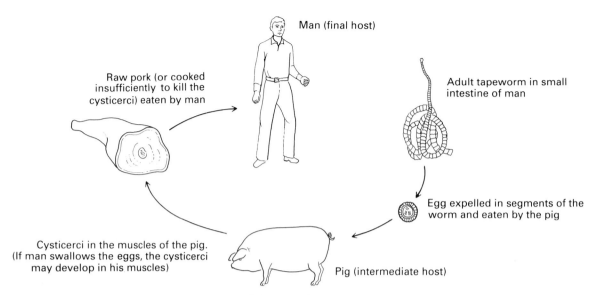

Man (final host)

Raw pork (or cooked insufficiently to kill the cysticerci) eaten by man

Adult tapeworm in small intestine of man

Egg expelled in segments of the worm and eaten by the pig

Cysticerci in the muscles of the pig. (If man swallows the eggs, the cysticerci may develop in his muscles)

Pig (intermediate host)

Figure 6.7 Diagrammatic representation of the life cycle of a human pork tapeworm

Tapeworms, like flukes, are hermaphrodites, and so the ova in one proglottis can potentially be fertilised by spermatozoa produced (a) from testes in the same proglottis, (b) from testes in a nearby proglottis or (c) from testes in a different worm. All three methods of fertilisation probably occur, although this is an aspect of tapeworm biology which has been very little studied - the technical problems of determining how parasites like tapeworms actually behave are formidable!

As a mature proglottis continues to pass backwards, the reproductive organs atrophy. Only the uterus remains. This eventually becomes swollen with eggs, and lateral branches develop which further increase its capacity. The proglottis is now called 'gravid' and may contain as many as 100 000 eggs. The gravid proglottides eventually detach from the posterior end; if they did not, the worm would continue growing indefinitely. There is nothing to stop a detached proglottis from being carried backwards down the intestine as a result of peristalsis, and eventually it will be expelled from the anus with the faeces.

Each proglottis is to all intents and purposes a discrete entity, since it has a complete set of reproductive organs. Nevertheless, a tapeworm has several organ systems which run the length of the worm and give cohesion to the whole, for example nerves and ducts used for excretion and probably osmoregulation.

Once a proglottis has been shed from the host, it begins to desiccate. This drying causes it to split, releasing the eggs. The eggs will develop further only if they are eaten by a suitable intermediate host (Fig.6.7). Pigs are the intermediate hosts for the pork tapeworm (this is the origin of the name). The eggs hatch in the small intestine, and the little larval stages which emerge bore their way through the gut wall, get into a blood capillary, and are carried by the bloodstream to the muscles. Here they grow to form hollow *cysticercus* or bladderworm larvae. A scolex develops within the cyst, although it is inside out. The cysticercus is now *infective*. If it is swallowed by a human, the cysticercus passes through the stomach, and in the intestine its wall (which contains smooth muscle) contracts. The scolex is pushed outwards (so that it's the right way round, with the suckers on the outside) and the hooks and suckers attach to the wall of the intestine. The cysticercus wall is then digested away. The remaining part of the worm - just the scolex - begins to grow, and soon becomes a large tapeworm. Tapeworms often have very rapid rates of growth.

 Can you work out some of the reasons why this should be so?

Although we have discussed the pork tapeworm you should note that neither it, nor the similar beef tapeworm, are common in places

where there is a good standard of meat inspection and hygiene. Not all tapeworm species utilise vertebrates as their intermediate hosts. *Dipylidium caninum*, for example, is found as an adult worm in dogs and cats, but the larvae are found in fleas and lice. Fleas feed on blood, and have sucking mouthparts; they never swallow eggs of the tapeworm. Flea larvae (see p.71) have biting mouthparts, however; they feed on organic debris, including dried blood and even the droppings of the adult fleas. They can therefore swallow eggs which have been released as a result of the drying and cracking of shed proglottides, as in the pork tapeworm. On being swallowed by a flea larva the egg hatches into a larval tapeworm, and this burrows into the body cavity of the flea larva. It survives the metamorphosis of the flea larva into an adult flea. If the flea is then swallowed by a dog or a cat (this usually happens during grooming), infection occurs.

■ PHYLUM NEMATODA

Nematodes are unsegmented worms. They have a gut with a mouth and anus; food passes through in a one-way direction. They are very abundant, in soil, humus, mud (both freshwater and marine) and elsewhere; the average suburban garden or one hectare of woodland or meadow contains many millions of these worms. Nematodes from these environments are called free-living, to distinguish them from parasitic forms. Free-living nematodes are usually less than 1 mm in length. Although they are ubiquitous, their importance in the habitats where they occur has not often been studied. Many are believed to feed on bacteria, small fungi or protozoans.

Parasitic nematodes are often larger than free-living ones. Some species are parasites of plants, in which they may transmit important diseases such as potato blight. Others are parasites of animals, including man. One of these is the pinworm, *Enterobius vermicularis*. These worms are 5-10 mm in length as adults; they live in the large intestine, and though found in most people at some time, are generally regarded as fairly harmless. Another is *Ascaris lumbricoides*. These worms may grow to 25 cm or more in length; they live in the small intestine. They may cause diarrhoea and reduce the general health of the person

infected. *A. lumbricoides* are now rare in the UK as human parasites, but they are still quite abundant in some tropical countries. They are also able to parasitise pigs, and are more commonly found in these hosts; many parasitologists think that the forms in pigs should be placed in a separate species.

Nematode worms have no structural skeleton. Their body wall has only longitudinal muscles (i.e. muscles in which the fibres run along the length of the body). The antagonist for these muscles is the incompressibility of the fluid which fills their body cavity. This is ensured by an inelastic external covering (the *cuticle*). When a portion of the longitudinal muscle contracts, the body of the worm bends into a C-shape. If the contraction moves backwards, to be followed by another backwardly moving contraction on the opposite side of the body, then the worm is bent into an S shape. (The muscles which contracted to form the first wave must, of course, relax when the second, opposite, wave is formed.) The backwardly moving waves, which are coordinated by the nervous sytem, cause the worm to move forwards.

■ PHYLUM ANNELIDA

The method of locomotion used by nematode worms, described above, is relatively simple. It could be made more effective if the body cavity were divided into a number of compartments, called *segments*. This has happened during the evolution of a group of worms called the annelids, which are placed in the phylum Annelida.

How such a locomotor system works can be understood by considering the movement of an earthworm such as the common species of fields and gardens, *Lumbricus terrestris* (a smaller species, *Allobophora chlorotica*, is almost equally common). There are two groups of muscles in the body wall of these animals. Some have the fibres running longitudinally, others have the fibres running in a ring around the body (circular muscle) - see Fig.6.8. If the circular muscle near the anterior end of the body contracts, and the longitudinal muscle relaxes, the fluid in the anterior segments is put under pressure. In a non-segmented worm, such as a nematode described above, the fluid could simply run backwards along the body. This is prevented in annelids by the bulkheads

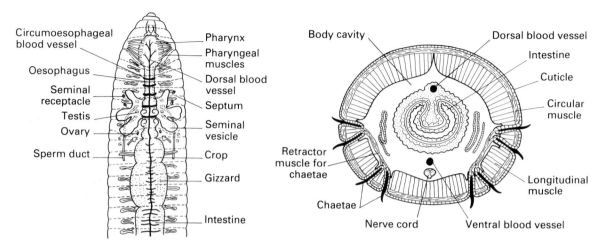

Figure 6.8 Left: anterior end of an earthworm dissected to show the internal anatomy; right: transverse section through the mid-region of an earthworm

of tissue dividing the segments - these are called *septa*. Since fluids are not compressible, the effect of the pressure is to cause the segments in which circular muscle contraction has occurred to lengthen (Fig.6.9). At the same time as this is happening, small spike-like projections from the body surface (called *chaetae*) are pushed outwards by the contraction of small muscles which are attached to their base, at the segments where the circular muscle has contracted. The chaetae push into the surrounding soil, and effectively anchor this part of the worm to the surrounding substrate. The effect of this is that the anterior part of the worm is pushed forwards. The chaetae at the very front end are then pushed out, and those at the rear of the area of movement pulled in. The longitudinal muscles then contract, pulling this part of the worm forwards. The whole process actually happens simultaneously in several different parts of the worm. As a result there are several regions of the worm moving forwards simultaneously. The overall consequence is that the entire worm moves forwards.

Movement of this kind would not be possible without a fairly complicated nervous system to coordinate it. There are other organ systems of annelids which are quite complex too. There is a blood circulatory system which is *closed*; the blood runs within distinct vessels and is carried to the tissues via *capillaries*. There is an excretory system in every segment. Although earthworms are hermaphroditic, reproduction

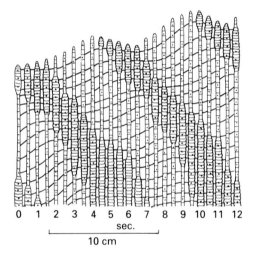

Figure 6.9 Earthworm. Diagram showing successive stages in movement. Each drawing (read them from left to right) shows the position of the worm at one second intervals

usually involves *cross-fertilisation*, as in *Paramecium* (p.18). In addition to testes and ovaries, there are organs for storing sperm (the seminal vesicles).

Earthworms are very important to farmers and gardeners because their burrows help to aerate the soil and to improve drainage. They also help roots of plants to penetrate downward; this is especially valuable in heavy clay soils. Many species of earthworms feed on dead or decaying leaves, which they drag into the burrows. Some species deposit their droppings on the surface as worm casts. Both feeding and defaecation increase the movement of materials within the soil, and so may help to improve fertility. These facts were first appreciated by Charles Darwin (best known as the main originator of the theory of evolution by natural selection) and explained in a most important book that he wrote in 1881 called *The Formation of Vegetable Mould by the Action of Worms with Observations on their Habits*. Earthworms may be very abundant. In a typical grass field on a farm in England there will usually be at least as great a weight of earthworms unseen beneath the soil as cattle or sheep on the surface. Each earthworm will weigh less than one or two grams; in total, there may be several million per hectare (a hectare measures 100 m × 100 m).

Not all annelids are burrowing animals. A group called ragworms live in the sea. Ragworms have a flap-like extension to each segment on either side of the body. Each functions a bit like a paddle and helps the animal to move over the surface or to swim in the water. Another group of annelids, called lugworms, look rather like earthworms. They burrow in muddy sand in the intertidal zone, especially at the edges of estuaries. They are well known to anglers who dig up large numbers to use as bait. There are several species of ragworms which live in intertidal mudflats too; intertidal ragworms and lugworms are an important source of food for larger wading birds such as curlews.

Leeches are annelids which have developed suckers at the front and rear ends of the body. Although the well-known medicinal leech feeds on the blood of vertebrates, most leeches are predators of other invertebrates such as insects and snails.

A marine worm
(*Nereis*)

■ PHYLUM ARTHROPODA

The Arthropoda is the biggest phylum of animals. More than one million species have been described, and it is thought that there are at least as many more which remain to be discovered, especially in the tropics. The phylum includes the classes Chilopoda (centipedes), Diplopoda (millipedes), Insecta (sometimes called Hexapoda, the insects), Crustacea (crustaceans) and Arachnida (arachnids). Some authorities think that the phylum Arthropoda is too big, and they divide it into a number of separate phyla; textbooks do not always agree on this matter.

The success of the arthropods is due largely to the fact that they have an *exoskeleton*. The outer covering of the body is composed partly of a material called *chitin* (Fig.6.10). This is a long-chain polysaccharide, a complex molecule made up of subunits based on six-carbon rings called n-acetyl glucosamines. These are bound together into long chains by covalent bonds; because of this structure, chitin is tough and resistant. It is usually hardened because of the presence of proteins called *sclerotins*.

Figure 6.10 Small part of a chitin molecule showing two acetyl-glucosamine units connected by a covalent bond

The exoskeleton is not a continuous covering; it is divided into plates which are joined together by softer cuticle, so that they can move (a suit of armour worn by a mediaeval knight, which acts as a kind of exoskeleton but is made of metal, must also have joints for the same reason). Unlike worms, arthropods have legs which are constructed of tubes of chitin, also connected by pliable cuticle so that they can move. They are jointed. As well as serving for protection, the exoskeleton prevents loss of water from the body by evaporation (desiccation). Some groups of arthropods are therefore able to live in very dry places, such as hot deserts.

The earliest arthropods, which evolved more than 400 million years ago, were probably rather similar to ragworms (p.67) but with jointed legs instead of parapodia. Modern centipedes (class Chilopoda) still retain this kind of organisation. Centipedes are carnivorous, feeding mostly on smaller arthropods. *Lithobius forficatus*, a reddish-brown centipede which is often found in gardens in the UK, is an example. Millipedes are quite similar to centipedes, but each external segment has two pairs of legs instead of the single pair per segment of centipedes (N.B. Centipedes do not have 100 legs; usually they have 17 pairs, and millipedes usually have 34 pairs.)

The most numerous and successful arthropods are insects. They have fewer segments than centipedes or millipedes, and segments in different parts of the body have become specialised for different functions (Fig.6.11). The first six segments have become totally fused; they form the *head*. The next three segments each have a pair of legs; they form the *thorax*. All insects have six legs, one pair attached to the ventral surface of each thoracic segment. Many insects have wings, which are also made of chitin. There are two pairs, except in the two-winged flies (order Diptera) in which the second pair has become modified into little organs which look like car gear sticks and are used for balance. The wings, if they are present, are attached to the first and second segments of the thorax. The remaining segments of the insect form the *abdomen*; these have no legs or wings. Most insects have eleven abdominal segments.

The head contains the mouth and surrounding structures which help an insect to manipulate its food. In insects which chew their food, such as locusts and cockroaches, the main mouthparts are *mandibles* (which do the cutting), *maxillae* and the *labium* (which manipulate the food). Insects with more specialised feeding habits have different mouthparts. Butterflies, for example, which suck nectar from flowers, have a long tube called a *proboscis*. This is coiled when not in use. Mosquitos, which feed on the blood of vertebrates, also have a proboscis (but this is never coiled). The head is also the site of major sense organs such as the *compound eyes* and *antennae*. Internally it is the site of aggregations of nerve cells which function as a brain. The thorax contains the muscles which activate the legs, and the wings if they are present. The abdomen contains the main parts of the digestive system, and other organ systems such as those for nitrogenous excretion (the *Malpighian tubules* - see Fig.6.12) and reproduction. Each of the segments of the abdomen has a small hole on either side. These are the *spiracles*, which are the openings of tubes which ramify through the tissues of the animal, carrying oxygen in and carbon dioxide out. These tubes are called *tracheae*. They are lined by chitin, except where they reach the tissues, where they become very small, fluid-filled and intercellular. Here they are called *tracheoles*. Diffusion of oxygen and carbon dioxide between tissues and the lumen of the tracheae takes place through the fluid in the tracheoles.

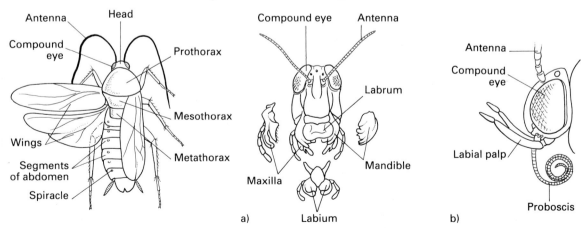

Figure 6.11 Left: dorsal view of a cockroach (*Periplaneta americana*).
The wings on the left-hand side have been moved sideways to show the underlying abdomen.
Right: mouthparts of (a) a grasshopper (which feeds on leaves) and (b) a butterfly (which feeds on nectar)

Running along the length of an insect on the ventral floor of the body cavity are bundles of nerve cells (neurones) which form the *ventral nerve cord*. The cell bodies of the neurones are aggregated together into *ganglia* (Fig.6.12), which can be seen as swellings in the longitudinal nerve. There is one ganglion in each segment (the longitudinal nerve cords and ganglia are actually paired structures, but in many arthropods the two sides are fused). The peripheral nerves join the longitudinal nerve cord at the ganglia.

Although they all have this basic body plan, there is enormous diversity in the detailed structure of insects. Fourteen of the more important orders are illustrated in Fig.6.16 and listed on p.72.

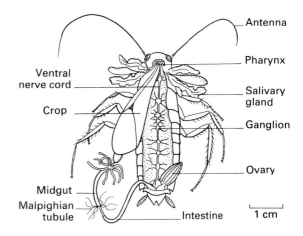

Figure 6.12 Cockroach, dissected from the dorsal surface to show the internal anatomy

BEHAVIOUR FILE

LOCUST FLIGHT

The rhythmic down and up beating of insect wings in flight is caused by contractions of muscles in the thorax. Depressor muscles cause the down beat and elevator muscles the up beat. Their contractions are stimulated by motor neurones carrying regular bursts of impulses from the thoracic ganglia. Locusts have been intensively studied to discover the neural circuits which generate this rhythm. The circuit shown has been determined by recording electric impulses from individual neurones in live locusts. The locusts performed normal flight movements while harnessed to a frame. A puff of air to the head stimulated them to flap their wings. The mechanism is by no means fully understood but enough is known of the positions of neurones, their connections and their effects on one another to suggest how a regular cycle of impulses is generated.

There are several hundreds of neurones in the thoracic ganglia and the interaction of two of them (A and B in Fig.6.13) forms the core of an oscillating circuit, alternately switching on and off. Figure 6.13 shows how A stimulates B and B inhibits A. A switches on B which switches off A. When A is off it no longer stimulates B so that it can no longer inhibit A. A therefore turns on again.

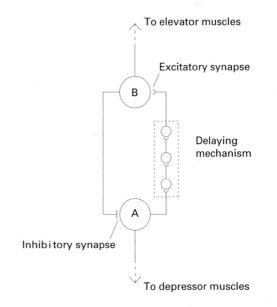

Figure 6.13 Locust flight. An oscillating circuit which produces bursts of action potentials alternately to the depressor and elevator flight muscles

The series of neurones between A and B creates a time delay which allows A to fire action potentials for a few milliseconds before being switched off by B. Other neurones feed these regular pulses of activity alternately to the depressor and elevator muscles to produce flight movements.

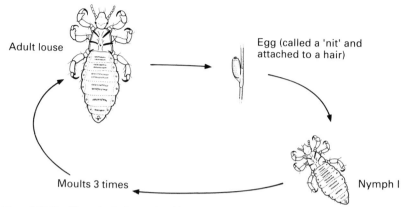

Figure 6.14 The life cycle of a human head louse

Most insects lay eggs. These have a shell made of chitin which protects the developing embryo. In many insects the young form which hatches from the egg looks very like the adult, but is smaller and has no wings. It is called a *nymph*. As a nymph begins to feed, it grows. The cuticle will not be able to expand, however, because it is rigid. What happens? The answer is that the nymph secretes a new cuticle beneath the original. At first this is soft and pliable, and at this stage the old cuticle splits and is cast off. The new cuticle underneath expands (so that the nymph increases in size), and only then does it harden. This process is called *moulting*. Insects which have a life cycle involving a number of nymphs are said to have *incomplete metamorphosis*; they are sometimes classified as *exopterygotes*. The stages between each moult are called *instars*. The life cycle of a human sucking louse (the head louse, *Pediculus humanus*), which has incomplete metamorphosis, is shown in Fig.6.14.

There are other insects which have a more complex life cycle (called *complete metamorphosis*); these are classified as *endopterygotes*. The form which hatches from the egg does not look like the adult; it is called a *larva*. Some larvae have no legs, and are called *maggots* (if they are the larvae of two-winged flies) or grubs (if they are the larvae of fleas, bees, wasps, ants and their allies, see Table 6.1).

Larvae of beetles, which have three small pairs of thoracic legs, are also called grubs. The larvae of butterflies and moths have two sorts of legs - six jointed legs at the anterior end and usually ten *prolegs* near the posterior end. Prolegs are not jointed. Each has a flat base which has small recurved hooks around its edge. These help the leg to attach to the substrate by catching in microscopic crevices or projections at the surface (this is the principle on which velcro tape works). These larvae are called *caterpillars*. When the time has come for a larva to transform into the adult insect, a

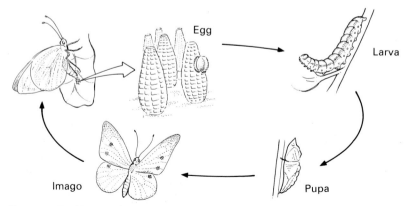

Figure 6.15 The life cycle of the cabbage white butterfly

resting stage called a *pupa* intervenes (Fig.6.15). Pupae (the plural of pupa) are protected by a particularly thick covering of chitin; they do not move about. The pupal stage of butterflies and moths is called a *chrysalis*.

Why do some insects have a complete metamorphosis? The answer is that the larvae and adults can specialise in completely different ways of life, and so each can exploit the resources of the environment with the greatest efficiency. Caterpillars feed on the leaves of plants, and have jaws to enable them to cut off fragments and chew them. Adult butterflies and moths, on the other hand, feed on nectar. Caddis-flies have larvae which live in ponds, rivers or streams. In many species these larvae cover themselves with a case of dead leaves or small stones for protection. The larva can retract fully into the case, but the head and thorax (with the legs) emerge when the animal moves. Usually the food source exploited by larvae is more abundant and nutritious than the food taken by the adults (because the larvae need a great deal of energy to grow). Some adult insects do not feed at all (mayflies are a well-known example). They fly for only a few days to mate, whereas the larvae may survive for a year or more.

Many insects are of economic or medical importance. Honeybees (*Apis mellifera*: order Hymenoptera) for example, are important because they produce honey. They live in colonies in a nest, and beekeepers make an artificial nest, the hive. Most of the bees in a colony are non-reproducing *workers*, but each colony also contains a female and one or more males. The females are called *queens*. They control the activities of the workers by secreting chemicals, called *pheromones*, which influence their behaviour. The workers construct chambers in the nest from a waxy material. The queens lay their eggs in the chambers, and the grubs develop there. Honey is a material which is manufactured by the workers (from the pollen and nectar of plants, mixed with their own saliva) which is placed in the cells; it is a highly nutritious food for the grubs. (For further details on bees and honey production see *Biology Advanced Studies - Food Production*.)

Other insects are *pests*: they consume material which could otherwise be used for food, destroy man-made structures, or transmit diseases. Locusts (order Orthoptera) are an example in the first group. They live in Africa and the Middle East, and from time to time form vast swarms which destroy crops, grass and trees. Aphids (order Hemiptera) are both pests and *vectors* (i.e. transmitters) of disease. As in butterflies and moths, the mouth is a proboscis; it is inserted into plants to suck the sap. If large numbers of aphids are present the amount of sap removed can harm the plant. Diseases such as that caused by the potato leaf roll virus are transmitted from the saliva of an aphid which was contaminated when it fed on an infected plant to other, previously uninfected, plants to which the animal may move to feed. Mosquitos (order Diptera) are two-winged flies which act as vectors for a wide range of human diseases, for example malaria (which is caused by protozoan parasites in the red blood cells - see p.21), dengue and yellow fever (which are caused by viruses).

BEHAVIOUR FILE

ROTHENBUHLER'S BEES

Larval honeybees (*Apis mellifera*) are sometimes killed by a bacterial disease called American foulbrood, which can spread throughout the hive if dead grubs are not removed. Some strains of bees, known as 'hygienic', show an adaptation to this risk. The worker bees open the comb cells and remove dead larvae. Other strains are 'unhygienic' and do not remove larvae. In the 1960s, Rothenbuhler did an elegant series of cross-breeding experiments producing, amongst others, workers that would open comb cells but not remove the contents, and workers which would not open cells but would remove dead grubs if the cells were opened for them. The precise ratios of each type of offspring (the details do not matter here) showed him that the behaviour was affected by two genes: one for opening the comb cells, and one for removing the contents. (If you have already done any genetics in your course, you should be able to work out what cross-breeding experiments Rothenbuhler did, using the following information: alleles causing 'unhygienic' behaviour, both not opening cells and not removing dead larvae, are *dominant* to their 'hygienic' equivalents.)

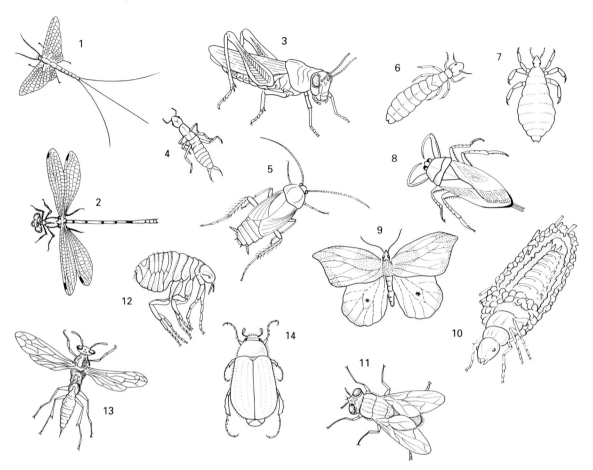

Figure 6.16 Some representatives of the major insect orders - 10 is the larva, all others are adults (not drawn to scale)

English name	Scientific name (name)	Development	Name of larval stage	Wings
Mayflies	1 Ephemeroptera	Incomplete	–	Yes
Dragonflies	2 Odonata	Incomplete	–	Yes
Grasshoppers	3 Orthoptera	Incomplete	–	Yes
Earwigs	4 Dermaptera	Incomplete	–	Yes
Cockroaches	5 Dictyoptera	Incomplete	–	Yes
Biting lice	6 Mallophaga	Incomplete	–	No
Sucking lice	7 Anoplura	Incomplete	–	No
Bugs	8 Hemiptera	Incomplete	–	Yes
Butterflies and moths	9 Lepidoptera	Complete	Caterpillar	Yes
Caddis-flies	10 Trichoptera	Complete	Larva	Yes
Two-winged flies	11 Diptera	Complete	Maggot	Yes
Fleas	12 Siphonaptera	Complete	Grub	No
Bees, wasps and ants	13 Hymenoptera	Complete	Grub	Yes
Beetles	14 Coleoptera	Complete	Grub	Yes

Table 6.1 Summary classification of insects (not all of the orders of insects are included in this table)

Evolution of the insects involved a reduction in the number of segments from the condition in early arthropods, and specialisation of segments in different parts of the body for different functions. This process has also occurred on other occasions during the evolution of arthropod groups, and in some of them animals which represent different stages in the process are still alive today. Within the class Crustacea, for example, one can find animals with many segments, and animals with few.

The characteristics which define the class Crustacea (see Table 6.2) are mainly technical features of their internal anatomy and the structure of their legs, but there is one external feature which is common to them all. This is the presence of two pairs of antennae. Insects, centipedes and millipedes have one pair of antennae, arachnids (see p.75) have none. The outer covering of crustaceans is hardened by calcium salts, not by sclerotin (see p.67). The group contains a wide variety of animals. Brine shrimps (*Artemia salina*) are amongst the simplest of crustaceans. They have eleven pairs of legs. Brine shrimps are often bred in large numbers by people who keep tropical fish as a hobby, because they produce large numbers of nymphs which make a convenient source of food for tiny hatchling fishes which will only take living prey. Woodlice have seven pairs of legs (see p.7) and are abundant in most gardens, feeding on dead and decaying plant material and moulds.

Crabs have only five pairs of legs, and only four are used for walking and swimming. The first pair have large *chelae* (pincers) which are used for handling food and for defence. *Cyclops* species have four pairs of legs, which are used for filter feeding (see p.57). Swimming is accomplished mainly by rowing movements of the large first pair of antennae. This is also the case in *Daphnia* species (the water fleas). *Daphnia* are also filter feeders; they are very abundant in some ponds and ditches. *Argulus foliaceus*, the fish louse, is a parasite on the surface of freshwater fishes (parasites which live on the outside of their hosts are called *ectoparasites*). One pair of mouthparts in fish lice has become modified as suckers, which help the animals to attach to the scales and avoid being swept away by the passage of water over the body as the fish swims through the water.

Barnacles live as adults permanently attached to rocks in shallow seas or in sheltered areas in the intertidal zone. They are encased in hard plates called *valves*. These can be opened to allow the animal to extrude six pairs of legs which are swept through the water to trap small suspended particles. Barnacles are filter feeders. They have larvae which swim freely in the sea, enabling these otherwise sessile animals to colonise new places.

BEHAVIOUR FILE

CRUSTACEA

Woodlice, e.g. *Porcellio scaber*, *Armadillidium vulgare*

Lift a piece of bark from a rotting log and you are quite likely to find a cluster of woodlice underneath. For a moment they are still, but then they run in all directions until in a few seconds they have disappeared under the remaining bark. They can be found in other places, too, such as under stones, inside piles of rotting vegetation and even in our homes, particularly beneath old floor coverings and in outhouses. What these habitats have in common is that they are damp with fungal moulds growing. Woodlice feed on the mould while the moisture prevents them from dehydrating (since their exoskeletons are permeable to water), supports their external gills and provides the moisture layer essential to all gas exchange surfaces (see *Biology Advanced Studies - Human Systems*). If their covered habitat is disturbed, such as by you lifting the bark, the conditions suddenly change. It is flooded by light and begins to dry out. It is no longer a favourable habitat. Any woodlice which remain would dehydrate by losing water through the exoskeleton and suffocate through the collapse of their gills. Light in itself is not a threat but it correlates with being uncovered and therefore dry. Woodlice keep themselves in damp habitats by means of behaviour known as taxes and kineses (see p.129).

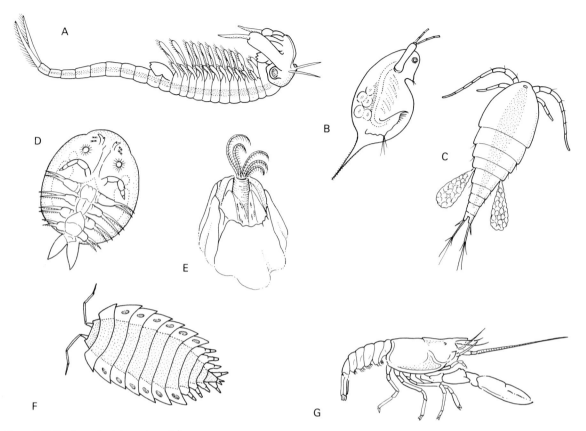

Figure 6.17 Crustacea (not drawn to scale)

English name	Group[1]	Habitat
Brine shrimps	A Branchiopoda, Anostraca	Brackish and sea water
Water fleas	B Branchiopoda, Cladocera	Fresh water
Copepods	C Copepoda	Fresh water and marine
Fish lice	D Branchiura	Fresh water
Barnacles	E Cirripedia	Marine
Woodlice	F Malacostraca, Isopoda	Terrestrial[2]
Crabs, lobsters, shrimps	G Malacostraca, Decapoda	Marine, a few in freshwater

[1] There is disagreement about the classification of Crustacea. Some authorities believe that they should be regarded as a class, in which case the groups listed here are orders. Others think that the Crustacea should be a subphylum, and that the groups listed here should therefore be classes.
[2] Some isopoda are found in marine and freshwater environments.

Table 6.2 Summary classification of crustaceans (not all of the groups of crustaceans are included in this table)

There is one final class of arthropods, the Arachnida. These have four pairs of walking legs and no antennae. As with crustaceans, there are forms with varying numbers of abdominal segments; some have many, some have none.

Scorpions (order Scorpionida) have an elongated abdomen with 12 segments and a sting at the posterior end. They have a pair of chelae ('pincers') at the anterior end, like crabs; but whereas in crabs the chelae are borne by the first pair of legs, in scorpions they are part of the mouthparts. This is an example of convergent evolution. Scorpions are not found in the UK, but there are similar animals to be found in leaf litter. They are rarely more than 3-4 mm in length and have relatively shorter abdomens than true scorpions, with fewer segments, and are called pseudoscorpions.

Scorpion, Sri Lanka

Spiders are the most familiar arachnids to many people, because they often produce a prominent *web*. Webs are made from a silky protein secreted from glands in the abdomen. They are used as traps to catch insects, on which the spider then feeds by sucking out the body fluids. Orb webs have spokes and spiral strands, and the flat surface is vertical. The spider usually sits near the middle. Sheet webs are flat and usually horizontal, while funnel webs are tubular. Not all spiders produce a web. Some are active hunters, running around on the ground in search of other small invertebrate prey. The larger ones are called wolf spiders. These are common in gardens during the summer months; they look rather like tarantulas. Although they do not make a web, they do have silk glands. They use the silk as a safety rope to enable them to climb back up if they fall from a height - something which can easily happen to an animal which is only a few millimetres in length - in rather the same way as a mountaineer uses a rope when abseiling down the side of a cliff.

Some fascinating research shows how injecting spiders with hallucinogenic drugs such as opium causes the webs to be constructed incorrectly. Spider silk is very strong and in thicker strands could be used to make a tough fabric. Current work uses genetic engineering to try to induce bacteria to synthesise spider silk; there is talk of producing bullet-proof garments from spider silk!

The body of a spider is divided into two major parts, the cephalothorax and abdomen; there are no obvious segments. Ticks and mites have a similar structure. They are placed in several different orders - the differences between them depend mainly on details of the respiratory system. Ticks are always ectoparasites, feeding on the blood of vertebrates. Like most blood-sucking animals, they may transmit diseases. Redwater (its formal name is babesiosis) is an infection of cattle, especially common in the western parts of the UK, and is caused by a parasitic protozoan in the red blood corpuscles. Lyme disease is caused by a spirochaete (see Fig.2.2), and is of concern to public health authorities because its incidence in the UK is increasing. Most tick species have adult stages which are 5-10 mm in length.

Mites, which are usually 2-3 mm in length, have a wider variety of lifestyles. Some, like ticks, are ectoparasites. Mites which parasitise vertebrates may produce a skin disease called mange (when mange is found on people it is called scabies). Other mites parasitise invertebrates. They can often be found attached to the undersides of large beetles or bumblebees, e.g. *Acarapis woodi*, which live in the tracheal system and cause serious disease in honey bees. Many species of mites are free-living. Terrestrial free-living mites are often very abundant; they are amongst the commonest of small invertebrate animals in suburban gardens. In fields and woods, free-living mites may achieve populations of more than 10 million per hectare. They may act as intermediate hosts for tapeworms (see p.63). The commonest tapeworms in sheep, cattle and horses in the UK all utilise mites as their intermediate hosts. Free-living mites are also found in fresh water.

Free-living mites may be present in large numbers in homes, and it is now believed that they may be a major cause of diseases such as asthma.

Who's sleeping in your bed?

Many common allergic diseases are triggered by the millions of mites in the comfortable British home, writes Nigel Hawkes.

Don't look now, but you are probably going to bed with two million eight-legged creatures. Invisible, thank heavens, to the naked eye, they are house dust mites which live on scales of dead skin. Carpets, curtains, upholstered chairs and, above all, beds provide a nourishing habitat for the mites. Up to 10 per cent of the weight of an average pillow consists of dead skin and house dust mites. Doctors believe that a large proportion of allergic diseases, including asthma, eczema, and rhinitis, are caused by the mites, or rather by their droppings.

A digestive enzyme, known as Derp 1, is the villain of the piece. Excreted by the mites in their faeces, Derp 1 floats around as light as a pollen grain. Conventional vacuum cleaners simply blow it out with the exhaust air, spreading it far and wide, because it is too small to be caught by the filters.

The modern home, warm, humid, and well-supplied with soft furnishings, has played into the hands of the dust mite. Dr Matthew Colloff, an acarologist (or student of mites) at Stobhill Hospital in Glasgow, says that mites originally lived in the nests of birds or small mammals. Ten thousand years ago, as early man civilised his cave, the mites siezed their chance.

'A house-martin's nest is not so different from a bed,' says Dr Colloff. 'It's warm, cosy, and well-supplied with scales of skin. So it wasn't difficult for the mites to make the shift. They aren't vital to us - we could live quite happily without them.'

They are not insects but arachnids, having eight legs and being more closely related to spiders, ticks and scorpions. Across the world, pole to pole, on land and in the sea, there are at least 60,000 different species of mite.

Among the house mite's many interesting features is its laborious method of procreation. Mites reproduce sexually, but not in a very intimate fashion. They lie back to back, the male on top manipulating a long, curved penis fashioned like the spout of a coffee pot. So tiny is the opening to this sexual organ - one thousandth of a millimetre - that the sperm can flow through it only in single file.

As a result, it takes the male mite 48 hours to

The house dust mite feeds off scales of dead skin and finds carpets, curtains and bedding a nourishing habitat

complete the operation, expelling the sperm one by one, while the female wanders around with him on her back. 'There's no other organism in the whole of creation that does that' says Dr Colloff triumphantly.

He doubts that mites are really any commoner today than they have ever been, though warmer homes and fitted carpets have helped, and the abandonment of carpet-beating must have given the mites a quieter life. The real change has been in the growing recognition of the damage that the mites can do, particularly in triggering allergic disease in children.

Among patients at Bart's, skin tests have shown that up to a third of people are allergic to house dust mites. A survey, carried out for the foundation by MORI, put the number among adults at one in four, or more than 11 million people in Britain as a whole. While it is questionable how accurate such a survey can hope to be, 80 per cent of asthmatic children have been shown to be allergic to house dust mites.

Nigel Hawkes, *The Times*, 21 September 1993
© Times Newspapers Ltd 1993

■ PHYLUM MOLLUSCA

The Molluscs are a very diverse phylum. Snails and slugs are probably the most familiar members, but limpets, cockles, squid and octopuses are also molluscs. There is no single major feature that all of these organisms share; they are defined by a combination of characteristics.

Molluscs are bilaterally symmetrical, like annelids and arthropods, but they are not externally segmented. It is believed, however, that molluscs evolved from segmented ancestors and that the segmentation has become lost. Loss of characters has occurred frequently during the course of evolution. Snakes, for example, evolved from lizard-like reptiles which had legs. Can you think of other examples?

The most important characteristic of molluscs, however, is that they either have a *shell* - which is formed from secreted calcium salts - or they are derived from ancestors which did (here is another example of the loss of a characteristic during evolution). In octopuses, squid and cuttlefish (class Cephalopoda) the shell is internal, and has been modified to form a buoyancy mechanism called cuttlebone. This is a porous material with large numbers of holes in it (a bit like Aero chocolate, but the holes are much smaller). The animal is able to secrete gas into the holes, or to absorb it; the amount of gas determines whether the creature floats or sinks. Cuttlebone is very rich in calcium. (It can be bought in petshops as a convenient source of the mineral for captive birds, which will peck at it avidly.)

Snails belong to a class of molluscs called the Gastropoda. Many species feed on plant material, rasping the food with a strip of tissue bearing rows of chitinous teeth called a *radula*. The action of the radula can easily be observed when a freshwater snail is crawling over the inside of the front pane of glass or plastic of an aquarium (it will be feeding on algae or bacteria attached to the surface). The shell in most gastropods is coiled. Dogwhelks (*Nucella lapillus*) and limpets are gastropods in which the shell is not coiled, but is a simple conical structure (rather like a Chinese coolie hat). Slugs are also gastropods, but in most species the

Dogwhelks (*Nucella lapillus*) feeding on barnacles

shell is small and internal, so it cannot be seen unless the animal is dissected. Terrestrial slugs are familiar animals in most gardens, where they are pests. Sea slugs, as their name implies, are marine, many being extremely colourful. *Aplysia punctata*, the sea hare, is red in colour when young. As it grows it turns brown, and finally becomes olive green, sometimes with brown or reddish spots, when it is adult. Many species of sea slugs feed on cnidarians (p.57). They do not digest the nematocysts, but incorporate them into their own epidermis; thus they do not only acquire nutrients from their food, they get a pre-formed defence mechanism as well.

Gastropods move by creeping over the surface. The ventral part of the body in contact with the ground is formed into a series of small ridges, which move along the length of the animal (they are caused by the movements of muscles in the underlying tissues). Locomotion is aided by the secretion of mucus from glands which open at the anterior end near the mouth. In some gastropods the ridges move forwards; the mucus causes each crest to adhere to the ground, and so the principles of the movement are rather similar to those of an earthworm (p.66) or a python when moving by rectilinear locomotion (p.89). In others, the ridges move backwards, and in this case it is the thrust which they exert against the mucus or small projections from the substrate which propel the mollusc forwards. 'Trails' are often observed when a snail has crawled by; they are the remains of the mucus over which the animal has moved.

DOGWHELKS

The dogwhelk *Nucella lapillus* lives on Atlantic rocky shores. It is usually found in the lower part of the middle shore zone. It is a predator of slow moving and sedentary animals with hard exteriors, such as mussels, limpets and barnacles. Extracting the food takes several hours or even days. The dogwhelk climbs on top of its prey and bores a tiny hole through the shell, using enzymes from an organ near its mouth and by scraping with its radula. It pushes a proboscis through the hole and injects a narcotic which paralyses the prey. It secretes enzymes which digest the tissues and sucks the liquidised food back up through the proboscis.

Whilst feeding, part of the body must protrude from the shell. If the tide goes out whilst it is feeding the body becomes exposed to the air and starts to lose water by evaporation. In response it retracts into the shell and avoids desiccation; but in so doing it has to let go of its prey. It follows that dogwhelks can feed only in places where they are covered by water for a good length of time, that is, low on the shore.

On most shores dogwhelks have a choice between prey species and between eating large or small individuals. Do they feed on whatever they happen to find or do they reject some prey in favour of something else that they prefer? The theory of *optimal foraging* (see p.112) predicts that if there were a choice of prey a dogwhelk would choose to eat the one which provided it with the greatest amount of energy compared with the amount of energy it would have to use up getting the food out.

That is, it would choose the most profitable prey. There is some evidence to suggest that dogwhelks are optimal foragers. Firstly they do seem to be able to distinguish between prey species. Table 6.3 shows dogwhelks in that study eating a particular type of barnacle (adult *Semibalanus balanoides*) in preference to other types. A calculation of energy yield (see below) from mussels and from barnacles has shown that barnacles provide the greater profit; so we would predict that dogwhelks should choose barnacles rather than mussels.

Reports in the literature do suggest that the most favoured food is the barnacle *Semibalanus balanoides* while the second is the mussel *Mytilus edulis*, confirming the prediction; however the third and fourth favourites are types of barnacle again, confusing the issue. As to size, within one prey species they tend to go for larger rather than smaller individuals; perhaps because for the same effort and risk they offer the greater prize of energy. But this is only apparent in good weather conditions. When their foraging time is restricted by the buffeting of high seas, or the danger of desiccation when the tide is out in summer, they will eat whatever size of prey they first come upon, snatching the chance of a meal before retreating to the safety of a crevice in the rocks. At the beginning of a spell of unfavourable weather they might eat the larger specimens within safe foraging distance of their crevice but eventually only the smaller ones will be left and they will have no choice.

Prey species	% of all barnacles present	% eaten
Semibalanus balanoides (adult)	7.6	52.5
Semibalanus balanoides (immature)	77.7	7.5
Elminius modestus	11.7	37.5
Chthamalus montagui	2.6	2.5
Chthamalus stellatus	0.3	0.0

Calculating the energy yield from prey:

$$\text{energy yield} = \frac{(\text{dry weight of edible parts}) \times (\text{joule value of the dried flesh})}{(\text{time expended})}$$

Table 6.3 Prey preferences among barnacles shown by *Nucella lapillus* in West Angle Bay (Milford Haven). Data collected by Colchester Girls' School and published by The Field Studies Council.

LIMPETS

Limpets live in the middle shore zone of rocky sea shores. They cling to the rock by suction with a large, muscular foot and, when covered by the tide, move across the rock feeding on a surface film of microscopic algae. When the tide is out and they are left uncovered they pull the wide based conical shell tightly against the rock, trapping water underneath which keeps the tissues moist. They frequently have a 'home' to which they return before the tide recedes. This is a place where the shell has grown to fit perfectly to the contours of the rock, thus forming a tight seal. The close match is created over a long time by the animal grinding the shell against the rock, wearing away both shell and rock, with tiny twisting movements.

At night, even when they are not covered by the sea, limpets graze the rock by rubbing off algae with short rasping licks of the radula. As they advance, slowly swinging the head from side to side, they sweep out a zig-zag pattern. You can often see where limpets have grazed by the trail of radula marks they have left behind. If you follow one of these trails you can sometimes trace it back to the limpet which made it, perhaps the previous night. The photograph on the right shows a limpet with trails which tell the story of its most recent foray. It grazed its way in long winding loops, ending up where it began.

It is possible to identify limpets with their homes by marking the shell and the adjacent rock with paint. You can tell whether or not a limpet returns home after a foraging session. Using this simple technique one

An experiment by Selwood Middle School (1985) in which limpets are identified with their homes by spots of paint

can seek answers to questions such as: do all limpets have homes; do they have only one home; do they always return home? The photograph above shows the results of such an investigation. Five have returned home and two of them are marked with two spots suggesting that they have at least two homes.

Limpet with grazing trails

Cockles are an example of molluscs which have two shells (called *valves*) which are joined together by a hinge. The soft parts of the body are immediately inside the hinge. The valves can be closed by the contraction of powerful *adductor muscles* (Fig.6.18). When the valves are closed the mollusc is very well protected, both from predators and from desiccation - the latter is particularly important for intertidal species. Molluscs with two halves are called bivalves or lamellibranchs (order Bivalvia).

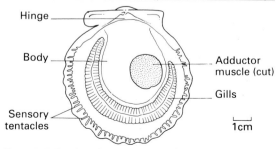

Figure 6.18 Drawing of a bivalve mollusc (*Pecten maximus*, the scallop). One valve of the shell has been removed and the adductor muscle has been cut

Bivalves have a pair of *gills*, which hang down from the main part of the body like a pair of thick curtains with small holes in them. The gills are covered with cilia, which by their movements produce currents of water which pass through the holes. These currents carry oxygenated water to the gills, and also small organisms such as bacteria and algae which are suspended in the water and become trapped in sticky mucus. This is carried in turn by cilia (which beat in appropriate directions) to the mouth, which is at the base of the gills. The gills are therefore used for both respiration and feeding; bivalves are filter-feeders (see p.57).

If pollutants or harmful bacteria are present in water in which bivalves are feeding, they may be concentrated in the bodies of the molluscs as a result of filter-feeding. As a consequence, bivalves are often a cause of food poisoning. Care should be taken to ensure that cockles, mussels, oysters and other bivalves which are eaten come from clean, unpolluted water.

■ PHYLUM ECHINODERMATA

These are animals which have *pentaradiate symmetry*: they have five identical sides. Starfishes are probably the best-known echinoderms. They have five *arms* which radiate outwards from the centre. The animal is covered with an endoskeleton of *ossicles*, which are plates of tissue which have become hardened with various calcium salts. How does such an 'armour-plated' animal move? The answer is that there are large numbers of hollow, thin-walled projections on the under surface, called *tube feet*, which project through small spaces in the ossicles. They are connected by a water-filled 'plumbing' system. Movement is achieved partly by muscles, and partly by pumping water into and out of the tube feet. This is a hydraulic system, and operates in a similar way to the mechanism which raises and lowers the shovel of a mechanical digger (in the latter case, the fluid is oil).

BEHAVIOUR FILE

LEARNING IN APLYSIA

Aplysia is a shell-less, marine snail up to 30 cm long and much used in neurophysiological work because of its simple nervous system with relatively large neurons. Amongst other simple behaviours, Aplysia shows a rapid withdrawal of its gills when a strong stimulus is applied to the tail (e.g. a predator grabbing it or, in the laboratory, a small electric shock). This is a simple reflex (like eye-blinking or the knee-jerk in humans) and involves only two nerve cells, a *sensory neurone* from the tail and a *motor neurone* to the gills. A much weaker gill-withdrawal response is given if the mantle or siphon is stimulated. However, if the shock to the tail is preceded by touching the mantle or siphon, and this pairing of stimuli is repeated several times, the Aplysia will soon start to withdraw its gills strongly even when the siphon or mantle alone is touched. It has changed its behaviour, and has learned to respond to mantle or siphon stimulation as if it were a shock to the tail. This ability to learn makes biological sense, as here the mantle stimulus predicts the (much worse) attack to the tail. This changing response to a previously irrelevant stimulus (touching the mantle) has all the ingredients of *classical conditioning*; compare it to the example of Pavlov's dogs on p.137. Which are the *unconditional stimulus, conditional stimulus* and *conditional response*?

Starfishes are marine, as are all other echinoderms; the group includes sea urchins and brittle stars. Echinoderms must have evolved from ancestors which were bilaterally symmetrical (see p.57), and they have a ciliated larval stage which, unlike the adults, has bilateral and not pentaradiate symmetry.

CHAPTER 7

THE ANIMALS: VERTEBRATES

All of the animals described in the previous chapter are *invertebrates* because they do not have a *backbone* (sometimes called a *vertebral column*). *Vertebrate* animals are those which do have a backbone. They are important because they are generally considered to be the most advanced animals. (Of course we are vertebrates. It will be a great help to you in your studies to make frequent comparisons with the situation in humans.) In this chapter there are frequent references to *Biology Advanced Studies - Human Systems* (HS) and *Biology Advanced Studies - Biochemistry* (B).

The backbone is dorsal, i.e. it lies along the top of the animal. It has two major components: one is the *dorsal nerve cord*, often called the *spinal cord*, with the *brain* at the anterior (front) end; and in primitive forms, and in the early embryos of all vertebrates, there is also a rod of cartilage, lying above the dorsal nerve cord, which provides support (the structure of cartilage is explained in HS p.28). The rod is called a *notochord*. Animals with a notochord are placed in the phylum Chordata.

During the development of the embryo of most Chordata, the cartilaginous rod is replaced by a series of segmental bones which entirely surround the nerve cord to protect it; these are the *vertebrae* (Fig.2.8 in HS). Chordates with fully developed vertebrae - and these are the majority - are placed in the sub-phylum Vertebrata. (We can consider vertebrates and chordates to be *almost* the same thing since the other sub-phyla contain fairly obscure marine animals, such as sea-squirts.) The bones around the brain do not form vertebrae; they are fused together to form the *skull*.

One of the puzzles of biology is to determine from what kind of animals the vertebrates evolved. There have been many theories; the most widely accepted is that vertebrate ancestors were rather like echinoderms. The reasons, however, are complex and involve a detailed understanding of comparative anatomy, embryology and biochemistry.

All vertebrates have a coelom (p.60). They also all share the characteristic that the dorsal nerve cord is hollow. Nerves carrying sensory input enter the spinal cord dorsally; those carrying motor output leave it ventrally (see HS, p.83).

■ CLASS AGNATHA

The first three classes of vertebrates listed in Table 7.1 are all fishes of various kinds, and it is reasonable to wonder why it should be necessary to make separate classes. The answer is that although the animals in these classes look superficially quite similar to one another, they actually have quite fundamental differences. The class Agnatha is small, and contains rather primitive eel-like fishes which do not have either jaws, or pectoral and pelvic fins (p.82).

Class	Common name
Agnatha	Lampreys and hagfishes
Osteichthyes	Bony fishes
Chondrichthyes	Cartilaginous fishes (sharks and rays)
Amphibia	Amphibians
Reptilia	Reptiles
Aves	Birds
Mammalia	Mammals

Table 7.1 The seven classes of living animals within the sub-phylum Vertebrata (there are a number of further classes, mainly of fishes, which are now extinct)

Lampreys have a funnel-shaped sucker at the anterior end which is lined with sharp, horny teeth (but these do not have the same structure as the teeth of mammals described in HS, p.73; they are much simpler). Lampreys use their sucker and teeth to attach themselves to other fishes, cutting the skin and flesh and feeding on the blood and bits of tissue which seep from the wound. The blood flow from the prey can be maintained for a long time because the lamprey secretes an *anticoagulant* which prevents clotting. Three species are found around the UK. One lives permanently in fresh water and two migrate between fresh water where they breed and the sea where most of their feeding takes place.

Lamprey

Hagfishes are similar to lampreys, but the sucker is not so well developed and they feed mainly on dead or injured fishes - they are scavengers. Hagfishes are marine, and only one species is found in the seas around the UK, although there are many more in the tropics.

■ CLASS OSTEICHTHYES

These are fishes with jaws. The class contains all such fishes in which the skeleton is made of bone (others have a skeleton made of cartilage, and are placed in the class Chondrichthyes,

p.86). Osteichthyes are the most abundant of all the classes of vertebrates; about 25 000 species have been described.

A typical bony fish, such as a trout or perch, has skin which is covered with protective *scales*, made of bony plates surrounded by epidermal cells. Swimming efficiency and stability in the water are aided by *fins*, which are raised areas of skin, without scales but supported by bony rods called *fin rays*. Most bony fishes have seven or eight fins (Fig.7.1). The *caudal fin* provides the main thrust for propulsion when it is moved from side to side. Paired *pectoral fins* (there is one on each side of the body), paired *pelvic fins*, an *anal fin* and one or two *dorsal fins* provide stability when the animal is moving and help it to change direction and position itself - they function rather like the tail and wing flaps of an aeroplane.

Respiration in fishes is by means of *gills*. There are usually five pairs in Osteichthyes. They are covered by a flap of the body wall, attached at the front and supported by an underlying plate of bone, the *operculum*. Movements of the operculum help to pump water into the mouth, across the gills and out through the opercular opening.

One of the most important features of bony fishes is the *swim bladder*. This is a hollow structure containing gas, which makes the fish buoyant so that it floats in the water. If more gas is secreted into the swim bladder (from the bloodstream) the fish rises; if gas is absorbed back into the blood, it sinks. The swimbladder

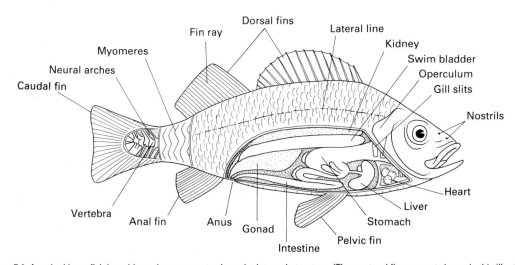

Figure 7.1 A typical bony fish (perch), partly cut away to show the internal structure. (The pectoral fins are not shown in this illustration.)

is placed at the centre of gravity of the fish, and its position in the vertical plane is such that the main line of force generated by the movement of the tail fin passes directly through it. The fish is therefore stable; it remains horizontal both when it is swimming and when it is floating motionless in the water.

Swimming requires the expenditure of a great deal of energy, and so a high proportion of the body of a fish is composed of muscle. The muscle fibres (HS, Ch.2) are arranged in segmental blocks, separated by thick sheets of connective tissue. This gives the flesh of fishes a characteristic structure, easily observed if the batter is scraped off a fillet of cod from a helping of fish and chips, or by opening a tin of tuna. The blocks have a complicated shape (they look rather like a W in a fillet of cod when viewed from the side), which has evolved to maximise the efficiency by which muscle contractions are converted into lateral bending of the body and so produce forward thrust. Tuna flesh is red, cod flesh is mostly white. This is because tuna muscles have more mitochondria and myoglobin (the protein that stores oxygen in muscle). Most fishes actually have a mixture of red and white muscle - it is the proportions that differ. Cod, for example, have a thin strip of red muscle along the midline immediately beneath the skin; this red muscle can be seen particularly easily in smoked mackerel.

Why do fishes have two sorts of muscle? The answer is that red muscle is aerobic (see B, Ch.6) and is used for slow, sustained swimming. White muscle is used for short bursts of fast swimming, the energy for which is produced mainly anaerobically. A cod normally cruises fairly slowly in the sea, using mainly the red muscle for movement. If a larger predator such as a shark appears in view, the white muscle will come into use, and with luck will enable the potential prey to make a fast escape.

The majority of fishes are *ectotherms*; this means that they have no physiological control over their body temperature (all invertebrates are ectotherms - the term has replaced the old idea of 'cold bloodedness'). The heat which is generated by muscle contraction is quickly lost to the environment, because there is no insulating layer of fur or feathers to conserve it (see HS, pp.79-80). Some fishes, however, have a limited degree of temperature control.

This is developed best in tunas, in which the blood vessels are arranged in such a way that the arteries carrying oxygenated blood from the gills to the muscles run alongside the veins carrying blood at a low oxygen tension away from the muscles. Blood is heated as it passes through the actively contracting muscles; some of this heat is transferred by diffusion back to the incoming blood, so conserving it. By this mechanism (which is technically called a countercurrent heat exchanger) a swimming tuna can maintain the temperature of its deeper muscles as much as 10 °C above that of the surrounding sea. This is of great benefit to the fish, because muscles work more efficiently at higher temperatures.

Bony fishes have an enormous range of shapes and sizes. They are found in the sea and in fresh-water environments, and some such as salmon, sea trout and eels, migrate between the two. Salmon and sea trout are examples of fishes that live primarily in the sea, but migrate to fresh water to breed. Eels do the reverse; they inhabit rivers and lakes for most of their lives, but breed in the sea. For many years biologists did not know just where eels went to breed, and this is perhaps not surprising because it has now been discovered that they go to the depths of the Sargasso Sea (in the western part of the North Atlantic Ocean). It is still not fully understood how they are able to navigate there (see Navigation, p.132), or why this kind of migration is of advantage to the species. Returning is rather easier; the little eels simply drift with the Gulf Stream. Many millions used to be caught at the season when they were moving through estuaries towards their breeding rivers, as the eels at this stage (which are called elvers) are a delicacy. It is a characteristic of bony fish that eggs are laid and then fertilised in the water; they have external fertilisation, unlike cartilaginous fish (see p.86), which have internal fertilisation.

Many other species of bony fishes act as a source of food for humans. Until recently most food fishes were captured with nets from boats, but fish farming is becoming increasingly important. Gene technology (see *Biology Advanced Studies - Microbiology and Biotechnology*) is likely to lead to an increase in the number of species which are domesticated in this way, and to improvements in their productivity and resistance to disease.

REPRODUCTIVE BEHAVIOUR OF THE THREE-SPINED STICKLEBACK

Three-spined sticklebacks (*Gasterosteus aculeatus*) live in fresh water streams and ponds in northern Europe. For most of the year both sexes look similar in size, shape and silvery colour, and individuals live solitary lives. Only in the spring do the sexes come together to mate. At this time their appearance changes significantly; the abdomens of the females swell with eggs and the males become brightly coloured with a green back, turquoise eyes and bright red belly and throat.

A male selects an area at the bottom of the stream and builds a nest. It is a dome of algae with a tunnel through it, held together with a sticky secretion from the stickleback's cloaca. Other males may sometimes swim into the area. If they are not in their breeding colours, the resident male ignores them; but if the other male is in breeding condition, displaying his red underside, the resident male defends his territory. He swims vigorously to attack the intruder, biting and chasing him away.

When a swollen female approaches the nest area, the male begins a courtship ritual. He repeatedly swoops towards and away from her in a display known as the *zig-zag dance*. After several zig-zags the female might swim close to him with her head up. If she does, he swims to his nest and hovers close to it with his snout pointing to the entrance. She follows. If not, he returns to zig-zag dancing and pointing to the nest until she does.

Eventually the female swims through the nest entrance and comes to rest inside with her tail sticking out. The male vibrates his snout against her side at the base of her tail until she is stimulated to shed her eggs. Then he pushes his way in, edging the female out, and sheds his sperm on to the eggs. He then swims out himself and chases the now flat-bellied female away.

Inside the nest the sperms fertilise the eggs, and development begins. The male stays close to the nest, threatening and chasing other males who intrude into the territory. Periodically, he fans a current of water through the nest with his pectoral fins, maintaining a flow of oxygen to the developing larvae.

After 6-10 days the young fish swim out of the nest to start their independent lives. The male loses his bright colours and returns to his solitary life.

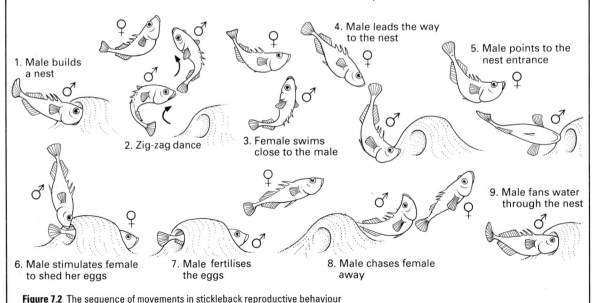

1. Male builds a nest

2. Zig-zag dance

3. Female swims close to the male

4. Male leads the way to the nest

5. Male points to the nest entrance

6. Male stimulates female to shed her eggs

7. Male fertilises the eggs

8. Male chases female away

9. Male fans water through the nest

Figure 7.2 The sequence of movements in stickleback reproductive behaviour

Scientists create 'mutant' salmon for the high street

Salmon that have been genetically altered to make them sterile have gone on sale in supermarkets without any labelling to help shoppers identify them.

More than 4000 tonnes of 'mutant' salmon will be produced for the British market this year, following government research which pioneered a technique to stop them developing ovaries.

In contrast to the salmon's 'natural' image, the genetically altered variety is deprived of its instinct to migrate upriver from the sea to spawn. Such fish would stay put and grow to twice the normal size of farmed fish.

The disclosure that shoppers are buying the salmon unwittingly has provoked criticism from consumer groups, who claim there has been a 'conspiracy of silence' about its introduction. Labour is to demand an explanation from ministers this week.

Producers admitted that genetically altered salmon, which are cheaper to rear, first reached the shops three years ago and already account for more than 10% of sales.

Michael Young, director of the Food Safety Advisory Centre, an independent body funded by supermarkets, said the government should have announced their arrival on the market and encouraged a public debate. 'Furtive discussion is not going to inspire confidence,' he said.

Stephen Locke, policy director of the Consumers' Association, called for labelling so that anyone opposed to genetic interference could avoid the new salmon. 'It is a classic case of scientists deciding everything is all right and consumers do not need to worry their heads about it,' he said. 'We are not saying this salmon is unsafe, but many consumers will have moral and ethical concerns. The industry should deal with that concern, not try and shove it under the carpet.'

More than 10 years of research have gone into producing 'triploid' salmon, so-called because they have three sets of chromosomes instead of the normal two. The chromosomes - tiny rod-like structures carrying genes - are added by a technique known as pressure shock, which is applied to fish eggs in containers of water.

The effect is to prevent the salmon reaching sexual maturity, which causes deterioration. Instead, they go on growing and keep their silver appearance, which commands top prices.

Ray Johnstone, the scientist who developed the technique at the Scottish Office's marine laboratory in Aberdeen, said it replicated a rare 'triploidisation' phenomenon in wild fish. 'As long as the products are of the quality that purchasers desire, I think people should be quite happy to eat them.'

Sean Ryan, *Sunday Times*, 26 September 1993.
© Times Newspapers Ltd 1993

Q Why do you think the headline writer used the incorrect term 'mutant' when the fish are, in fact, triploid?

One group of bony fishes, the *lungfishes*, helps to provide clues about how land vertebrates might have evolved. They are otherwise a rather obscure group; there are only three living genera, found in muddy swamps and rivers in the tropics. The swimbladder has been replaced by lungs (or one lung in the case of *Neoceratodus* from Australia), which are used for breathing at times when the water becomes so stagnant that it contains little oxygen. The fishes cannot then use their gills, and have to come up to the surface at intervals to breathe, by gulping air into the lungs.

Lungfish (*Protopherus aethiopicus*)

■ CLASS CHONDRICHTHYES

Fishes in this class (e.g. sharks and dogfishes) have a skeleton made of cartilage. They are not so abundant and varied as bony fish - there are only about 3500 species - and they are almost all marine. Unlike bony fishes they have no swimbladder. In order to maintain their position in the water they must keep swimming. The pectoral fins act as hydrofoils, providing lift (this is the same basic principle as that by which an aeroplane flies - if an aeroplane stops moving it crashes, if a shark stops swimming it sinks). The upward forces on the pectoral fins which provide the lift act in front of the centre of gravity. As a result a turning moment is produced. This must be counteracted; otherwise the head would continually move upwards and the fish would 'loop the loop'. This does not happen because the tail fin is asymmetrical (Fig.7.3); the dorsal lobe is bigger than the ventral lobe. As a result, most of the thrust force generated by the tail acts above the centre of gravity. This produces a turning moment which counteracts the moment due to lift, and the fish is in dynamic equilibrium.

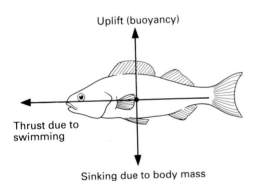

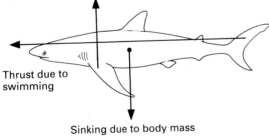

Figure 7.3 Major forces acting on a swimming bony fish (above) and cartilaginous fish (below). See text for detailed explanation

Bull shark

Many cartilaginous fishes, such as sharks, swim actively for most of the time and so rarely sink. Others, however, have become adapted for living on the bottom. These are the skates and rays, which are often called flatfishes. They are flattened in a dorsoventral plane, i.e. an individual looks a bit like a shark which has been squashed from above. There are bottom-living bony fishes which are also flattened, for example plaice and flounder, but in these the flattening is lateral, i.e. it is from side to side. The body is therefore 'on its side' and asymmetrical when viewed from above. During the course of embryonic development one eye migrates so that it comes to lie on the same side of the head as the other; this is kept upwards as the topside of the fish.

Cartilaginous fishes do not have an operculum; five *gill slits* can be seen on either side of the body.

Plaice (*Pleuronectes platessa*)

■ CLASS AMPHIBIA

At some time during the Devonian geological period, about 400 million years ago, a group of fishes emerged from freshwater swamps and began to live on land. This required enormous changes in structure and physiology. Animals on land cannot swim, and so where limb-like structures developed they were selected for over a period of time. These were very different from the jointed limbs of arthropods (p.67). They were formed from pectoral and pelvic fins, and had an internal skeleton of bones. Where the top bones of the limbs articulated (joined) with the backbone, *pectoral* and *pelvic girdles* developed to form attachments for the limb muscles. All terrestrial vertebrates are *tetrapods*: they have two pairs of limbs (which may be modified as wings or flippers, as in birds, bats, whales and seals, or lost altogether). Breathing in these Devonian tetrapods was partly by means of lungs, as in lungfishes (p.85), and partly through the skin. The blood system became more complicated; there was a *double circulation* (Fig.7.4). What this means is that any blood corpuscle travels through the heart twice before it begins again on the route at which it started.

The modern animals which retain the kind of organisation of these Devonian ancestors are called amphibians. They have lungs and a double circulation, but neither is efficient enough to supply all of the oxygen that an individual needs to fuel its metabolism. The shortfall is made up from oxygen which diffuses into the body through the skin. This can occur only if the skin is thin and kept moist; amphibians have *mucus gland*s in the skin which help to prevent them drying out (Fig.7.5). Amphibians are therefore mostly confined to living in damp places. A few have colonised arid environments such as deserts, but their activity must be confined to the short periods during or immediately after rain. For the rest of the time they remain immobile in deep burrows or caked in dry mud.

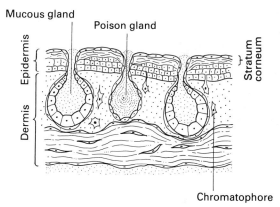

Figure 7.5 Vertical section through amphibian skin

There is a second reason why amphibians are associated with water. They reproduce by laying eggs which have no means for preventing loss of water if they are in a dry place. They are therefore almost invariably laid in water. They hatch as larvae, which have gills and are called *tadpoles*. Tadpoles undergo a period of growth in the water, and only then do they develop lungs, lose their gills, and emerge on land. This process is called amphibian *metamorphosis*.

There are a number of intriguing adaptations by means of which some amphibians avoid the limitations of this kind of life cycle. Foam-nesting frogs in the tropics lay their eggs on land, but surround them with a protective layer of foamy mucus. The eggs are almost always placed in a branch of a tree overhanging a pond or river. When a tadpole hatches, it drops

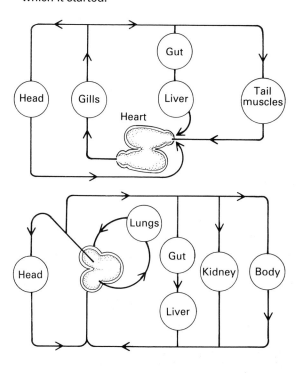

Figure 7.4 Diagram showing a single circulation (as in a fish) and a double circulation (in an amphibian)

into the water. The female Surinam toad, *Pipa pipa*, develops a thick spongy layer of skin (which retains water) on her back during the breeding season. The male toad pushes the eggs into this when they are laid, and both the eggs and the tadpoles develop there.

Three major groups of amphibians have survived to the present day. Newts and salamanders (order Urodela) are closest in appearance to the earliest amphibians. In temperate climates their migrations to the water to breed are seasonal, usually taking place in the spring. In some species an elaborate courtship takes place in the water, and there may be intense competition between males, which often develop *secondary sexual characters*, which include a dorsal crest and brightly coloured body pattern. Chemical stimuli may also be involved in this kind of behaviour; the male smooth newt, *Triturus vulgaris*, wafts a current of water towards the female by fanning with his tail, and this transmits chemicals which are an integral part of the courtship sequence. Other urodeles, such as the European fire salamander, have *warning coloration* because some of their skin glands produce foul-tasting chemicals which are toxic to potential prey.

Male smooth newt (*Triturus vulgaris*) showing courtship colours and crests

Frogs and toads (order Anura) have relatively shorter bodies than urodeles, and they have no tail. Many can jump, because the back legs are elongated and muscular. Courtship and inter-male rivalry start *before* they enter the water to breed. Both behaviours are based almost exclusively on sound rather than visual or chemical signals. Sound is transmitted on land better than under water, whereas chemical communication is less effective on land. Visual communication would

Common frogs and spawn

not be very effective because most amphibian activity takes place after dark when it is cooler and the risk of desiccation is reduced. Calling frogs or toads can be so loud that people living nearby find them a nuisance.

The third group of amphibians are called caecilians (order Gymnophiona). They have lost their legs entirely and are worm-like in appearance and habits. Caecilians are not found in Europe.

■ CLASS REPTILIA

With the evolution of reptiles, which occurred during the Carboniferous period about 330 million years ago, many of the problems which are faced by amphibians were overcome.

How this was achieved can be illustrated by comparing an amphibian such as a newt with a reptile such as a small lizard. These animals look superficially very similar - Carl Linnaeus, when he first classified animals in the eighteenth century (see p.1), did not distinguish between them. They can often be found in the same habitats, although newts are nocturnal (when they are on land) and lizards are diurnal.

Lizard, Oman

In what ways do they differ? First of all, the lizard has a *scaly skin*. The epidermis is thickened by plates of *keratin*, a protein containing a great deal of the amino acid cysteine, which has the formula $CH_2SH.CHNH_2.COOH$. The $-SH$ groups in adjacent cysteine molecules become oxidised and link together as in Fig.7.6. A large, stable and very inert molecule is formed. Keratin is found in many structures which must resist wear, such as scales, feathers, hair and horn.

$$...NH.CH.CO... \qquad ...NH.CH.CO...$$
$$| \qquad\qquad\qquad |$$
$$CH.SH_2 \qquad\qquad CH_2S$$
$$\qquad\longrightarrow\qquad |$$
$$CH.SH_2 \qquad\qquad CH_2S$$
$$| \qquad\qquad\qquad |$$
$$...NH.CH.CO... \qquad ...NH.CH.CO...$$

Figure 7.6

Because of the scales, the rate at which water is lost from the skin is much slower than in an amphibian. The skin of the lizard is dry, and so cannot be used as a respiratory organ. There have consequently been improvements over amphibians in the efficiency of the lungs and blood circulation of reptiles.

The second way in which a lizard differs from a newt is that the lizard is able to lay its eggs on land. A shell has developed which prevents loss of water. This has resulted in the lizard embryo completing its development within the egg. There is no need for an aquatic tadpole stage. In isolation, however, this would create a problem: how is the embryo to be fed? This is achieved by the provision of a nutritious material, the *yolk*. This is stored in a 'bag' of tissue, the *yolk sac*. A second such 'bag' is used to store the material produced by nitrogenous excretion (see *Biology Advanced Studies - Biochemistry*, p.83 and *Biology Advanced Studies - Human Systems*, p.58) and is called the *allantois*. The yolk sack and the allantois are two of the *egg membranes*; other egg membranes are the *chorion* and the *amnion*, which are used primarily to hold fluid which encircles the embryo and protects it from mechanical shock and desiccation.

Reptiles, like amphibians, are ectotherms (p.83). Since they are resistant to water loss, however, they are able to survive if their bodies are warm - an amphibian under these conditions would dry up very rapidly. Many reptiles actively regulate their body temperatures. They warm themselves by placing their bodies in the direct rays of the sun or on sun-warmed rocks or bark. This is called *basking*. If they get too hot they go into the shade or drop into nearby water. This kind of temperature control is called *behavioural thermoregulation* (to distinguish the process from *physiological thermoregulation* of the kind seen in endothermic birds and mammals, and described, for humans, in *Biology Advanced Studies - Human Systems*, pp.79-80). Because it can maintain a high body temperature (but only when the sun is shining), a lizard can be much more active than a newt. It moves faster, and is more alert and intelligent.

About 4000 species of living reptiles are known. Lizards are placed in the order Squamata, together with snakes. Snakes evolved from lizards by elongation of the body, loss of legs and the development of a jaw mechanism which enables them to swallow prey which are even bigger in diameter than themselves. Snakes move mainly by flexing the body into a series of waves, which move backwards and so produce a thrust force against any projections from the surface. The principles are the same as those governing the locomotion of nematode worms (see p.65). Occasionally alternative means of locomotion are seen. A python on a smooth surface will move by creating a series of ridges on the ventral surface, using the muscles of the body wall and the ribs. This is called rectlinear locomotion; the principles are similar to those described for a gastropod mollusc (see p.77). Crocodiles and alligators are placed in a separate order, the Crocodilia, mainly because the skull is constructed in a different way. Tortoises, terrapins and turtles (order Chelonia) have an exoskeleton, the shell, which is constructed of plates made of bone (on the inside) and horny skin (on the outside).

Galapagos giant tortoise

Galapagos land iguana

At one time reptiles were more abundant than they are today, and the entire Mesozoic era, from about 230 to 65 million years ago, is often called 'The Age of Reptiles'. Amongst the groups which thrived at that time were the well-known dinosaurs (Fig.7.7). *Brachiosaurus* was a dinosaur which could reach a weight of 80 tonnes. This is more than the weight of 12 elephants; *Brachiosaurus* was the biggest land vertebrate ever to have lived. Other groups included the marine plesiosaurs and ichthyosaurs, and the pterosaurs which could fly.

■ CLASS AVES

Birds (class Aves) evolved from reptiles during the Jurassic period, about 200 million years ago, but they did not become abundant until much later. Their two most important features are that they can fly (there are a few exceptions, such as ostriches and kiwis) and that they are *endothermic* (see *Biology Advanced Studies - Human Systems*, p.79). Birds share this characteristic with mammals - both can generate heat internally and regulate the body temperature within narrow limits. This constancy of temperature is known as *homoiothermy* (other animals are ectothermic and poikilothermic).

The bodies of birds have become greatly modified for flight. The forelimbs have evolved into *wings*, and the pectoral (shoulder) girdle has enlarged to support the massive *pectoralis muscles* which flap the wings and so provide propulsion (it is the pectoralis muscles which are the 'breast' of a chicken). A bird needs to be as light as possible, and many of the bones are therefore thin-walled with large marrow cavities. Their nitrogenous excretion is

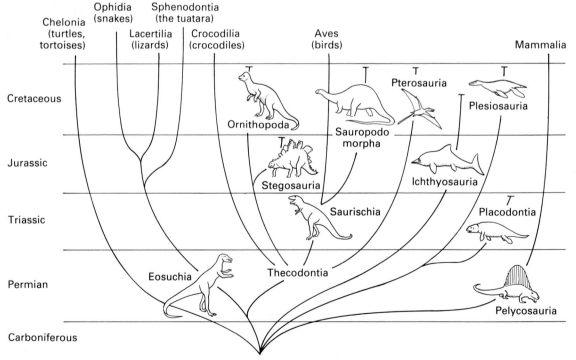

Figure 7.7 Simplified diagram of the evolutionary history of reptiles. Only the animals that evolved from Thecodontia in the Permian period are dinosaurs, although many other reptiles (such as Pelycosaurs) looked rather like them. Note that five major groups became extinct during the Cretaceous period. Lines which continue to the top of the figure show groups of higher vertebrates which are still alive today

mainly in the form of *uric acid* (see *Biology Advanced Studies - Biochemistry*, p.83); this is relatively non-toxic and so does not need a great deal of water to dilute it, unlike the urea of mammals. The respiratory system is very efficient; in addition to the lungs there are a number of air sacs which allow a one-way flow of air across the respiratory surfaces (the system in mammals, in which there is a two-way flow of air, is described in *Biology Advanced Studies - Human Systems*, pp.47-8). The parts of the brain concerned with vision and coordination (the optic lobes and the cerebellum) are well developed; effective flight would be impossible without these capacities. Other parts of the brain, including the frontal lobes (which are the main centre for intelligence), are relatively smaller. Much of the behaviour of birds is therefore based on instinct rather than intelligence; *sign stimuli*, such as the red breast of the robin, are particularly important in their behaviour.

Birds evolved from reptiles, which have a scaly skin (see p.89). Scales in modern birds are found only on the legs; elsewhere they have become modified to form *feathers*. Feathers are made mainly of keratin and have a quite complicated structure (Fig.7.8). The central shaft of a feather is called the *rachis*; this grows from a *follicle* in the skin, which is similar to the hair follicle in mammals. The rachis has two rows of *barbs*, and these are kept in contact by small interlocking projections called *barbules* (which function rather like 'velcro'). When a bird is preening, one of the things it is doing is smoothing the feathers so that barbs which have become detached from one another are rejoined. Feathers are important for flight, since they streamline the bird and the large *primaries* and *secondaries* on a wing increase its surface area. Feathers are also important for *insulation*; endothermic animals can only maintain high body temperatures if the heat which is produced in their bodies can be retained. Garden birds like robins often look particularly fat during very cold weather. This is partly because they *are* fat in the literal sense - they have laid down a layer of storage fat beneath the skin and metabolising this can then be used to tide them over short periods when food might be difficult to obtain. However, it is mainly because they have puffed out their feathers, thus increasing the thickness of the insulating layer of air which is trapped between the feathers and the underlying skin.

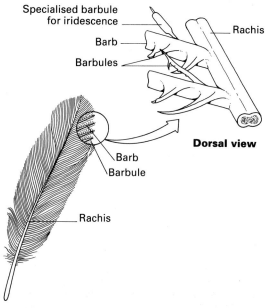

Specialised barbule for iridescence

Barb

Barbules

Rachis

Dorsal view

Barb

Barbule

Rachis

Figure 7.8 Structure of a bird feather

TERRITORY ECONOMICS IN A NECTAR-EATING BIRD

Sunbirds are the Old World equivalent of the New World hummingbirds. They live almost exclusively on nectar (*nectarivorous*), and sometimes defend exclusive territories containing the flowers they need. (Why only sometimes?) The golden-winged sunbird (*Nectarinia reichenowi*), in East Africa, has been studied in some detail by Gill and Wolf. When the flowers have lots of nectar, birds can spend less time per day foraging and more time resting, safe from predators. Gill and Wolf estimated the time needed for foraging per day from observations of wild birds:

Nectar volume per flower/cm^3	Foraging time per day/h
1	8.0
2	4.0
3	2.7

This suggests that by defending a territory, and stopping other birds drinking the nectar, a sunbird can increase the amount of nectar available for itself and save time foraging. An increase from 2 to 3 cm^3 would result in (4.0 - 2.7) = 1.3 extra hours per day. But territorial defence is more costly than sitting around or foraging, as the bird has to fly around searching for and chasing intruders. Gill and Wolf used laboratory measurements of energetic expenditure to estimate these costs:

Activity	Cost/kJh^{-1}
Foraging	4.18
Sitting	1.67
Territorial defence	12.54

Golden-winged sunbird

Field observations indicate that birds spend about 0.28 h per day on defence. So, to raise the average nectar content per flower from 2 to 3 cm^3, a territorial bird would have to spend (12.54 × 0.28) kJ per day, as opposed to a non-territorial bird which would spend (1.67 × 0.28) kJ per day sitting around. The energetic cost of defence is thus:

(12.54 × 0.28) − (1.67 × 0.28) = 3.04 kJ.

A territorial bird which did this would, remember, gain an extra 1.3 h per day for sitting rather than foraging. Sitting only costs 1.67 kJ per hour rather than 4.18 per hour for foraging. So the energetic saving is:

(4.18 × 1.3) − (1.67 × 1.3) = 3.26 kJ.

So, defending a territory is only just economically worthwhile (benefit = 3.26 kJ, cost = 3.04 kJ) if it increases available nectar from 2 to 3 cm^3 per flower. The sunbirds are on a tight budget!

Birds lay *eggs*, usually within a *nest*. The eggs are basically similar to those of reptiles, although they always have a shell which is hardened by the inclusion of calcium salts (the shells of reptile eggs are often leathery). In addition to the yolk they contain large amounts of the protein *albumen*. This is the 'white' part of a hen's egg. The precise functions of albumen are still not fully understood, although a great deal is known about its biochemical structure.

The forelimbs of birds are used as wings, and the hind limbs for walking; birds cannot therefore use their forelimbs to manipulate food or other objects such as nesting material. For this purpose a keratinous *bill* has evolved. The structure of the bill is adapted to the ecology, and particularly to the feeding habits, of a species. One of the major influences on the thinking of Charles Darwin, which led him to formulate the concept of evolution by natural selection, was observing the variety of bills in finches on the Galapagos Islands in the Pacific Ocean off the coast of Ecuador. All of the forms are derived from one ancestral species; and although some of them have retained a finch-like bill (which is adapted for eating seeds), others have developed different bill shapes, which adapt them for feeding on other things (Fig.7.9).

■ CLASS MAMMALIA

Mammals, like birds, evolved from reptiles. The first mammals appeared near the beginning of the Mesozoic era, about 230 million years ago. They were relatively scarce for almost the whole of the 'Age of Reptiles', however, and it was not until 60-70 million years ago that they began to dominate.

Mammals and birds are *endothermic*; most maintain body temperatures of 37-38 °C. The insulation which helps to keep the metabolically-produced heat within the body is in mammals mainly provided by a layer of *fur*, which is made up of large numbers of *hairs*. Hairs, like feathers, are derived from reptilian scales, and they too are composed largely of keratin. They grow from specialised structures in the skin called *hair follicles* (see *Biology Advanced Studies - Human Systems*, p.12).

Mammals differ from birds in two further very profound ways. The first is that the majority do not fly (bats, of course, are an exception). The second is in their method of reproduction. Mammals do not lay eggs (with the exception of monotremes, see p.94). They retain the embryos within the uterus, where each is nourished via a *placenta* (see HS, p.110). When the embryos are finally born, they continue to be nourished by the mother with *milk* from the *mammary glands*.

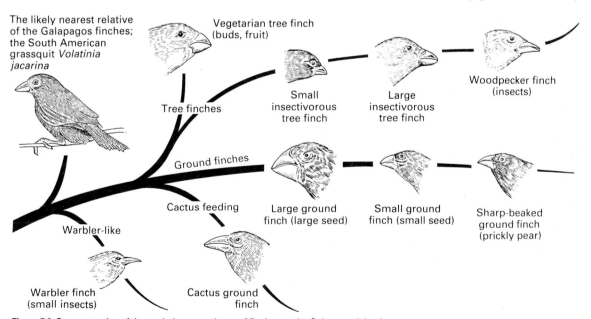

Figure 7.9 Reconstruction of the evolutionary pathway of finches on the Galapagos Islands ('Darwin's finches') showing how a wide range of bill types have evolved in response to different feeding habits

Subclass	Infra-class	Order	English name
Prototheria	–	Monotremata	Monotremes (duck-billed platypus and echidna)
Theria	Metatheria	Marsupialia	Marsupials (kangaroos and their relatives)
Theria	Eutheria	Many orders	Eutherian or placental mammals (including mice, whales and humans)

Table 7.2 Classification of monotremes, marsupials and eutherian mammals (not all authorities agree about the appropriate hierarchical level for some of these taxa)

Two sorts of mammals, the duck-billed platypus and the echidna from Australia and New Guinea, do lay eggs. They do not have a placenta. They are collectively called *monotremes* (order Monotremata). Monotremes are so different from all other mammals that, together with some extinct forms, they are placed in a separate subclass, the Prototheria (Table 7.2).

Mammals which do not lay eggs but which also do not have a placenta formed from the allantois are called marsupials (order Marsupialia), and include kangaroos and opossums. The embryos begin their development in the uterus, where they are nourished partly by yolk and partly by secretions from the uterine wall. When they are born, very immature and minute, they crawl from the opening of the uterus to a special *pouch* (the *marsupium*) on the abdomen, where they develop and grow further. The pouch contains the nipples of the mammary glands, and young marsupials remain there until they have grown quite large. Marsupial mammals are found mostly in Australia and New Guinea, although there are some species in South and Central America, and opossums extend northwards as far as the USA. Together with some fossil forms, they are placed in the infra-class Metatheria.

All remaining mammals are placed in the infra-class Eutheria; they are often called *eutherian* or *placental* mammals (Table 7.3). The placenta is derived from the egg membranes of reptiles, and especially from the allantois. It is attached to the wall of the uterus, allowing nutrients and oxygen to pass into the embryo, and carbon dioxide and nitrogenous waste to be removed from it.

Red-necked wallaby (*Macropus rufogriseus*) with young in marsupium

Order	Examples
Insectivora	Shrew, mole, hedgehog
Carnivora	Dog, cat, bear, badger
Pinnipedia*	Seal
Chiroptera	Bat
Rodentia	Mouse, rat, squirrel
Lagomorpha	Rabbit, hare
Artiodactyla	Pig, cow, sheep, deer
Perissodactyla	Horse, rhinoceros, tapir
Cetacea	Whale, dolphin
Proboscidea	Elephant
Primates	Monkey, gorilla, man

* Some authorities consider that seals should be placed in the order Carnivora.

Table 7.3 The major orders of eutherian mammals

Mammals have well-developed brains, and the *cerebral hemispheres* (which contain the *frontal lobes*) are especially large. The cerebral hemispheres are particularly concerned with learning and intelligence. Mammals are usually more intelligent than birds, and their behaviour is much more flexible. They rely on a wider range of senses for communication than birds; smell, for example, is important for many mammals. When a dog 'follows a trail' it is detecting chemicals left in the environment by another animal. If it 'cocks its leg' it is marking lamp-posts with its urine, which contains chemicals called pheromones. (See p.72 for an account of pheromones in insects.) These signal to another dog that it has passed by; it has scent-marked its territory.

■ Order Insectivora

These are sometimes considered to be the most primitive mammals. Their teeth are grouped as incisors, canines, premolars and molars (see *Biology Advanced Studies - Human Systems*, pp.72-3), but none of them are very specialised (Fig.7.10). Insectivores feed on a wide variety of invertebrates and not just insects as the name implies. Hedgehogs have some of their body hairs modified to form spines. Moles are adapted for burrowing in the soil; they have powerful forelimbs to help them to dig effectively, and they feed predominantly on earthworms.

Figure 7.10 An insectivore (hedgehog) and its skull, showing the relatively unspecialised teeth. Can you identify the different types of teeth?

■ Order Carnivora

Carnivora are flesh-eating mammals. They have the canine teeth enlarged to help them to grip their prey and tear its tissue. The eyes face forwards, giving them good binocular vision, which is important for efficient hunting. Some carnivores, such as leopards, cheetahs and the domestic cat, usually hunt their prey singly. Others, such as wolves and hyaenas, hunt in social groups called *packs*. Lions may use either strategy.

Not all carnivores hunt large, fast-moving prey, and some have a varied diet which can include invertebrates and plants. Badgers eat large numbers of earthworms, but they collect these when they are at the surface; they do not dig for them. Otters hunt fish underwater, but they can also move efficiently on land.

■ Order Pinnipedia

Seals and sealions are closely related to carnivores, but have become adapted for living in the sea (and a very small number of species live in fresh water). They feed on fish and cephalopods. Their limbs have become *flippers* and their circulatory and respiratory systems have become modified so that they can hold their breath and dive for long periods. The blood contains a high concentration of haemoglobin and the muscles have eight times more myoglobin than an equivalent weight of beef. Weddell seals from the Antarctic have been recorded as diving for nearly 45 minutes without coming to the surface to take a breath. They have been known to go to a depth of 600 metres.

■ Order Chiroptera

Bats make up almost a quarter of the 4200 known species of mammals, but it is often not appreciated just how common they are because most species are nocturnal. The bones of the forelimbs are elongated; a membrane of hairless skin stretches between the limb-bones and the sides of the body, and this forms the wing (Fig.7.11). Bats do not fly as strongly as most birds, as their flight muscles account for only 10% of their body weight, one half the equivalent figure for birds. Most species of bats are comparatively small and feed on insects. Some tropical species feed on fruit, and vampire bats feed on the blood of other vertebrates. Vampire bats have very sharp incisor and canine teeth, which they use to make a wound from which the blood flows especially freely because the saliva contains a anticoagulant which inhibits clotting.

Many bats produce *ultrasounds*, which are usually at frequencies too high to be detected by the human ear. They are used for communication and for echolocation. The sounds are reflected by surfaces, and sensing the reflected sound waves enables a bat to locate trees and other obstacles in the environment, and to find the flying insects on which it feeds. Vampire bats and fruit-eating bats do not use echolocation.

BEHAVIOUR FILE

RECIPROCAL BLOOD-SHARING IN VAMPIRE BATS

Vampire bats, particularly females, live in communal roosts of a dozen or more, often in old hollow trees. They get almost all their nourishment from lapping the blood of large vertebrates such as cattle and, sometimes, humans. (This is in fact quite painless, but since the bats can carry rabies, their bite could be fatal.) Interestingly, if a particular bat is unsuccessful in *foraging* (see p.111) for blood, some of its roostmates may regurgitate part of their meal. This unselfish, or *altruistic* (p.118), behaviour is very important to the receiver of a blood 'gift'; a few nights without blood and a vampire bat would die. But why are the donors so generous? Wouldn't a selfish bat do better by keeping its meal to itself (see p.109)? The answer is that bats form small alliances, so a 'blood donor' tends only to share blood with a bat that had been generous to it in the past (you scratch my back and I'll scratch yours!) As bats can readily recognise each other by smell, a selfish 'cheat' would soon be spotted and excluded from the roost.

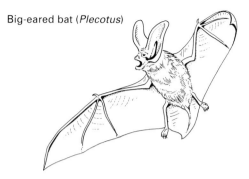

Big-eared bat (*Plecotus*)

Figure 7.11 A bat in flight, showing the membranous wings

■ Order Rodentia

More than one third of all mammals are rodents. The key to their success is their dentition (teeth). Rodents have large middle incisors which continue growing throughout their lives; as the cutting edges of these teeth are worn, they are replaced by growth from the base (Fig.7.12). Relatively hard materials like seeds (including cereal grains), nuts and bark can therefore be used as food. Rodents are able to separate the nutritious and the indigestible parts of their food; nutritious material is swallowed, the indigestible part - for example husks of grain - are passed out sideways from the mouth through a gap between the incisors and the premolars (rodents have no canines).

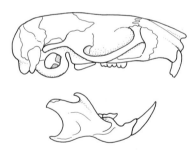

Figure 7.12 Skull of a rodent (a mouse) showing the large incisor teeth

Many species of rodents, such as rats and mice, are serious pests. They eat stored foods, contaminating and spoiling it; and they spread diseases.

■ Order Lagomorpha

Lagomorphs, such as rabbits and hares, also have well-developed incisors. They are placed in a separate order from rodents because they are believed to have evolved independently.

■ Order Artiodactyla

This is the order which contains cattle, sheep and deer. These animals feed almost exclusively on plants; they are herbivores. Plant cells are much more difficult to digest than animal cells because they have thick walls containing resistant polymers such as cellulose, hemicelluloses and lignins (see B,p.19). Vertebrate enzymes cannot deal with these molecules, and so can only digest the material within plant cells when these have been broken up. However, some vertebrates contain symbiotic bacteria and protozoans within their digestive tracts which *can* digest plant cell walls. In many Artiodactyla the symbiotic micro-organisms inhabit the stomach, which is divided into four chambers. In order from the oesophagus, these are called the *reticulum*, *rumen*, *abomasum* and *omasum*. The rumen is the largest of these, and contains most of the symbionts. Its contents have a neutral pH. Food is partly digested in the rumen, but is then returned to the mouth where it is chewed for a second time, breaking the cells up still further. This is called *rumination* or chewing the cud; the animals which do it are *ruminants*. A cow may spend more than eight hours per day ruminating after it has been feeding on relatively indigestible and fibrous materials such as hay. The contents of the abomasum are acid, this organ is equivalent to the stomach of most other mammals. Not all Artiodactyla ruminate; pigs and hippopotamuses are examples of mammals in this order which do not.

The teeth of Artiodactyla are specialised for the diet of plant material. The upper incisors are replaced in many species by a hard pad of thick skin, and the lower incisors cut against this (Fig.7.13). The canines are small, but the premolars and molars are large and are used to grind the food and so break it up.

Herbivorous mammals form a major part of the diet of large carnivores (see p.95). Many species have developed long legs to enable them to run as fast as possible, to give them the opportunity to escape. Several adaptations increase the efficiency of this process. Horny *hooves* have developed at the ends of the legs, to help withstand the wear which results from fast running. Animals with hooves are called *ungulates*. They stand on their toes (this is technically called a *digitigrade stance*). Only two of the original five digits (fingers or toes) remain in Artiodactyla; the remaining three have been reduced or lost during the course of their evolution. Because there are two hooves on each leg, artiodactyls are sometimes called even-toed ungulates. There are other ungulates in which three or only one digit remain; these are called odd-toed ungulates and are placed in the order Perissodactyla (Fig.7.14).

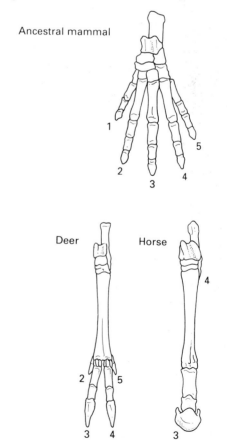

Figure 7.14 Bones at the ends of a limb of an even-toed ungulate (a deer, left, with two hooves) and an odd-toed ungulate (a horse, right, with one hoof)

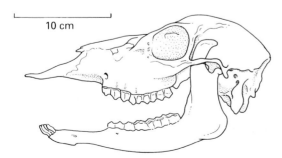

Figure 7.13 Skull of an artiodactyl (a deer)

■ Order Perissodactyla

These are the ungulates which are odd-toed. Rhinoceroses have three remaining digits, and so three hooves on each foot. Horses and zebras have only one. Perissodactyls do not ruminate. The symbiotic micro-organisms which help them to digest plant material are found in the caecum and colon of the large intestine (see *Biology Advanced Studies - Human Systems*, p.75).

■ Order Cetacea

This order contains the whales, porpoises and dolphins. They are all highly adapted for living in the sea, which they never leave. The forelimbs are modified as *flippers* and the hind-limbs, together with most of the pelvic girdle, have been lost. There is a pair of horizontal fins, which are called *flukes* (do not confuse these with the parasitic flatworms having the same name, described on p.61). The flukes are at the posterior end of the body, and provide most of the thrust for swimming.

There are two major groups of cetaceans. Toothed whales feed mainly on fish and cephalopods (see p.77). Whalebone, or *baleen*, whales lose their teeth during embryonic development, and develop instead a series of plates of keratin at the sides of the mouth. These are used to filter planktonic plants and animals, on which the whales feed. The blue whale (*Balaenoptera musculus*), which is the largest animal in the world, is a whalebone whale. There is some uncertainty what is the maximum size of these animals, but specimens weighing more than 130 tonnes have been reliably recorded.

■ Order Proboscidea

This is the order to which elephants belong. Modern elephants are now confined to Africa and tropical Asia. They are the largest living land vertebrates, but are very much smaller than blue whales or the extinct dinosaur *Brachiosaurus* (see p.90); very few reach a weight larger than five tonnes. They have a *trunk*, which is formed by the fusion and elongation of the upper lip and nose. The trunk is used to handle food. Elephants can be trained to carry out hard work and they are able to 'use tools' - see box on page opposite.

■ Order Primates

Primates first appeared at the end of the Cretaceous period, about 65 million years ago.

The earliest primates probably fed on insects and other invertebrates, but species with a dentition which adapted them for feeding on a wider range of foods (omnivores) evolved quite rapidly.

Many early primates also became adapted for living in trees, and this important series of events shaped the subsequent evolution of the group. The crucial sense for arboreal (tree-dwelling) mammals is sight - good vision is essential, or an individual might miss its footing while leaping from branch to branch, fall and die. As a result of this intense selection pressure, the eyes of primates are large and face forwards to give a wide field with binocular vision. The sense of smell is relatively less important for arboreal mammals, and during primate evolution the snout has become progressively reduced; most primates have a flat face.

The cerebral hemispheres (see *Biology Advanced Studies - Human Systems*, p.84) became enlarged to enable the brain to process the increased amount and complexity of sensory input resulting from rapid movement through the trees, and to convert and coordinate this to appropriate muscular action. There has been a progressive increase in the relative size of the brain during the course of primate evolution (Fig.7.15). Primates are the most intelligent mammals, and man - who is a primate - is the most intelligent of all.

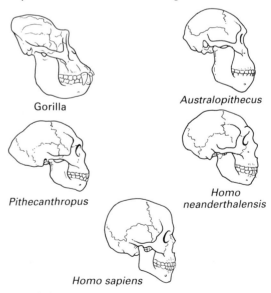

Figure 7.15 Skulls of a gorilla, three extinct examples of man-like creatures (*Australopithecus*, *Pithecanthropus* and Neanderthal man) and a modern human, showing the progressive increase in the relative volume of the brain case

POWER-PACK PACHYDERMS

Elephants are resourceful creatures and they solve problems in highly original ways. Here is one recipe for demolishing a fence, elephant style: first find a little elephant, pick it up and throw it against the fence. Walk through the hole. Alternative method: pile large branches on top of the fence until it collapses.

This extraordinary behaviour came to light during a recent study of elephants and their use of 'tools'. In this context, a tool is any external object wielded for a specific purpose, so an elephant's nipper counts as a tool, every bit as much as a pair of nippers from a mechanic's toolbox. Here are some more tricks of the trade, as practised by the tooled-up elephant.

To block a road used by the park service for elephant-culling: collect tree branches and dump them on the road. To hit a human: pick up a stick in a trunk and advance menacingly - or simply lob the stick. (The elephant packs a mean trunk and it often hits its target.) If sticks are in short supply, pick up a dollop of dung and throw that instead. To stop a bird eating your dinner: take a trunk full of air and just blow the bird away.

To get rid of a leech in the armpit: find a fence post, trim it to length and prod the leech until it drops off. To get rid of troublesome flies, just suck up some earth with the trunk ... and zap. To cool off: suck up water or mud and take a quick shower. (If you can't find any fresh water, just regurgitate stomach contents into trunk and drench your ears.)

Uses for grass, hay and other vegetation: (1) for scratching ears - although carrots will do just as well; (2) for wiping cuts; (3) for placing on the back as a fly screen; (4) for sweeping the floor; (5) for twisting into decorative shapes, such as balls, ropes and rings. Special note for advanced users needing to scratch back legs: seize hay with trunk, pass the hay backwards, grab it with tail and rub it up and down.

This latest catalogue of elephant ingenuity is the work of Suzanne Chevalier-Skolnikoff of the University of California and Jo Liska of the University of Colorado. Their research confirms that elephants richly deserve their place in the tool-using fraternity, alongside various primates and a few other mammals, such as the sea otter, a winsome creature that smashes shells on stones held on its chest.

Elephants use tools in a number of contexts, but most involve bodycare - cooling off, scratching and fly-swatting, for instance - or violence. Yet sometimes their trunkcraft reaches a loftier, more creative plane. They have even dabbled in the world of art. One artistic heavyweight by the name of Carol painted canvases that fetched up to $500 apiece, while elephants without access to the studio have been known to draw on the ground with sticks. Talent will out - and elephants have it by the ton.

Stephen Young, *The Guardian*, 30 September 1993

The order Primates is divided into two suborders: bushbabies, tarsiers, lemurs and several other species of nocturnal primates from the Old World tropics are placed in the suborder Prosimii; monkeys, marmosets, apes and man, which have flatter faces and larger brains, are placed in the suborder Anthropoidea. Monkeys are a large and diverse group; the baboon illustrated on p.122 is a monkey. Monkeys mostly have a *quadrupedal* gait, i.e. like most other mammals, they walk on all four legs. Apes - seven species of gibbons, the orang-utan, chimpanzee and two species of gorillas - have very long forelimbs. Gibbons use these mainly for swinging from branches, but chimpanzees and gorillas show the beginnings of a *bipedal* gait; they frequently walk on their hind legs, using the forelegs for balance, resting the knuckles on the ground. Man is completely bipedal; the forelimbs are shorter than those of gorillas and chimpanzees.

IS HUMAN BEHAVIOUR UNIQUE AMONG THE PRIMATES? - A DIALOGUE

A *Humans are certainly primates but we can do things which no other primate can. Humans are unique.*

B Admittedly humans can do many things far better than other primates but several behaviours which were once thought to be uniquely human have now been seen, in a rudimentary form, in monkeys and apes.

A *Only humans use tools.*

B But Jane Goodall reported how chimpanzees use sticks to catch termites for food by poking them into the termite mound and waiting for the insects to climb up. (See also 'Power-pack Pachyderms' on p.99.)

A *Perhaps humans are different in being able to make tools to fit the job?*

B Chimpanzees select sticks of just the right thickness and break them to a comfortable length and even chew the end to make it fan out like a brush so as to sweep up the termites.

A *Well maybe the difference is that humans can plan ahead how they are going to use a tool?*

B Some chimpanzees crack nuts with stones, resting the nut in a depression in a large stone and hitting it with a smaller one. They carry their nutcrackers to the trees with the nuts. They know that they are going to use the nutcracker at that tree and plan for it.

A *Humans are more intelligent than the other primates.*

B True.

A *And we use our intelligence to find new solutions to problems; we invent new ways of doing things.*

B Some Japanese macaque monkeys living near a seashore were regularly fed rice by the scientists who studied them. Some grains always fell into the sand, giving the monkeys a gritty snack. One three-year-old female (named Imo by the scientists) threw a handful of sand mixed with rice into the shallow edge of the sea. The sand sank, the rice floated and she scooped up the clean rice from the surface of the water. From then on Imo continued to use her discovery to obtain a sand-free meal.

A *But humans are able to pass on their discoveries to others. We have culture, ways of doing things which we learn from others through the generations.*

B Imo had also discovered a new food preparation technique earlier, when she was eighteen months old. She was the first in her troop to use sea water to wash sand off sweet potatoes. Imo's mother copied her, so did her young playmates; and their mothers copied them. Later when Imo and friends had infants of their own those youngsters picked up the habit, too. In a few generations the practice was widespread. Imo's rice-separating technique spread in the same way. Both behaviours became part of the troop's culture.

A *Language is where humans excel. We can communicate ideas and information to others. Surely other primates can only express their emotions.*

B True there is nothing to match the subtlety and complexity of human language but vervet monkeys have been observed to use predator alarm calls which not only express their fear, and so tell others of general danger, but also specify which predator it is. The 'snake' alarm is a chattering rattle; the 'eagle' alarm is a high barking, coughing trill; and the 'leopard' alarm is a harsh barking gobble. The monkeys hearing another's alarm respond differently, and appropriately, to the different calls. (See Table 7.4.)

A *But that may be little more than signalling different degrees of fear. Humans can express their thoughts in code: words and writing.*

B It is true that only humans can represent their ideas in speech but several chimpanzees have been taught to use symbols to name objects and express their wishes. In different research projects the symbols have been American Sign Language (one of the hand signal languages used by deaf people in America), plastic shapes which are laid out in a sequence or coloured symbols printed on a board which are pointed to and symbols on a computer keyboard. Chimpanzees can learn to use a vocabulary of around two hundred symbols, putting them together in sequences like short sentences, to greet people, ask for particular food and, a favourite request, to be tickled!

A *Perhaps it isn't true language. Human infants don't have to be taught to speak, they just pick it up. And the chimpanzees might just be learning long sequences of tricks rather than understanding the meaning of the symbols. What is more, a true language is flexible - you can invent new phrases.*

B One female common chimpanzee (Washoe) saw for the first time a big white bird swimming on a river. She had not learnt the American Sign Language symbol for 'swan'. So she signalled to her human companion the symbols for 'water' and 'bird'. Doesn't that mean that she recognised relationships between the swan and other birds, and between the swan and the water, and furthermore that she understood that these relationships could be represented by symbols? In another study while the researchers worked with a female pygmy chimpanzee named Matata, her baby, Kanzi, used to play around them, apparently interested in the board of symbols only as a plaything. In this study the symbols were used in conjunction with spoken English to see if chimpanzees could learn to understand spoken words. Eventually the researchers got the feeling that Kanzi knew what the conversations were about and when

they tested him discovered that he did indeed understand some symbols and English words. He had not been taught, he had picked up the language being used around him.

A *Humans understand what is going on in the minds of others. Surely other primates aren't sophisticated enough to know what others are thinking?*

B Returning to vervets and their predator alarms, some have been observed to gain an advantage by 'lying', that is signalling deceptively. For example, when one individual had food, another gave the leopard alarm so that the other dropped the food and ran up the nearest tree. This could mean that the deceiver had predicted what the other monkey would do because it knew what the other would think.

A *Or it could have been merely a trick learnt by trial and error without true understanding.*

B But the fact that such deceptions are often arranged quite tactically, when the target is looking the other way, might suggest that vervet monkeys are more sophisticated than that.

A *Perhaps, then, we should say that in some respects monkeys and apes can be like humans?*

B It would be more meaningful to say that humans are primates and share with other primates a heritage of behaviour.

| Vervet on the ground | | | | | |
| | | | Responses | | |
Alarm type	Run up tree	Run into bushes	Look up	Look down	Approach predator
Leopard	20	1			
Eagle	6	26	64		
Snake	1	2		8	7

| Vervet in trees | | | | | |
| | | | Responses | | |
Alarm type	Run higher in tree	Run out of tree	Look up	Look down	Approach predator
Leopard	2				
Eagle	1	2	10		
Snake				8	9

Table 7.4 Responses to vervet alarm calls. The number of occasions when at least one individual showed a particular response to a given type of alarm call

8 VIRUSES

Viruses are not included in the Five Kingdom system of classification as they do not have a cellular structure; they are described as *akaryotic*. Traditionally, they have been included amongst the micro-organisms, and most scientists believe that they have evolved from the genetic material of living organisms, although a few still regard them as very simple structures, intermediate between living and non-living matter.

The existence of viruses as agents of disease was first shown by a Russian botanist, Iwanowski, in 1892. He was trying to find out what caused the tobacco mosaic disease and had extracted a juice from the leaves of some diseased plants. He passed this extract through a bacterial filter, but found that it was still capable of producing the symptoms of the disease in healthy plants. He concluded that the disease was due to a living organism smaller than a bacterium and one which was not visible under the microscope. Other workers repeated his experiments, and also tried to kill off the organisms by treating the extract with alcohol. To their surprise, the alcohol had no effect. The term *virus*, derived from the Greek for poisonous fluid, was given to these organisms, and even more confusion arose when, in 1935, Stanley purified the tobacco mosaic virus (TMV) and obtained it in crystalline form. In 1937, Bawden and Pirie showed that TMV was made up of ribonucleoprotein and subsequently other workers identified the type of nucleic acid present in a number of different viruses.

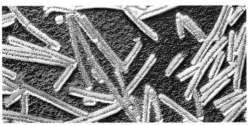

Electron micrograph of tobacco mosaic virus (magnification × 66 000)

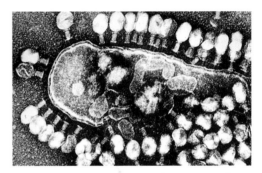

Electron micrograph of T4 bacteriophages surrounding an *Escherichia coli* bacterium

The discovery of *bacteriophages*, viruses which attack bacteria, generated a great deal of interest, particularly in the medical world, as doctors became interested in their potential use in the treatment of bacterial infections. Their behaviour was studied intensively and several significant facts about viral behaviour were established. It was found that the bacteriophages were specific to their host cells, that they entered the cells and took over their hosts' mechanisms for synthesising nucleic acids and proteins. This resulted in a multiplication phase within the host cell, where large numbers of new virus particles were assembled, to be released by rupture of the host cell wall. In 1929, Burnet demonstrated that in 20 minutes, one bacteriophage infecting a bacterial cell could produce more than a hundred new particles.

It had not been possible to determine the shape or form of viruses, until the development of the electron microscope, as only the largest were visible at the limits of resolution of the best light microscopes. Viruses were obvious candidates for investigation by the high resolution made possible by the electron microscope, and we now know the form and dimensions of most. They usually range in size from 20-300 nm though a few viruses can be as small as 6 nm in diameter while some of the largest poxviruses can be up to 800 nm (0.8 μm).

There are three basic forms (Fig.8.1):
• *helical* - as shown by TMV and the influenza virus
• *polyhedral* - as shown by the polio and herpes virus
• *complex* - as shown by the bacteriophages T2, T4 and λ.

a)

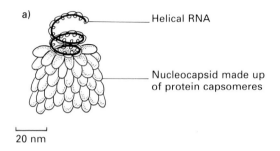

20 nm

b)

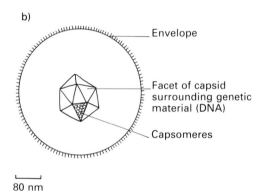

80 nm

c)

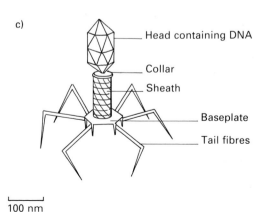

100 nm

Figure 8.1 (a) TMV (Tobacco Mosaic Virus) - an example of a helical virus, (b) Herpes - an example of a polyhedral virus, (c) T2 phage (infects *Escherichia coli*) - an example of a bacteriophage

All viruses consist of a core of genetic material, either DNA (deoxyribonucleic acid) or RNA (ribonucleic acid), surrounded by a protective coat of protein called a *capsid*. The capsid is made up of sub-units called *capsomeres*. In addition, some viruses have an envelope of carbohydrate or lipoprotein around the capsid (Fig.8.2).

Range in size from 20-300 nm

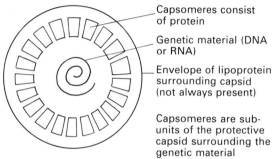

Figure 8.2 Typical virus structure

The genetic material in cells always consists of double-stranded DNA, but that of viruses can be either RNA or DNA, single- or double-stranded. The viruses which have single- or double-stranded RNA and single-stranded DNA consist of from 2 to 30 genes and are typically smaller than those with double-stranded DNA.

The capsomeres which make up the capsid appear in the form of angular prisms and are composed of protein molecules. The function of the capsid is to protect the genetic material, and it also reacts with surface molecules on the cell wall or cell membrane of the host cells, ensuring that the virus only enters its specific host. Some of the proteins in the capsid may help the virus to gain entry by digesting the cell wall or cell membrane. In the bacteriophages, successful penetration of the bacterial cell wall is achieved by means of the contractile sheath acting like a syringe and injecting the viral nucleic acid, in this case DNA, into the cytoplasm of the host cell.

The infection cycle of the T2 or T4 bacteriophage lasts 20 minutes from the penetration of the host cell by the virus to its bursting open, or *lysis*. The cycle is often referred to as a *lytic cycle* and the virus is said to be virulent whilst it is undergoing such cycles (Fig.8.3). Some strains of bacteria can produce anti-viral enzymes (endonucleases) which are capable of destroying the viral DNA.

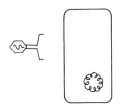

1. Virus approaches bacterial cell

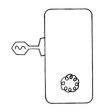

2. Tail fibres attach to receptor site on cell membrane

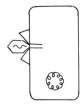

3. Tail sheath contracts, DNA injected into bacterium together with enzymes

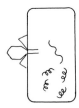

4. Phage enzymes break down bacterial DNA

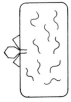

5. Phage DNA incorporated into bacterial DNA and takes over. Phage DNA replicates and codes for new proteins

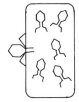

6. New phages are assembled. Phage DNA codes for lysozyme

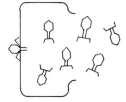

7. Build up of lysozyme causes lysis of bacterial cell. Phages released. Can be up to 1000 and cycle takes about 30 minutes to complete

Figure 8.3 Lytic cycle of T2 bacteriophage

Temperate bacteriophages, such as the λ phage of *E. coli*, may undergo lytic cycles, but they can also enter host cells and become integrated into the bacterial chromosome. An enzyme, *λ-integrase*, is necessary to make the attachment and to join the DNA of the bacteriophage to the DNA of the host cell. In this state, it is called a prophage, or provirus, and can remain attached for a long time, replicating each time the bacterial DNA replicates. This is termed the *lysogenic phase*. It has the potential to become virulent, by synthesising more λ-integrase and detaching its DNA from the host chromosome. Temperate phages usually enter a lysogenic phase when the bacterial colony is growing rapidly, changing to a lytic cycle as the colony gets older.

Mumps is caused by a helical, single-stranded RNA virus, which enters the respiratory tract, where it multiplies, causing the parotid glands (salivary glands just in front of the ear) to swell up. Virus particles appear in the saliva and the disease can be spread by droplet infection as a result of the infected person coughing or sneezing when in close contact with another person. The spread of the disease is favoured by crowded, moist and warm conditions. Normally, the infected person would recover after 14 to 21 days, but complications, which include inflammation of the ovaries or testes and the membranes around the brain, can be serious.

The influenza virus causes epidemics in which many people die. The virus is a rounded, ovoid with a diameter of 80-100 nm. It has eight helical capsids, coiled inside a membrane, which is derived from its host. The virus identifies the host cells and enters them, where it moves into the nucleus through a pore in the nuclear envelope. It undergoes a replication phase making more viral RNA in the host nucleus and capsid protein in the cytoplasm. The capsid protein enters the nucleus and new virus particles are assembled. These move into the cytoplasm and then to the cell surface where they leave by means of exocytosis, surrounded by host cell membrane (Fig.8.4).

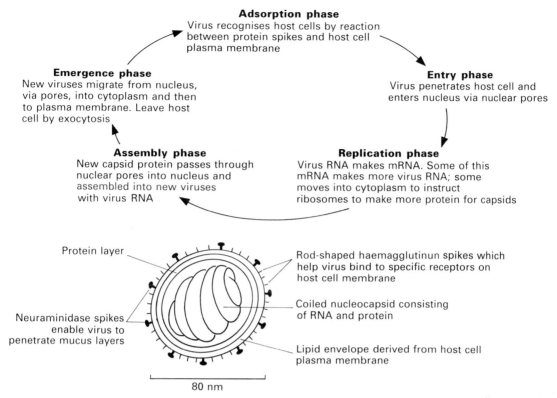

Adsorption phase
Virus recognises host cells by reaction between protein spikes and host cell plasma membrane

Emergence phase
New viruses migrate from nucleus, via pores, into cytoplasm and then to plasma membrane. Leave host cell by exocytosis

Entry phase
Virus penetrates host cell and enters nucleus via nuclear pores

Assembly phase
New capsid protein passes through nuclear pores into nucleus and assembled into new viruses with virus RNA

Replication phase
Virus RNA makes mRNA. Some of this mRNA makes more virus RNA; some moves into cytoplasm to instruct ribosomes to make more protein for capsids

Protein layer

Rod-shaped haemagglutinun spikes which help virus bind to specific receptors on host cell membrane

Coiled nucleocapsid consisting of RNA and protein

Neuraminidase spikes enable virus to penetrate mucus layers

Lipid envelope derived from host cell plasma membrane

80 nm

Figure 8.4 Cycle of influenza virus - a single strand RNA helical virus, which can manufacture mRNA directly

Retroviruses (Fig.8.5) are RNA viruses, possessing the enzyme reverse transcriptase in their capsules. The viral genetic material enters the host cell nucleus and the enzyme enables the synthesis of a strand of DNA from the strand of RNA, and then a complementary strand of DNA to form a circular chromosome, which is inserted into the host cell DNA. This group of viruses has become well-known because the human immuno-deficiency virus (HIV) is a retrovirus, and could be the cause of AIDS (acquired immuno-deficiency syndrome).

Viroids consist of small, single strands of RNA, with no surrounding protein capsids, found only in plants as yet. The first to be identified as a pathogen was PSTV (potato spindle tuber viroid). It has its RNA in the form of rods or closed circles, about 50 nm long. PSTV is found in the nucleus of infected cells and is thought to interfere with the switching on and off of the host cell genes. Infected tissue has been found to contain larger amounts of certain proteins than healthy tissue.

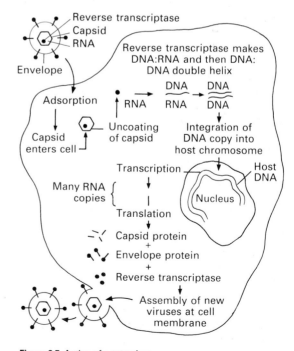

Reverse transcriptase
Capsid
RNA
Envelope

Reverse transcriptase makes DNA:RNA and then DNA: DNA double helix

Adsorption

DNA
RNA
RNA
DNA
DNA

Capsid enters cell

Uncoating of capsid

Integration of DNA copy into host chromosome

Transcription

Host DNA

Many RNA copies

Nucleus

Translation

Capsid protein
+
Envelope protein
+
Reverse transcriptase

Assembly of new viruses at cell membrane

Figure 8.5 Action of a retrovirus

BEHAVIOUR

CHAPTER 9

> '...it is far more satisfactory to look at such instincts as the young cuckoo ejecting its foster-brothers, ants making slaves (of other species), the larvae of ichneumonidae (parasitic wasps) feeding within the live bodies of caterpillars, not as specially endowed or created instincts, but as small consequences of one general law, leading to the advancement of all organic beings, namely multiply, vary, let the strongest live and the weakest die'. (Darwin 1859, in *On the Origin of Species*; bracketed text inserted)

Charles Darwin (1809-82) was the first person to make animal behaviour a legitimate object for scientific study. Until the latter half of the 19th century only hunters and farmers were keenly interested in animal behaviour, and our knowledge of behaviour depended very much on anecdotal, if detailed, observations by country squires, parsons and others with the leisure time to observe nature. Darwin realised that, just like their physical form, the behaviours of animals are adapted to their lifestyles and that similarities can be seen between evolutionarily related species. However, biologists were slow to take Darwin's lead on behaviour, concentrating instead on comparisons of anatomy and physiology. The first big strides in our understanding of behaviour came not from biologists at all, but from *comparative psychologists*. We will note later their contribution to the study of animal *learning*. It wasn't until the middle of the 20th century that biologists began to investigate behaviour in wild animals. Perhaps the most influential of these was the Dutchman Niko Tinbergen (who shared the 1973 Novel Prize with two other well-known animal behaviour scientists, the German Karl von Frisch and the Austrian Konrad Lorenz). He made the useful distinction between *proximate* explanations of behaviour (how the behaviour develops and is produced in the individual's lifetime) and *ultimate* explanations (why the behaviour evolved in the first place). Biologists

Tree pipit feeding cuckoo in nest

who study behaviour are called *ethologists* (from the Greek ethos = behaviour) or, if they concentrate solely on evolutionary and ecological questions about behaviour, *behavioural ecologists*. Animal behaviour can be studied from many perspectives, ranging from the neurobiological and psychological, where the *proximate* causes are investigated, to the evolutionary and ecological, where the *ultimate* causes are of interest.

Tinbergen took the question, 'Why does an animal do that?' and listed four ways in which it could be answered!

The *proximate* answers are in terms of:
1. *development* (How does the behaviour develop over the lifetime of the individual?) and
2. *mechanism* or *causation* (What causes the behaviour to happen in the short term?)

The *ultimate* answers are in terms of:
3. *function* (What is it for? Its current survival value or contribution to the animal's 'Darwinian fitness')
and
4. *evolution* (What were the origins of the behaviour in the evolutionary ancestors of the species?)

The difference between Tinbergen's 'four why questions' can be seen when one asks, 'Why do birds sing in spring?' Answers could include: because increasing daylength stimulates release of sex hormones, which in turn promote song and other sexual displays (a developmental explanation); because heightened territorial activity increases the number of challenges to a territory holder (a mechanistic explanation); because song attracts mates and spring is the best time to breed (a functional explanation); because, in birds' tree-dwelling ancestors, sounds were an efficient means of long-distance communication, and spring was the best time to breed (an evolutionary explanation). Try to ask your own questions that can be answered in terms of each of Tinbergen's 'four whys'. For example, why do you like sweet things? And why do skunks smell?

WHAT IS BEHAVIOUR?

The *Dictionary of Biology* (Collins) gives two definitions of behaviour: (1) the total activities of an animal, and (2) the measurable response of an organism to stimuli from the environment. Do you think these are adequate? Osmoregulation is an 'activity' of an animal, yet we would probably not want to include this as behaviour. Plants respond to stimuli (e.g. growth towards light), but is this behaviour? We might limit the definition to rapid responses (is the closure of a venus flytrap 'behaviour'?), or to responses involving a nervous sytem (so are an amoeba's movements in search of food not 'behaviour'?). In fact, it is probably wise to keep a very general definition in mind, but here we shall be referring exclusively to animals. In terms of *function*, the parasitism of mistletoe on an oak tree and a louse on a human, share many similarities. In terms of *mechanism* of parasitic attack, the plant and animal differ markedly. So depending on which of Tinbergen's 'why' questions you are attempting to answer, what one calls 'behaviour' may change.

■ WHY STUDY ANIMAL BEHAVIOUR?

Living things are the most complex objects we know of: capable of self-maintenance, growth, reproduction, interaction, and evolution, unlike inanimate objects. Understanding the complexity and design of the five kingdoms, of which the behavioural interactions are part, is a fascinating intellectual challenge. However, apart from the pure scientific appeal of expanding our knowledge of the world, the study of animal behaviour has many more direct applications to human life.

• There are applied benefits of commercial importance. These include control of pests (understanding how certain species are attracted to our crops, or how their natural predators can be used to control them), manipulation of livestock breeding schedules (e.g. changing patterns of the seasonal breeding that evolved in wild ancestors, but which are unproductive in domestic stock), and changing the behaviour of domestic breeds (e.g. less aggressive honey bees).

• As animal welfare becomes a more important issue, we need to understand not just the physical, but the emotional, needs of different species (e.g. in devising ways of keeping farm and zoo animals which allow them to perform natural behaviour - see 'The Ideal Indoor Pig Pen' on p.108).

• Understanding the behavioural interactions of individuals helps us understand complex higher-level processes, such as population changes and migration.

• We are animals, and an understanding of the mechanisms and evolution of animal behaviour can give us insights into those of our own species.

Jane Goodall studying the behaviour of wild chimpanzees in Tanzania

THE IDEAL INDOOR PIG PEN

The natural behaviour of farm animals is severely restricted in indoor intensive units. An ethological analysis of the behaviour of a group of pigs in a large field with hills, trees and bushes has enabled an 'enriched' pig pen to be designed which allows pigs to be kept at high density while providing them with opportunities for natural behaviour.

Natural pig behaviour:
• Feed, defecate and sleep in separate areas
• Uncover food by pushing up soft earth with the snout (rooting)
• Lever up fallen branches with the snout in search of food
• Mark points in the area with urine
• Rub against tree trunks, etc.
• Wallow in mud

• Build nests of sticks and grass for sleeping and giving birth
• Birthing nests built some way from the group but from where the female can see danger approaching
• Piglets forage, play and sleep in family groups.

Good husbandry practice:
• Feeding stalls reduce competition among piglets for food
• Creep rail allows piglets access to food but bars adults
• Farrowing rail keeps sow from rolling on newborn piglets.

The enriched pen:
• Good husbandry combined with ethology
• Several pens are arranged in a row, each with two sows and their piglets.

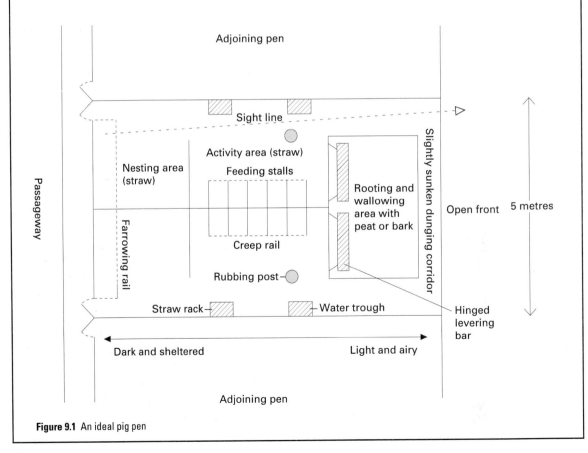

Figure 9.1 An ideal pig pen

■ ULTIMATE EXPLANATIONS OF BEHAVIOUR

■ Genes and behaviour

Is it possible that behaviour is inherited? Could it be 'in the genes'? Genes code for the synthesis of proteins. Enzymes, which are proteins, are the biological catalysts that determine and regulate all metabolism and development. Is it by this means that genes influence the biochemistry, physiology, anatomy, and behaviour of the organism containing them? (See *Biology Advanced Studies - Genetics and Evolution.*) Whilst it is easy to think of genes for eye colour having their effect through an enzyme controlling the synthesis of colour pigments, what about something as complex as behaviour? How can genes 'control' behaviour? In fact, it is best not to think of genes 'controlling' anything, not even eye colour; rather that they specify the 'recipe' for the resultant organism. Just as differently designed machines tend to act in different ways (compare a Formula One car with a tractor) so, by affecting rates of nervous system development, and timing and rates of hormone synthesis, genes can influence the likelihood of an organism behaving in a particular way. This will rarely be all-or-nothing ('if you have a particular gene you will definitely do a particular behaviour') - environmental influences on behaviour, such as through learning, can often be large. If we are interested in the development of behaviour (see p.133), we might want to try and separate genetic from environmental influences on behaviour. However, to investigate the function or evolution of a behaviour, it is only the genetic influences that matter, as genes are the hereditary material on which evolution acts.

THE IMMORTAL AND SELFISH GENE

Think of a friend, and now think of the shape of that friend's nose. It is very likely that several of the noses in the same family are similarly shaped (provided it is not that shape because of an injury). You might call it a characteristic family nose. The reason is that a nose develops according to information held in DNA molecules - the genes - and since copies of those genes are passed from parent to offspring down the generations, the members of a family have more 'nose genes' in common with each other than with people outside the family. You might have seen a photograph of a great-grandmother, sadly no longer alive, and the family nose was umistakable. Does that mean the nose is immortal and lives on in your friend? Clearly not literally. The nose tissue of the great grandmother is dead. Your friend's living nose tissue is just very like it. The nose itself was not passed from parent to offspring, but copies of the 'nose-shape' genes were. It is the information held in the DNA of those genes, the *sequence of organic bases*, which is passed down the generations.

Now think of all the other characteristics of your friend which were inherited from his/her parents. His/her body has been built from information held in the genes, the same information that contributed to the building of his/her ancestors as well as the other living members of the family. In our everyday lives we consider people to be important to us, not their DNA. But when we turn our attention to understanding evolution it is more useful to take a different viewpoint and focus on the genes. Genes build bodies which for a certain length of time keep them safe from damage by the world outside. Eventually the outside world takes its toll and the bodies die; but if the bodies survive long enough the genes make copies of themselves, packaged inside sperms and eggs, and become dispersed to make more bodies for their own protection. Genes whose contributions make a body more likely to survive and reproduce are more likely to be represented in the next generation.

Genes which are in existence today, if they are not new mutations, are copies of genes which existed in the past. The fact that they are here now means that they have successfully contributed to the building of bodies to protect and propagate themselves. Some genes contribute to the ability of those bodies to behave and thereby to survive. Animal behaviour is a mechanism created by genes which brings about the genes' own perpetuation. It is as if genes act *selfishly* by making bodies that will help them, the genes, survive.

What is the evidence for genes affecting behaviour? The fact that so many species-specific behaviours appear to be adaptive (i.e. suiting the organism to its environment), so must have evolved, is only weak, circumstantial evidence. So, too, is the occurrence of behaviour (e.g. the cuckoo's song) that appears to be *innate* (or inborn), requiring no environmental input. Geneticists usually rely on two main techniques:

• cross-breeding between stocks which show different characteristics and
• artificial selection (through selective breeding) for a particular characteristic.

Even if you have not yet studied genetics, the principals can be understood without knowing the formal theory.

■ Cross-breeding
The necklace and collared dove are two, very closely related, members of the pigeon family, and each has its own characteristic sexual display. Each type bows its head and coos to a potential mate at a different rate. However, if you cross-breed these two types of dove, the resultant hybrid has a bowing-and-cooing rate intermediate between those of its parents. By incubating the eggs and rearing the chicks in isolation, one can be sure that the display has not been learned as a mixture from the two parents; only genes have been passed on. Unfortunately, like the mule (the offspring of a horse and a donkey), the hybrid dove is sterile, so one cannot carry on further breeding experiments. Within-species breeding experiments are thus much more powerful (see the behaviour file on hygienic bees, p.72).

■ Artificial selection
Probably the most familiar everyday example of how behaviour can be altered by selective breeding is the different natures of various breeds of domestic dogs. Humans have selected many working dogs (such as sheepdogs, terriers and retrievers) for behavioural traits just as much as for physical attributes. This is not to say that upbringing and environment are not important (rottweilers can be soppy; labradors can be aggressive), but genetic differences undoubtedly affect a dog's potential for behaving in ways typical of its breed. Today's breeds result from artificial selection in the past, the historical details of which have not been recorded accurately. A clear example, where the details of selection were carefully recorded, comes from the geneticist's favourite animal, the fruit fly *Drosophila*. In any wild population of the species *Drosophila melanogaster*, some individuals tend to move upwards, whilst others have a tendency to move downwards (due to a negative or positive response to gravity - i.e. geotaxis - see p.129). To quantify the extent of negative rather than positive geotaxis, Jerry Hirsch and co-workers designed a vertical maze (Fig.9.2). The end-point reached by a fly reflected how often it had turned up rather than down. They then started an artificial selection experiment. They took flies that had ended at the top of the maze (extreme negative geotaxis) and bred from them alone, and they took flies from the bottom of the maze (extreme positive geotaxis) and used them as a separate breeding stock. They then took offspring from these separate breeding stocks, or lines, and

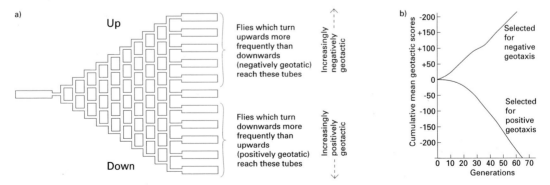

Figure 9.2 Hirsch's maze and results (a) Vertical maze for separating negatively from positively geotactic fruit flies (*Drosophila melanogaster*). Flies enter from the tube on the left and move through the maze, turning upwards or downwards at each choice point until they emerge into the tubes on the right. (b) Selection for negative and positive geotaxis. Over a number of generations, selected lines of fruit flies became progressively more extreme in their degree of geotaxis.

ran them through the maze. Once again they bred separately from the extreme negative and positive stocks, and ran their offspring through the maze. With each successive generation, the negative and positive stocks became more extreme in their respective geotaxis. As each insect ran the maze only once, there was no possibility of learning, and *Drosophila* do not teach their offspring which way to walk! The change between generations occurs only because the parents allowed to breed are genetically different from their original population: they have genes which promote more extreme geotaxis. This selection experiment is evolution in miniature, and it is behaviour (albeit a simple one) that is evolving.

■ Adaptive behaviour

As behaviour is influenced by genes, we would expect those behaviours which help an animal survive and reproduce to persist in the gene pool, whilst those that don't should be eliminated. This is evolution by natural selection and, over the hundreds or thousands of generations of a species' evolution, this leads to species showing those traits which make them particularly well-suited to their ecological circumstances - *adaptive* traits. Ultimate questions about the *function* of a behaviour are questions about *adaptation*.

When biologists see a behaviour and ask, 'What is it for?', they mean, 'How does it contribute to the animal's survival and reproductive success?', or more succinctly, 'How does it contribute to the animal's inclusive fitness?' (see Social behaviour, pp.116). So it is important that we should now consider some of the common classes of animal behaviour and ask these *functional* or *adaptive* questions.

■ ACQUIRING FOOD, SHELTER AND A PARTNER

Different species employ different behaviours to acquire resources but, irrespective of the details, they boil down to certain basic tasks.

Successful animals (defined as those which survive to maturity and have offspring) succeed because they manage to acquire and use enough vital resources. They eat enough of the appropriate foods to be healthy, and find shelter from extremes of weather and from predators. They find a partner of the same species and opposite sex and then mate. Having produced offspring, they may provide food and shelter for the young to survive until they can look after themselves. But not every individual succeeds. Resources are always finite and populations usually grow until there is not enough to go round. All animals compete with others of their species for what is available and those best adapted succeed to leave behind offspring which carry their genes into the future.

WHAT IS FOOD?

Food is the complex organic molecules used by organisms as raw material for building and repairing their cells and as fuel to provide energy for driving the workings of those cells. Plants, some protoctista and some bacteria make their own food from simple molecules. They are the *producers*. Animals are *consumers*; they cannot make the complex molecules for themselves but eat (consume) plants or other animals. To put that another way, animals are thieves; they steal the molecules they need by eating other organisms (see *Biology Advanced Studies - Environment and Ecology*).

■ Foraging

Most animals spend a large proportion of their waking time *foraging*, that is, detecting, acquiring and consuming food. (See 'A Cat Goes Hunting' on p.112, 'Dogwhelks' on p.78, 'Limpets' on p.79, and 'Territory Economics in a Nectar-eating Bird' on p.92.) Sometimes choices must be made. From a variety of foods an animal might select the most profitable one; that is the food which provides the greatest benefit (energy and nutrients) for the least cost (risk and effort). This is *optimal foraging*.

■ Reproduction

It takes energy to make offspring and so an animal will only have reproductive success if it does not waste too much energy in fruitless behaviour (such as attempting to mate with another species or with the wrong sex). Animals reduce such wastage by 'cueing-in' on signals which reveal potential partners' species, sex, maturity and whether or not they are fertile.

Typically, an animal detects, locates and orientates itself towards a potential mate. A period of *courtship* behaviour follows during which each partner gains information about the other's suitability; not only as to species, sex and maturity but also whether he or she is healthy and likely to be an effective parent. Once a choice has been made the two orientate their bodies so that their genitals are in the right positions and then, if fertilisation is internal, they copulate or, if it is external, they synchronously shed their gametes.

Common frogs mating

■ MATE CHOICE, SEXUAL SELECTION AND SIGNALS

Birds sing, frogs croak, grasshoppers chirp, red deer bellow, and gorillas slap their chest; yet it is nearly always the male of the species that performs these displays. Why do males spend so much time showing off? Such displays are not only costly in terms of time and energy, but may attract predators or result in injury from direct combat. These common sex differences in display behaviour are often matched by differences in costly ornamentation, such as the peacock's tail or a stag's antlers. This puzzled Darwin; he had explained evolution by natural selection as 'survival of the fittest', yet here are features of animals which actually reduce survival. These sex

A CAT GOES HUNTING

A farm cat left the farmyard and ran along a path until it reached a meadow. Once there it walked slowly, zig-zagging its way across the field, looking down, searching the ground. Occasionally it stood still, looking up as if to check what was happening further away, then down would go its head and on it would prowl. Eventually it came across a small hole, a mouse burrow. With its body held low to the ground, its eyes fixed on the burrow, it slowly and quietly crept closer. At the mouth of the burrow it continued to crouch and stare. When after a few minutes no mouse had appeared the cat stood up, looked around for a couple of seconds and continued its search. At last, finding another burrow, it approached, crouched and stared once more. This time a mouse appeared and, not seeing the motionless cat, left the burrow. The cat waited, eyes fixed on the mouse, its muscles becoming more and more tense in its crouching posture, until the mouse was some distance from the entrance. Then it pounced, leaping forward and aiming its killing bite at the mouse's neck. The cat ate the mouse entirely, head first, so that the hair did not catch in its throat.

The cat continued its search of the field until its attention was drawn by a movement in the hedgerow. It was a small bird on a low branch. It had not seen the cat, which began slowly to stalk its new prey, keeping its head and body low and its eyes constantly on the bird. Whenever the bird moved, the cat 'froze'. Once or twice it became hidden by a clump of leaves and then the cat sprinted forward until, seeing the bird once more, it froze again. Finally the cat was within pouncing range of the bird, but it did not pounce straight away. Instead, as with the mouse, it waited for a moment, crouching and tense. Then it pounced. But too late; during that final wait the bird saw the cat and flew away.

(Freely adapted from *Hunting Behaviour of the Domestic Cat* by D.C. Turner and D. Meister, in *The Domestic Cat, the Biology of its Behaviour* edited by D.C. Turner and P. Bateson, Cambridge University Press 1988.)

Male peacock displaying tail

differences, or *secondary sexual characters*, go far beyond what is necessary simply to ensure reproduction. Darwin's explanation was that all such features, whilst they do not aid survival, benefit males in reproductive competition, either in direct conflict with rival males or through attracting females. He called this process *sexual selection*, to distinguish it from natural selection, which concerns features that aid survival or rearing offspring. Today, some evolutionary biologists accept Darwin's distinction but most view sexual selection as simply one form of natural selection, as it still acts by promoting the replication and survival of genes.

You may have asked two important questions about sexual selection:

• *Why is it usually males (and not females) that possess ornaments and perform displays?*
The more-or-less fundamental distinction between the sexes of any species is that males produce large numbers of small gametes (sperm), whereas females produce small numbers of large gametes (eggs). This has two main consequences. First, the cost of a 'bad' mating is higher for females; at worst, if a female mates with the wrong species she may waste her entire season's egg production, whilst a male can replenish sperm supplies rapidly. This means that females should be more choosey than males at mating, and may explain why many secondary sexual characters (e.g. the peacock's tail) are directed toward impressing females. Second, a male's reproductive capacity is much higher than a female's, as he can produce more gametes. However, for every male that is successful at mating several times, there are other males who father no offspring. This means there is the potential for great competition

between males, and any features that aid competition will be favoured.

• *Why does reproductive competition favour ornaments and displays?*
It is easy to understand how large body size, enlarged canines, horns and antlers, might be beneficial in male-male competition. But why are the elaborate feathers of a peacock attractive to the female peahen? Darwin himself couldn't explain why females of some species had particular preferences, be they for bright plumage or beautiful song. (As a typical Victorian English gentleman, he simply accepted that females had inexplicable 'whims' and left it at that!) Today, although the topic is still controversial, most biologists now realise that songs and ornaments are used in display precisely because they are costly. They are handicaps, and only the best males can afford the cost. For example, take bird song. A male cannot sing and feed at the same time, and singing uses up the energy reserves which are vital for overnight survival. So only males who are good at finding food, or who have good territories, can afford to sing a lot. A male that sings too much runs the risk of starvation so, in the long term, song output is a cheat-proof signal of male quality. This argument can also be applied to aggressive displays directed at rival males. Red deer stags have roaring contests, with only the healthiest strongest males having the stamina to continue for any length of time. Only closely matched stags actually come to fighting, where roaring ability cannot differentiate between them. It is very tempting to apply the logic of the 'handicap principle' to humans: how much adolescent male behaviour consists of performing risky, dangerous, stunts to show fellow males, and females, that you are tough enough to take it?

Over a long period of evolutionary time, signals and displays can become so modified that they no longer resemble the original behaviour that was used to assess the health or quality of the signaller. For example some waterfowl such as grebe, *Podiceps cristatus*, wave vegetation at each other, presumably originating from nest-building behaviour. Many ducks have pecking and head-turning displays which probably evolved from preening (feather-maintenance) behaviour. This process of elaboration of simple behaviours into elaborate displays is known as *ritualisation*.

■ PARENTAL CARE

Humans have few children. You are unlikely to have more than eight brothers and sisters! As a foetus your mother fed you through the placenta; as a baby your parents, or other adults, ensured your survival by providing your food and drink as mother's milk (or a similar food made up to a formula). They kept you warm, protected you from injury and showed you how, eventually, to look after yourself. In caring for children in this way humans behave as typical mammals. By contrast, a fish such as cod has tens of thousands or even millions of offspring each year but does nothing to help them survive. These examples represent two extreme options which put simplistically are:
• produce a great many offspring so that even though most will die a reasonable number will survive to maturity
• produce few offspring but look after them so that each one is more likely to survive to maturity.

Both of these strategies result in the parents' genes being adequately represented in the next generation.

■ LIFESTYLES - SOLITARY TO SOCIAL

All animals at some stage in their lives spend time with others of the same species. Those which meet only for sexual reproduction are generally termed *solitary*, while those which spend longer in groups interacting with others are said to be *social*, and the behaviour they perform in response to one another, *social behaviour* (Table 9.1).

The selfish gene idea is particularly useful when trying to understand the adaptive advantages of different life styles. Since both solitary and social lifestyles exist, we must conclude that they both have their advantages, perhaps under different ecological circumstances. But which?

 What are the advantages and disadvantages of solitary and social living?

r AND K SELECTION

There is an equation used to describe the rate of growth of populations (the details of which need not bother us here) which has two variables, r and K, whose values depend on the species under consideration. Species whose r value is high are said to be *r-selected*. They are adapted for rapid population growth and are characterised by short life span, large numbers of offspring and little or no parental care. Species with a high K value are *K-selected*. They are adapted for maintaining populations at an already high level with relatively long lives and few offspring which they look after. Species which are r-selected invest energy into producing large numbers of young. K-selected species invest energy into caring for a small number of young. Which of the following are r-selected and which are K-selected?
• Birds provide a lot of yolk in their eggs, build nests to protect eggs and chicks, use the heat of their bodies to incubate the egg and warm the chicks, and feed the growing chicks on food which they forage.
• Digger wasps (*Sphex ichneumonias*) invest energy in digging a burrow, stocking it with grasshoppers which they have paralysed with a sting, and then laying eggs inside the grasshoppers. When the larvae hatch they eat the grasshoppers.
• Some birds, such as the ringed plover, will lead a predator away from its nest of chicks by fluttering on the ground as if it were injured. It risks being killed itself but it is a risk worth taking in exchange for the survival of its offspring.
• Some cichlid fish from lakes in East Africa carry their fertilised eggs in their mouth. After they hatch the young fish swim close to the mother but, when a predator approaches, hide in her mouth again.
• Fruit flies can lay 20 eggs per day in rotting fruit until about 900 are laid. The larvae feed on the fruit.

 Is the three-spined stickleback r- or K-selected?

Types of grouping	Example
• Solitary - males and females come together only to mate • Aggregations - accidental groupings attracted only by the habitat • Colony of physically joined organisms • Anonymous shoals and herds - but attracted by others of the same species • Colony of separate individuals with distinct roles (castes) • Single sex groups - non-breeding • Family group - offspring leave at maturity • Extended family group - offspring remain after maturity • Multi-male, multi-female societies with many families	Sticklebacks Earthworms *Obelia*, coral Wildebeest Ants Male red deer Swans Foxes Baboons

Table 9.1 Types of grouping

Pay attention to the way that genes responsible for behaviour could, through that behaviour, increase the chances of copies of themselves existing in future generations. Now check through Table 9.2. There are costs and benefits associated with any lifestyle, social or solitary. A given species in a given habitat has a certain repertoire of behaviour by which it extracts from the habitat energy and other resources to maintain its health and growth, and ultimately to reproduce. It uses energy to power its behaviour and is always at some risk of predation, injury and disease. If in the long term the energy and nutrient value of food which it takes from the habitat (benefit) is greater than the energy it uses up in getting it (cost), and the probability of reaching maturity and having offspring (benefit) is greater than the probability of dying early or becoming disabled (cost), then benefits outweigh costs

	Benefits	Costs
Group	• Protection from predators • Sexual partners near at hand • Food is more likely to be found when several individuals are searching for it • Several individuals can cooperate in hunting and so catch larger or faster prey than a single individual could cope with • The opportunity to observe others and learn from them • Temperature regulation, e.g. a group can huddle together to reduce heat loss • Opportunity for related individuals to help each other survive and reproduce, therefore increasing the chance of their genes surviving into the next generation (increasing their inclusive fitness)	• Groups are more conspicuous than solitary individuals and attract predators • More competition for sexual partners • More competition for food • More competition for shelter • Increased chance of becoming infected by pathogens and parasites
Alone	• Inconspicuous to predators • Little competition for food • Little competition for shelter • Reduced chance of catching diseases and picking up parasites	• Vulnerable to predators, if detected • Sexual partners must be searched for • Food must be searched for alone • There is a limit to the size of prey a single individual can kill • Little opportunity to learn from others • No chance of help from others to survive or to rear young

Table 9.2

and that species will continue to live in that manner in that environment. This sort of *cost-benefit* reasoning is exactly analogous to that used to understand foraging or resource acquisition (see p.112). Let us see how it can help us understand an important aspect of social organisation: whether individuals defend exclusive areas, or *territories*, or whether they mix freely in large groups.

(a) Small antelope, such as the African dik-dik (genus *Madoqua*), live solitarily or in male-female pairs. They defend exclusive territories, marking the boundaries with scent from special glands around their face and genitals, and will attack any members of their species who ignore these 'keep out' signals.

(b) Larger antelope like the wildebeest (or gnu; genus *Connochaetes*) do not defend any particular area, and roam the African savanna in vast herds numbering tens of thousands.

Why do we see such different social organisations? Why is it important for the dik-dik to defend an area, and not the wildebeest? Why do some songbirds, such as finches and tits, defend exclusive territories in spring and summer, but not in winter? To understand these questions and why some species are territorial, and others not, we first have to discover what resource the animals are defending, and second we have to understand the concept of *economic defendability*. Put simply, whatever the resource (food, nest site, etc.), for evolution to have favoured territorial behaviour in a particular species, the benefits

of having the resource must be greater than the cost of defending it. Many animals defend territories to gain exclusive use of the food it contains, but the costs in time and energy of defending the territory increase with the size of the territory. So, if an animal's food is highly concentrated into rich patches (a clumped distribution), it will be relatively easy to patrol and defend the small area that contains the food. However, if the food is evenly spread through the habitat (a dispersed distribution), then it may require more time and energy defending an area large enough to supply daily needs than it gets from the food. This explains the difference between dik-dik and wildebeest social organisation. The dik-dik feeds on high-quality fruit and shoots, which have a patchy distribution in the forest; being small, the dik-dik can easily defend an area large enough to supply its needs. The wildebeest, on the other hand, is much larger and, feeding on low-quality grass, needs to range over a large area to meet its daily energy requirements. Defending such a vast area would take more time and energy than the grass could supply. The behaviour file on p.92 shows how this cost-benefit approach can be applied in a more quantitative manner to explain the size of sunbird territories. Not all animals defend territories for an exclusive food supply. For example, the blackbird has quite small territories (as small as 25 by 25 metres) and does most of its feeding off-territory. In this and many other songbirds, territories are slightly larger, and song activity greater, at the time females are fertile and laying eggs. It seems that many songbird territories are 'total exclusion zones', by which a male stops rivals sneaking in to mate with his female. Song is a keep-out signal that repels other males and thus defends his paternity of his female's chicks. (It has been said that bird song is a 'means of territorial declaration and sexual invitation'!)

■ **Social behaviour**

Truly social animals communicate with others of their group and are attracted preferentially towards them. But many animals accumulate in the same place not because of any positive response to one another but because of the nature of the place; they all orientate towards the same favourable habitat (e.g. earthworms in a compost heap move to the richest nutrients).

It is not useful to consider such aggregates as social groups. However, there may be positive benefits to an animal finding itself in an aggregation because the very presence of other animals might make the environment more favourable. Consider woodlice (*Porcellio scaber*) in a crevice between two stones. Water evaporating from their several bodies increases the humidity. They probably accumulated there accidentally by kineses and taxes (p.129), but each additional arrival benefits from the raised humidity.

Q Devise, and if possible carry out, an investigation to see if woodlice are attracted by other woodlice.

If a predator discovers a group of animals, each individual within that group is at less risk of being killed than if it had been discovered on its own. The reason is that in a group there are probably some others around which are closer to the predator and who are more likely to be taken. (The larger the group the greater is the probability that the predator will eat someone else rather than you!) Social animals frequently respond to the presence of predators by moving closer to one another or even attempting to get nearer to the centre of the group (selfish behaviour produced by selfish genes - see p.109). This results in the group contracting and becoming denser: a phenomenon described, for instance, in flocks of starlings attacked by a falcon or herds of antelope attacked by lions. The evolutionary biologist William Hamilton described this as the *selfish herd*.

Whereas a solitary animal must carry out all the tasks of living for itself, in a social group some tasks can be shared. Looking out for predators is one such task. In groups of feeding ostriches, at any one time a certain number of individuals have their heads down, eating, whilst others have their heads up, vigilant. Each individual spends some time feeding and some time on guard, and the larger the group the less time an individual needs to spend being vigilant (Fig.9.3).

Q Does the 'vigilance while feeding' behaviour also apply to humans? Devise, and if possible carry out, an investigation to find out if people look up more often from their food when dining in a large group than when dining with only a few people or alone.

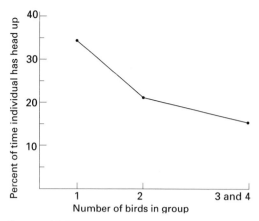

Figure 9.3 Vigilance in ostriches. An ostrich (*Struthio camelus*) spends a smaller proportion of its time scanning for predators when it is in a group

Ostriches do not take strict turns to look up, but still benefit from the shared vigilance. A property of truly social groups is *division of labour*, where different individuals specialise in particular roles. Active defence from attack by predators or members of other groups is frequently the role of the larger group members, usually male. When a troop of olive baboons (*Papio anubis*) is threatened, the adult and adolescent males are more likely to move to the edge to face the threat.

Q Why might males, rather than females, do the defending in this species? Think of the possible different *costs* and *benefits* for each sex in facing a predator.

Members of a social group can benefit from the efforts of others to find food. When one discovers a source of food it might communicate the position to others or it may have been watched by others who now know where to look.

The task of looking after infants can be shared between older members of a group. This is particularly prominent in primates. A baboon mother for most of the time keeps her newborn infant held close to her, but in time increasingly allows mature companions to carry and groom it while she feeds. In some primate species, such as langurs (*Presbytis*), mothers allow their infant to be carried from its earliest days by adult and adolescent females who frequently spend long periods of time passing the youngster around amongst themselves.

It is easy to see the adaptive advantage of division of labour to those individuals who receive help. A mother relieved for a while of the burden of her infant is given an opportunity to feed more efficiently, the benefit of which is passed on to the infant through her milk. The infant's survival chances are therefore enhanced so the chance of the mother's genes continuing through another generation is increased. But what benefit does the helper gain?

Any helpful action taken by an animal costs energy. That action could put the helper at risk of injury or death: facing up to a predator for instance. If an animal behaves *altruistically* (i.e. expends energy or risks its life in the help of others), does that not increase the chance of the others' genes continuing into the next generation at the expense of its own? How does this square with the notion of selfish genes? If there were genes for altruistic behaviour surely they would automatically decrease in the gene pool since individuals carrying them would be selected against: being less well fed and suffering more injuries than individuals who behaved totally selfishly. Put that way, it is difficult to see how altruistic behaviour could have evolved. This remained a paradox in ethology until fairly recently, when more and more long-term studies of social animals in their natural habitats showed a common theme. A large proportion of the members of social groups are closely related; so that when, for instance, an adult male baboon risks death defending his group he is risking it on behalf of his offspring, nephews, nieces, etc. Furthermore, when acts of altruism are directed towards specific individuals, the recipients of help tend to be close relatives of the helper. Helpers may put themselves in jeopardy, but in doing so they increase the chance of copies of their genes, carried in close relatives, continuing into the future. The evolution of altruistic behaviour through the indirect benefits of altruism to relatives, rather than direct benefits through one's own reproductive success, is by *kin selection*, to distinguish it from ordinary natural selection as Darwin described it. Altruistic behaviour can evolve by other means (see the behaviour file on p.96), but kin selection appears to be the most powerful force. Its most extreme expression is seen in *eusocial* animals.

A BIOLOGIST'S VIEW OF SOCIAL INTERACTIONS

The simplest sort of social interaction involves just two individuals. If one animal, the *actor*, does something to another, the *recipient*, there are four possible sorts of outcome: either both benefit, both suffer costs, the actor benefits at the recipient's expense, or vice versa. Costs and benefits are measured in terms of survival and reproductive success, or Darwinian *fitness*. We would expect evolution by natural selection to favour genes that cause the individuals carrying them to benefit. This makes altruism and spiteful behaviour hard to explain in simple Darwinian terms, but not when you consider altruism toward kin (see main text). Even cooperation, where both parties benefit, might be difficult to evolve if cheating is possible (but see p.96 on reciprocal altruism).

		Recipient	
		Benefit	Cost
Actor	Benefit	Cooperation	Selfishness
	Cost	Altruism	Spite

■ Eusociality

The peak of social organisation in the animal kingdom is found amongst the *social insects*: the ants, bees, wasps and termites. The first three are members of the order Hymenoptera (see p.71), whilst the termites form their own order, the Isoptera, closely related to cockroaches (p.68). An African Driver Ant's nest (*Dorylus wilverthi*) may contain over 22 000 000 individuals, together weighing 20 kg. There is strict division of labour, with morphologically distinct castes acting as food-gatherers, soldiers and 'child-carers'; yet the entire colony has been produced by only one egg-bearing female (the rest are sterile). Several million individuals working selflessly for the good of one is a level of cooperation and organisation not matched (even by human beings), but how could such a phenomenon have evolved? Many times in fact, perhaps as many as 11 times independently within the Hymenoptera and, aside from the termites, some aphids and spiders also have sterile workers which help a single female, the 'queen', reproduce. Amongst vertebrates, only two species of African rodents, called mole rats, have societies with sterile workers and a single breeding female. Such species are termed *eusocial* (eu is the Greek for true), defined as where there are morphologically distinct castes, sterile workers, and overlapping generations (many of the workers are themselves offspring of the queen). From the evolutionary point of view, the mystery is how sterility could have evolved: a sterile individual, by definition, leaves no offspring, so how can genes for sterility be passed on? If you have read the section on *kin selection* (p.118), you may guess. The secret is that in all eusocial species the members of a hive or nest are very closely related. Whilst the workers may not have offspring themselves, they are helping the queen, usually their mother, raise younger 'brothers' and 'sisters' who share copies of the same genes as themselves. In social aphids, the workers are produced by asexual reproduction (*parthenogenesis*), so are in fact genetically identical to each other and the queen. In termites and mole rats, once a new colony is founded there is much inbreeding, so average relatedness is high. In Hymenoptera (ants, bees and wasps), the story has an interesting twist, as these insects have an unusual means of sex determination. In humans, and many other organisms, sex is determined by special chromosomes, the sex chromosomes, of which there are two types, X and Y (see *Biology Advanced Studies - Genetics and Evolution*). Females have two X chromosomes, whilst males have one X and one Y. Hymenoptera, on the other hand, do not have sex chromosomes. Sex is determined by whether an egg is fertilised or not. If an egg is fertilised, it turns out female; if it is unfertilised, it turns out male (in humans an unfertilised egg would never develop at all). Because females are *diploid* (they have two sets of chromosomes, like us) whilst males are *haploid* (they have one set of chromosomes), this form of sex determination is referred to as *haplodiploidy*. As the queen stores enough sperm after mating to fertilise a lifetime's egg production, she can in fact determine the sex of her offspring simply by releasing sperm, or not, as an egg is laid! This has interesting consequences for genetic relatedness between

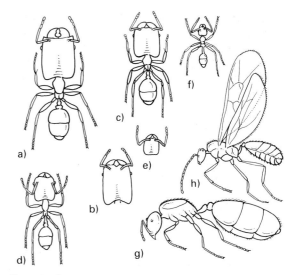

Figure 9.4 Castes in the ant, *Pheidole tepicana*. The queen (g), the male (h), and six worker subcastes, from the major worker (a), through several sizes of workers (b-e), to the minor worker (f)

family members. In humans, as we get 50% of our genes from our mother and 50% from our father, we are 50% genetically related to each parent, and likewise to our own children, if we have any. Similar reasoning (Fig.9.5) makes us 50% related to a full brother or sister. As hymenopteran queens produce eggs by meiosis, just like us, each egg contains half the genes of the mother, and relatedness between mother and offspring is also 50% (Fig.9.5). However, things are very different between sisters. A male develops from an unfertilised egg, so he has only one set of genes and thus all his sperm will be genetically identical. Thus two sisters, with the same father, will inherit identical genes from their father (100% related). For their mother's genes, as the egg is produced by meiosis, they only have a 50% chance of getting identical genes. Therefore, on average, two sisters are (100% + 50%)/2 = 75% related. In the hymenoptera, sisters are more closely related to each other than to their own daughters! William Hamilton, in the 1960s, realised that this unusual pattern of relatedness might explain why in ants, bees and wasps, the workers are always female. A female hymenopteran, in genetical terms, does better by helping her mother (the queen) raise younger sisters than she would by having her own offspring. Interestingly, termites, which are normal chromosomally sex-determined animals like ourselves, have both male and female workers. So do mole rats.

Humans (XX,XY sex determination)

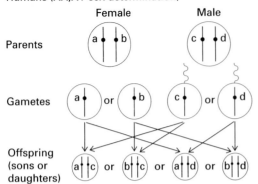

Bees (haplodiploid sex determination)

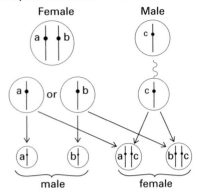

Figure 9.5 Relatedness in humans and bees. Humans, like most other animals, are diploid and sex is determined by possession of *sex chromosomes*. As gametes are formed by halving the chromosome number in meiosis, each offspring has 50% of either parent's genes, and has a 50% chance of having an identical gene to its brother or sister. In the drawing, the points a, b, c and d represent four versions of the same gene; only one pair of chromosomes is drawn for simplicity. In bees, and other hymenoptera, inheritance of maternal genes occurs in the same way but, as males have only one set of genes (they are haploid), daughters will be identical for the genes they inherit from their father. Two sisters can therefore, on average, be considered to be 75% related

■ Dominance hierarchies

You have no doubt heard someone describing their job in an organisation as being 'at a particular level in the *pecking order*'. This comes from a phenomenon first described in flocks of domestic poultry but which also occurs in natural groups of social birds. Let us identify three hens: A, B and C. A agressively pecks the other two but they do not peck her. B pecks C but not A. C is pecked by both A and B and does not peck back. We can describe their pecking order as A>B>C. When the poultry farmer first put them together in the enclosure these three hens did not know each other. Each one fought with the other two and either won or was beaten. Each hen therefore learnt who she could beat and who could beat her. All the hens probably benefit from having compared their fighting prowess with the others. Less time is spent fighting, leaving more time for feeding. If two hens attempt to pick up the same piece of food the *subordinate* (the poorer fighter) tends to be displaced by the *dominant* (the better fighter). Dominant hens get more food, but subordinates also benefit through learning how to avoid conflict by feeding away from more dominant hens. What is more, in wild populations, with less fighting they are more likely to remain together and gain the benefits of being in a group (Fig.9.6).

Social rank based on aggression is also found in groups of mammals. In wolves (*Canis lupus*) a dominant leader is submitted to by the rest of the pack. This probably allowed early humans to tame wolves by dominating them, eventually turning them into the domestic dog of today, which submits to its human master.

Primate societies have hierarchies, but they are rarely straightforward. In baboons, rhesus monkeys, chimpanzees and gorillas, for example, 'friends' form alliances and successfully threaten others whom, on their own, they would not be able to dominate. Some families rank higher than others so that any member of one family can displace any member of another. In rhesus monkey families (with a mother and several offspring) the mother is dominant to her daughters and in those daughters who have reached puberty, the younger they are the higher they rank: the youngest is dominant to her elder sisters.

It is an advantage for an animal to be able to beat others in fights or to cause them to submit when threatened, because by displacing others it can obtain more food, a safer site for shelter or first access to sexual partners. The significance of the latter for males is that the one who is the first to copulate with a female after she ovulates is the one whose sperm is most likely to fertilise the egg. The genes of a

A flock of five hens, each identified by a coloured plastic leg ring, was observed for several hours. The researcher recorded every occasion when one hen aggressively pecked or displaced another. The results are shown in the first table.

The dominance hierarchy of the flock was worked out by rearranging the table so that Green, who was never attacked or displaced, comes first and Blue, who was attacked or displaced by everyone else, comes last. The other hens were put into the order which gives the smallest numbers (0s) below the diagonal.

		Number of occasions when an individual was aggressively pecked or displaced by another				
		Red	Blue	Green	Yellow	White
Number of occasions when an individual pecked or displaced another	Red	–	22	0	31	11
	Blue	0	–	0	0	0
	Green	28	10	–	7	15
	Yellow	0	9	0	–	8
	White	0	4	0	0	–

		Number of occasions when an individual was aggressively pecked or displaced by another				
		Green	Red	Yellow	White	Blue
Number of occasions when an individual pecked or displaced another.	Green	–	28	7	15	10
	Red	0	–	31	11	22
	Yellow	0	0	–	8	9
	White	0	0	0	–	4
	Blue	0	0	0	0	–

The dominance hierarchy of the flock was therefore
Green → Red → Yellow → White → Blue

Figure 9.6 Working out the dominance hierarchy in a flock of domestic hens

dominant animal are therefore more likely to pass into the next generation than those of a subordinate. That is not to say that dominant animals have it all their own way. Subordinates can sneak food away from under the noses of more dominant animals if they are clever or agile enough; and low ranking males sometimes gain access to fertile females, even though they are at the end of the queue! Furthermore, dominance sometimes has costs. In sparrows, dominant males may father more young in any one breeding season, but seem to have lower life expectancy, perhaps due to the stress of maintaining their status. In red deer, dominant stags rarely maintain control of a harem of females for more than a few seasons, then they lose out to younger males.

■ Cohesion in social groups

Whether solitary or social, individuals are always in competition for limited resources and mates. In social groups this produces a paradox: competition leads to conflict which tends to make individuals move apart and disrupt the group; yet they need to stay together in order to gain the advantages of living in a group. How is group cohesion maintained?

Social animals tend to be attracted towards *conspecifics* (i.e. individuals of the same species). Rhesus monkeys have been shown to learn complex tasks for the sole reward of being able to see another rhesus through a window. In total isolation many animals show signs of physiological stress.

All-out fighting, as seen in a newly formed flock of hens, is relatively infrequent in natural societies. Most members of a group grow up together and settle their dominance relationships early on, perhaps by comparing strength and skill in the relatively safe context of play fighting (see p.134). Aggressive encounters are frequently just an exchange of threatening and submissive signals or ritualised trials of strength which stop before the loser is seriously hurt (Fig.9.7).

Olive baboons grooming

A behaviour which draws animals together and lowers arousal is social grooming. One animal licks, scratches and picks through the fur or feathers of another, removing dirt, loose skin and parasites. The one being groomed normally accepts this attention willingly, relaxing and shifting its body to facilitate the process even though the one doing the grooming is so close. In birds it is usual for the actor in a grooming pair to be dominant to the recipient. It is as if social grooming reassures the recipient and inhibits its tendency to escape. In primates it is more frequently the other way round: the subordinate grooms the dominant. Here it is as if grooming inhibits the dominant animal's tendency to attack.

In many primates, young infants are usually of a conspicuously different colour from adults. They are an almost irresistible attraction to both sexes and all ages, who attempt to get close to mothers and examine their infants. In some species (for instance Barbary macaques and olive baboons) males pick up and carry infants who are mature enough to leave their mothers. A male with an infant friend is able to stay closer to other more dominant males than he would on his own, particularly if the infant is from a high ranking family. Also, by advertising that he is 'good with young ones', he may attract prospective mates.

Rhesus monkey (*Macaca mulatta*): staring directly at its opponent with open mouth

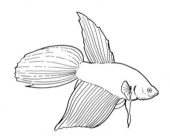

Siamese fighting fish (*Betta splendans*): broadside to its opponent, with the nearer pelvic fin extended downward

Great tit (*Parus major*): black ventral stripe and yellow belly displayed towards it opponent

Figure 9.7 Some threat postures

■ CAUSE AND DEVELOPMENT OF BEHAVIOUR

A female cat has a litter of kittens. She sits purring while they squirm and totter around her. Occasionally she sniffs at them or grooms them by licking their fur. When one wanders away she walks to it and retrieves it in her mouth. Now she flops on to her side allowing the kittens to suckle at her nipples. Eventually she stands up and, leaving her young behind in the nest, walks away to find food for herself.

We have already considered some of the functions of behaviour. Now we shall consider some of the causes. Let us use the scene of the cat and her kittens to raise questions about the mechanisms which cause behaviour and how behaviour changes during an animal's life.

What signals to the cat that these wriggling objects are kittens and, what is more, hers? This is a question about stimuli. How do the kittens find the nipples and how does the mother find her way back to the nest after being away? These are questions about *orientation* and *navigation*.

Notice that she does not always behave in the same way to the presence of the kittens. Sometimes she watches them, retrieves them, licks them and lets them suckle. Sometimes she ignores them and occasionally she even leaves them. Her changing responses might be due to short-term changes within her central nervous system. This raises questions about *motivation*.

The kittens' behaviour is certain to change as they get older. New behaviours will appear and old ones will disappear or improve. At any time it could be said that their behaviour had resulted from a sequence of developmental changes. But what causes behaviour to appear at a certain time? Is it instinctive, arising from the way the nervous system is constructed; or does the animal learn to behave that way? Perhaps more realistically the question should be: to what extent is behaviour instinctive or

learnt? Similar questions could be asked about the mother. At what age did she become capable of behaving maternally? Did she have to learn how to be a mother or did maternal behaviour come automatically to her when she gave birth? Will she learn from the experience of looking after these kittens and be an even better mother next time?

Q When you have read more about cause, motivation and development, return to these questions and suggest possible answers.

■ Stimuli

If an animal's behaviour appears to be influenced by the presence of objects or other animals, then questions can be asked about the stimuli causing the response. Considering all the possible stimuli (size, shape, colour, sounds, speed of movement, etc.), does the animal respond to them all together, to some, or only one of them?

No animal can respond to all the stimuli impinging on it at the same time. At any one time some stimuli are attended to whilst others are ignored. You have probably experienced *selective attention* yourself when in a crowd of noisy people. In the general hubbub of noise you cannot hear words clearly; but if someone says your name, your ears 'prick up'. You attend to that stimulus (your name) in preference to any other. This suggests that there is a mechanism which distinguishes relevant from irrelevant stimuli and causes you to respond only to relevant ones.

■ Sign stimuli

When an animal responds to just a very small part of the total complex of stimuli, that part is called a *sign stimulus*.

The male Robin (*Erithacus rubecula*), the small bird with a red breast, flies at other males intruding into its territory; pecking and scratching until the intruder is driven away. What stimulates this violent behaviour? It could be the intruder's shape, size, subtle details of its brown feathers, its red breast, its pattern of movement, or a combination of these things. It turns out that the red breast alone is sufficient. It has been shown by experiment that a male robin will attack a simple bunch of red feathers with just as much vigour as a real, complete bird. In fact, since the bunch of feathers cannot escape it gets ripped to pieces! The colour red is a sign stimulus which causes the aggressive response.

AGGRESSION AND COURTSHIP IN A FRESHWATER FISH: THE STICKLEBACK (GASTEROSTEUS ACULEATUS)

Niko Tinbergen performed experiments to discover the stimuli which cause male sticklebacks to attack other males and to court egg-laden females (see p.84). He made a series of stickleback models ranging from the very lifelike to coarse, only vaguely fish-like, blobs. During the breeding season, males were presented with models, one at a time. Even the roughest models elicited the same aggressive responses as the most lifelike ones, provided the underside was coloured red; and rough models were courted as intensely as lifelike ones provided they had a bulging underside. This showed that the red abdomen of a male stickleback and the bulging abdomen of an egg-laden female are sign stimuli which elicit aggressive and sexual behaviour, respectively, from males.

Tinbergen's sticklebacks demonstrated their response to the colour red even when it was not part of a stimulus model. In an aquarium which happened to be close to a window the fish regularly attacked the side of the tank next to the window at the same time every day. Tinbergen was greatly puzzled until it dawned on him that it always happened when the red post office van arrived to deliver the mail!

If sense organs are stimulated by a complex stream of stimuli, but the animal responds to only a portion of the total, then some part of the nervous system must act as a filter, blocking irrelevant information and allowing through only that which is relevant. Where the mechanism is built into the sense organ itself this is known as *peripheral filtering* and where it is a function of the central nervous system this is known as *central filtering*.

■ Peripheral filtering

All sense organs are sensitive to a restricted range of energy. For example, human eyes can detect only between approximately 400 nm and 700 nm wavelength of electromagnetic radiation - we call it visible light. We cannot see ultra-violet, infra-red, radio waves or X-rays. The same type of range restriction happens in relation to sound. The male mosquito (*Aedes aegypti*) is attracted to the female by the sound of her wings. They beat at a different frequency from his. Her frequency acts as a sign stimulus to which he responds by flying in her direction. He detects air vibrations by means of hairs on his antennae which are formed in such a way that they vibrate in sympathy with the female frequency. His nervous system therefore only receives nerve impulses corresponding to 'female in the vicinity' and not to 'presence of male'.

An example which involves neural circuits in the retina of the eye is that of the frog's 'bug detector'. Frogs feed by trapping insects on their long sticky tongues, which they shoot out as the insect flies within range. In experiments, frogs were shown patterns projected on to a screen while nerve impulses were recorded from electrodes placed into single axons in their optic nerves. Some axons were found which made no response either to large patterns or to a screen full of moving dots, but did respond to a single moving dot. It appears that the photoreceptor cells in the retina connect to the neurones in such a way that a small moving stimulus (such as a flying insect) causes an intense signal to reach the brain and trigger the shooting out of the tongue.

■ Central filtering

When an animal's response to stimuli varies with other complex factors (such as male sticklebacks attacking other red bellied males only when sexually active during spring) or when it responds to apparently complex stimuli (such as distinguishing conspecifics from other species, recognising individuals, or selecting particular foods), the analysis is assumed to be done by central filtering mechanisms in the brain.

Faces. Faces have special biological significance for many social mammals, and particularly for dependent young, as a means of individual recognition and of assessing the mood of the subject. Specific nerve cells in the sheep's brain have been shown to be active only when the animal sees another sheep's face and not any other object. They are specialised, centrally located, 'face-detector' cells!

Eyes. Some birds respond to the stimulus of eyes by rapid escape. This is adaptive, as the eyes might be those of a bird of prey fixating them. Some butterflies and moths have eye-spots in the wing patterns. They probably evolved as a defence mechanism against birds. A bird approaches a moth in order to eat it; the butterfly opens its wings, revealing two staring 'eyes'; the bird's central mechanism detects the eyes and triggers the escape response; the bird flies away. (How do cats respond if you stare at them?)

Eyed hawk moth (*Smerinthus ocellata*)

Foraging and search images. Many foraging animals are known not to consume different prey types in simple proportion to their abundance: rare prey appear in the diet even less than expected, and common prey much more than expected. Why? One explanation is that the forager needs to 'get its eye in'. More technically, it takes repeated experience of a (perhaps camouflaged) prey type before a central filter develops that is specific to the colour and shape of that prey. The central mechanism which decides which objects are 'food' becomes increasingly sensitive to the most abundant stimulus and causes the animal to select the abundant rather than the rare food. The animal is said to have developed a *search image* for the abundant food. It is an advantage to the animal because it reduces the time spent deciding whether an object is food or not and increases the time available for eating.

■ Stimulus chains

Apparently complex interactions between two individuals are sometimes the result of a chain of simple responses to stimuli. The response of one animal acts as the stimulus for the other (Fig.9.8).

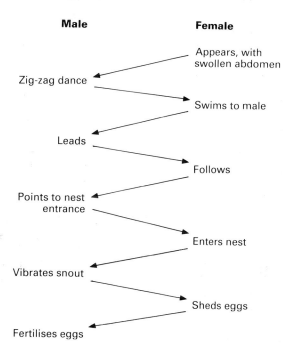

Figure 9.8 Stickleback courtship procedes from start to finish because the behaviour of each partner stimulates the other to perform the next act in the sequence (see the behaviour file on page 84). This is an example of a stimulus chain

■ MOTIVATION

When an animal meets a particular stimulus, it does not always respond to it in the same way (e.g. the cat's response to her kittens, p.123). The response depends on the animal's *motivation*, that is, the way the information is processed in the central nervous system (CNS). Each *motivational state* is presumed to be produced by mechanisms involving neurones and hormones, but scientists are a very long way from understanding the details of how they work.

■ Motivation is not the same as emotional feelings

In our everyday way of thinking and speaking, we frequently explain our behaviour by saying that it is caused by emotional feelings; for example, 'I ate a piece of bread because I felt hungry.' But that is not sufficient to explain the mechanism of motivation; it suggests nothing of what might be happening inside the brain.

It would be more useful to say that, 'Certain internal conditions (a motivational state) caused me to eat the bread.' We can then go on to ask how the motivation works; what parts of the CNS are involved, what information is processed, and how neurones and hormones are involved.

In the study of animal behaviour, motivational states are given commonsense names for convenience: for example feeding is motivated by a state called 'hunger' and fighting is motivated by 'aggression'; but we have to remember that behaviour is caused by mechanisms and not by any feelings which an animal might have.

This idea might become clearer if instead of an animal we examine a word-processor. The motivation to produce a particular image on the screen would be a combination of the electronic circuits and the program which is currently running (the instructions the machine is following). At the moment it is motivated (programmed) to display the letter 'p' when you press a particular key. You can change its motivation by altering the program slightly (perhaps by pressing the ALT key) so that when you press that key it responds with a π. It is obviously unhelpful to say that the machine produces a π because 'it feels like it'. But we could say that it is constructed and programmed to respond in this way, and from there we could ask how the program is designed and what electronic components are involved.

N.B. It would be wrong to say that animals do not have feelings. Although we cannot tell for certain whether they do or not, we should perhaps assume that they do, especially if we are responsible for their well-being, so that we are more likely to treat them with care and respect.

■ Analysing motivation by looking at behaviour

Ethologists attempt to identify the motivational systems which give rise to behaviour. Motivational states are produced as a result of an animal's physiological and social needs. Sometimes we can be

reasonably certain what motivates a behaviour. An animal lapping at water is probably motivated by thirst. But what of a bird pecking at a twig? It might be motivated by hunger, nest building or even aggression. Over a period of time an animal's motivation changes; and during that time it will perform a number of different behaviours. Behaviours which increase or decrease together are more likely to be driven by the same motivation than behaviours which change independently.

Strength of motivation is measured by depriving an animal of something it requires, such as food, water or a sexual partner and then observing its behaviour. It is assumed that motivation to feed, drink, mate, etc., will get stronger the longer the animal is deprived, but it cannot be measured absolutely; there are no SI units for motivation (like joules for energy or metres for distance). All we can do is to measure the intensity of the resulting behaviour and use that as an indirect measure of motivational strength.

Clues to the way that different motivational systems interact can be gained by watching an animal with conflicting motivations. For instance, if it is motivated to both attack and escape at the same time, what does it do? Sometimes birds peck irrelevantly at twigs or grass, or preen feathers. We too perform inappropriate behaviour at times - such as scratching the head or fiddling with a pencil. This irrelevant response when caught between conflicting motivation is known as *displacement behaviour.*

Figure 9.9 Displacement behaviour. Two herring gulls (*Larus argentatus*) are threatening each other at the boundary between their territories. Neither is giving way and one interrupts its aggressive behaviour to pull at some grass as if it were collecting material for a nest.

■ Models of motivation

In science we try to visualise difficult concepts by using metaphors to describe them. For instance we say that light travels in waves, like those on the surface of water when a stone is thrown into a pond. A number of metaphors, or models, have been used to visualise motivation.

Sometimes, if an animal has been prevented from behaving in a certain way (for instance eating or fighting) and then eventually does get an opportunity, the behaviour seems to come out in a rush as if it were water released from a cistern. What is more, the longer the animal is deprived, the less it needs to be stimulated to behave. This aspect of motivation was captured by Konrad Lorenz in his 'psycho-hydraulic' model (see Fig.9.10). He suggested that there is some kind of energy, represented by water, which produces behaviour; and every behaviour has its own 'action specific' energy. The energy builds up while the animal is *not* performing that behaviour and as time goes by it becomes easier to release the behaviour with weaker stimuli. Of course Lorenz knew that the mechanism involved neurones and nerve impulses. He did not suggest that there really were tanks, pipes and valves in the brain; they are only parts of his model.

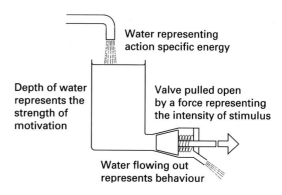

Figure 9.10 Lorenz's psycho-hydraulic model. Water flows from a spout (the animal behaves) when the valve is pulled open (there is a stimulus) or pushed open by the pressure of water (motivation is so strong that the animal behaves spontaneously without being stimulated - vacuum activity). The force required to open the valve (the intensity of stimulus required to release the behaviour) depends on the depth of the water (the strength of motivation).

Another model using action specific energy was that of Niko Tinbergen (see Fig.9.11). This proposed that there are areas or *centres* in the CNS responsible for releasing action patterns which are switched on when energy flows through them. The language is more like that used by neurophysiologists, and Tinbergen hoped that eventually parts of his model would be identified with real parts of the CNS. Unfortunately, his hope has not been realised.

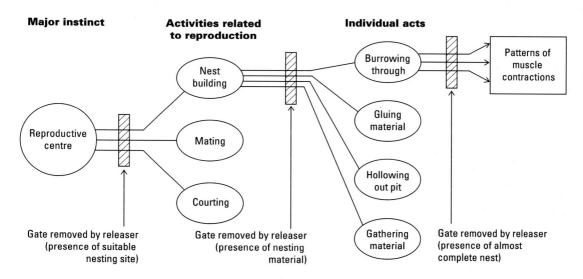

Figure 9.11 Tinbergen's hierarchical model. Animals possess instincts (reproduction, feeding, aggression, etc.), each with a major controlling centre in the brain. Energy flows from a major centre to lower centres controlling related activities when a gate is opened by the presence of a stimulus (a releaser). The centre controlling a particular behaviour related to the instinct is activated when a gate is opened by another releaser.

These 'energy' models assumed that behaviour begins when some internal impulse to behave builds up to a certain level and is released by a stimulus from the environment (or else simply 'overflows') and stops when it 'runs out'. More up-to-date models, known as *systems models*, are based on negative feed-back, a process which keeps conditions constant (maintains homeostasis - see *Biology Advanced Studies - Human Systems*). If an animal's internal environment (e.g. the glucose level of its body fluids) or its external environment (the situation in the world outside) is not ideal, then behaviour is stimulated which brings the state back to the norm or ideal. One advantage of such systems models is that they can be tested on a computer and the 'behaviour' produced by the model compared with the behaviour of the real animal. Figure 9.12 shows some of the elements of a typical systems model of motivation.

■ THE NEURAL BASIS OF BEHAVIOUR

Models of motivation attempt to describe the kinds of process going on inside the central nervous system, not the neural circuits involved. But there is some progress in that direction. Regions of the central nervous system can be studied very directly by recording their electrical activity while an animal is behaving, or by stimulating them with *tiny* electric currents and watching the resulting behaviour. Such studies show which regions, and sometimes even which neurones, are involved in producing behaviour.

Invertebrate nervous systems are composed of far fewer neurones than those of vertebrates, which makes them easier to study. Individual neurones can be identified because they are found in the same position in members of the same species and they are relatively easy to manipulate in a live animal

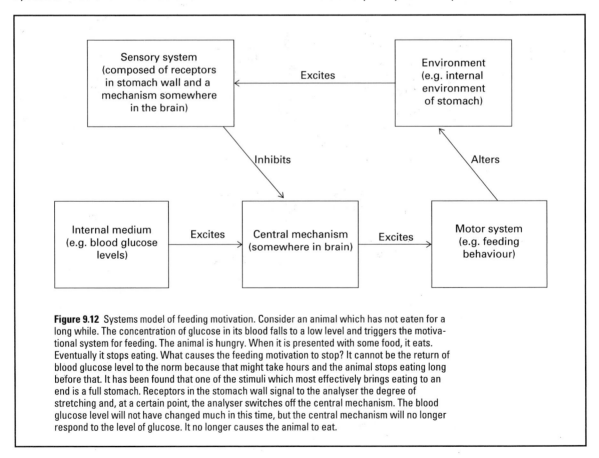

Figure 9.12 Systems model of feeding motivation. Consider an animal which has not eaten for a long while. The concentration of glucose in its blood falls to a low level and triggers the motiva-tional system for feeding. The animal is hungry. When it is presented with some food, it eats. Eventually it stops eating. What causes the feeding motivation to stop? It cannot be the return of blood glucose level to the norm because that might take hours and the animal stops eating long before that. It has been found that one of the stimuli which most effectively brings eating to an end is a full stomach. Receptors in the stomach wall signal to the analyser the degree of stretching and, at a certain point, the analyser switches off the central mechanism. The blood glucose level will not have changed much in this time, but the central mechanism will no longer respond to the level of glucose. It no longer causes the animal to eat.

because of their size. They are large enough for microelectrodes to be placed accurately on them for recording their electrical activity. By studying the simpler systems of invertebrates it is hoped to find out how small neural circuits function and to provide insights into the far more complex vertebrate systems (see accounts of locust wing beat, p.69, and learning in Aplysia, p.80).

■ HORMONES AND BEHAVIOUR

Hormones are chemicals produced by organs called endocrine glands and carried by body fluids throughout the body. Other organs, known as target organs, respond to changes in the concentration of specific hormones by altering their activity in some way (see *Biology Advanced Studies - Human Systems*).

There are several techniques used to investigate the role of hormones in causing behaviour. They involve correlating changes in behaviour with hormonal changes. The hormonal changes can be measured or brought about by:

• monitoring changes in the size of endocrine glands
• taking blood samples and analysing the concentration of hormones
• injecting known amounts of hormone into the blood
• surgically removing endocrine glands
• directly stimulating regions of the brain by implanting pellets containing a hormone.

The influence on sexual behaviour of oestrogen from the ovaries has been demonstrated in domestic cats. Female cats become receptive to males three times a year. They present themselves for copulation by crouching with hips raised, back bowed and tail to one side; a posture common in mammals and called *lordosis*. Cats which have had their ovaries removed, no longer respond to the presence of a male with lordosis; however, if they receive injections of oestrogen, lordosis returns. Experiments with oestrogen implants show that the hormone acts directly on the brain. Implants in the part of the brain known as the hypothalamus cause lordosis in the presence of male cats but elsewhere in the brain they have no effect. It is important to note that oestrogen itself does not trigger the neural activity which produces lordosis, a male cat has to be present as a stimulus. Oestrogen alters the female's response to the male; it changes her motivation.

Some hormones are produced by one animal but act on another and stimulate a direct physiological effect. These are *pheromones*.

■ ORIENTATION AND NAVIGATION

All animals have behaviour which gets them to, and keeps them in, a favourable environment. This orientation behaviour can involve simple reflexes such as in *taxes* and *kineses*, or complex processing of information such as in *navigation*.

■ Taxes
If an animal responds to a stimulus by orientating towards, away from, or at a set angle to the direction from which the stimulus comes, then its behaviour is a *taxis* (plural - *taxes*).

The direction of the stimulus is detected by swinging the head and hence the sense organs from side to side and comparing the intensity on each side, or by using paired sense organs to make the comparison simultaneously. In both cases, the animal orientates in the direction which produces equal stimulation on both sides (except for menotaxis, where a preferred difference in stimulation on the two sides will lead to the preferred angle of orientation).

Orientation towards a stimulus is called a *positive* taxis, orientation away is a *negative* taxis. Taxes are named according to the stimulus: *phototaxis* = light, *chemotaxis* = chemical, *geotaxis* = gravity, *thigmotaxis* = touch, *rheotaxis* = water or air current. For example, locomotion up a chemical concentration gradient (towards the source of the chemical) results from *positive chemotaxis*, locomotion away from a light source results in *negative phototaxis*. In some cases, the response is to orientate the body at a particular angle to the direction of the stimulus. This is *menotaxis*, an example of which is the 'light compass' reaction of some insects.

Orientation by swinging sense organs from side to side is *klinotaxis*. Orientation by simultaneously comparing the stimulus intensity on both sides is *tropotaxis*.

■ Kineses

If an animal responds to the *intensity* of a stimulus by changing its *speed* of *locomotion* or *rate of returning*, then its behaviour is a *kinesis*. Different species vary in detail but in general kineses work as follows.

In a favourable environment the animal moves slowly or is stationary. It is therefore more likely to remain where it is. In an unfavourable environment the animal moves quickly and turns frequently. This increases the chances of it reaching a different place; and anywhere else is likely to be more beneficial than where it is at present.

More subtly, if an animal strays out of a favourable area into an unfavourable area its increased speed of movement and turning rate should bring it back into safety. But if that fails and it remains in a harmful area, the kinesis adapts after a time and the rate of turning diminishes. The animal then moves in a straighter path which takes it further away. If where it is now is very bad, then the chances are that somewhere else will be better.

Q Here are some descriptions of invertebrate orientation behaviour. What types of orientation are they showing?

1. Maggots (larvae of flies such as the bluebottle *Calliphora erythrocephala*), a few days before pupation, swing their heads, bearing photoreceptors, from left to right and move toward the darker side.
2. Flatworms such as *Planaria* and *Dendrocoelum* approach food in a long winding path. When a few centimetres away they move more directly towards the food, swinging the anterior region from side to side.
3. The flatworm *Dendrocoelum* increases its rate of turning with increased light intensity. But after several minutes it turns less frequently and it moves in longer, straighter stretches.
4. The pill bug (woodlouse) *Armadillidium* normally stays in a dark moist environment under stones or bark. If it becomes badly dehydrated or lacking in food it moves fairly directly towards a source of light.

■ Turn alternation

When an invertebrate such as a woodlouse finds itself in an unfavourable environment (for a woodlouse that might be dry and light) it usually escapes by means of its tactic and kinetic responses. But what if its path is blocked by an obstacle such as a twig and it is forced to turn, let us say, left? When it reaches the end of the twig it is most likely to turn right and continue in roughly its original direction. With this tendency to turn in the opposite direction from a previous forced turn the animal has a greater chance of escaping the unfavourable environment. Random turning could keep it trapped there for longer. Experiments show that woodlice detect the direction of a turn by comparing the distance walked by the legs on each side (on a left turn the legs on the right side walk further than those on the left) and respond by speeding up the steps of the, formerly, inside legs.

EXPERIMENTS ON TAXES, KINESES AND TURN ALTERATION

Responses of flatworms to light and food

Place a flatworm, in water, in a petri dish. Observe it in dim light and describe its behaviour in terms of speed of locomotion, rate of turning and movements of its anterior region. Try to quantify your observations; it helps to put a sheet of graph paper under the petri dish.

Illuminate it from above with a bench lamp.

Can you find evidence of photokinesis? Now illuminate it from the side. Is there any evidence of phototaxis?

Put a small piece of fresh liver in the dish with the flatworm. Is there any evidence of chemo-taxis or chemo-kinesis?

It is possible to show the mucus trail left by a flatworm, after it has been removed from the dish, by sprinkling a fine, coloured powder (e.g. borax carmine) over the bottom of the dish. It sticks to the mucus.

Responses of woodlice to humidity and light

Construct a choice chamber as shown in Fig.9.13 (ready-made choice chambers are available commercially).

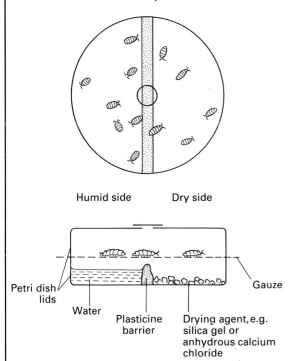

Humid side   **Dry side**

Figure 9.13 A choice chamber

A choice chamber can be used to investigate animals' response to pairs of contrasting conditions. In the diagram, the choice is between humid and dry environments. A choice between light and dark can be set up by illuminating one side and covering the other with a card. It is important to ensure, as far as possible, that the animals' behaviour is not influenced by conditions other than those you are investigating. For instance, if you are interested in the effect of humidity, make sure that light intensity is constant and does not come from a particular direction.

Place a number of woodlice at the centre and cover the hole. At regular intervals record the number of woodlice in one half of the chamber. How can you display your data graphically? Do the woodlice respond adaptively to the conditions in the choice chamber?

Devise ways of recording behaviour or presenting the stimuli such that you can distinguish between kineses and taxes.

Turn alternation in woodlice

Make a T-shaped channel from card and paper as in Fig.9.14.

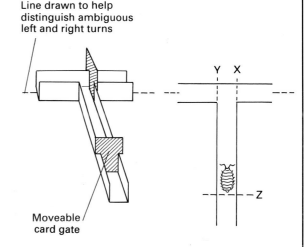

Line drawn to help distinguish ambiguous left and right turns

Moveable card gate

Figure 9.14 Turn alternation in woodlice

Put gates at positions Z and X. Allow a woodlouse to run along the channel. It will be forced to turn left. Record the direction it turns when it emerges, left or right of the centre line. Put gates at Z and Y and force the next woodlouse to turn right. Record the direction it turns when it emerges. It is useful to record the data as 'same direction' or 'opposite direction' to the forced turn. Run as many woodlice as is practicable (equal numbers of 'forced lefts' and 'forced rights'). Ensure as far as possible that the animals' behaviour is not influenced by extraneous stimuli such as the direction of light, noise, draughts, etc. Do your results suggest a tendency to turn in the opposite direction from a previous forced turn?

The phenomenon can be further investigated by modifying the apparatus and procedure.

• Does the memory of the forced turn fade? Vary the length of the channel after the forced turn.

• Does the angle through which woodlice turn when they emerge vary with the angle through which they were forced? Build several channels with different angles of forced turn.

• Is the tendency to alternate related to the state of dehydration? Compare woodlice kept in dry petri dishes for different lengths of time.

■ Navigation

How do you find your way about? With familiar routes, you might use landmarks: conspicuous features of the environment which you have memorised. With repeatedly used routes, such as when you go to the toilet in the middle of the night, you might even be so familiar with the numbers of paces between left and right turns that you can retrace the route 'blind'. For unfamiliar routes you might use a combination of landmarks and distance, perhaps aided by a map. In this instance, you would need to know which way was north, so compass information can also be useful in navigation. But how do animals find their way around? Do they memorise landmarks, and if so, which sort? Do they have inbuilt compasses or maps in their heads? If so, what sort of compass information do they use? The navigation feats of some species are truly remarkable. The Arctic tern breeds in the Arctic and over-winters in the Antarctic, so it migrates halfway round the world, twice a year. When they return to breed each year, pairs often nest in exactly the same spot. Salmon and eels spawn in the rivers in which they were born, yet in between birth and breeding migrate to the ocean to grow and mature. Cuckoos, raised by foster parents, migrate to Africa for the winter and return to breed the following summer, yet they plainly cannot have been taught the route by their own parents. Even some insects migrate long distances: the monarch butterfly breeds in North Amrica, yet over-winters in South and Central America. On a smaller scale, homing pigeons can be transported to unfamiliar release sites over a hundred kilometres from home, yet find their way back to the loft.

It is convenient to break navigation systems into three main types: *pilotage*, where orientation is derived from familiar landmarks without the need of compass (north-south) information; *vector navigation*, where compass and distance information tell the animal in which direction to go and for how long to travel; and *bi-coordinate* (or 'true') *navigation*, where the animal has a sense of absolute latitude and longitude. The latter system, which we humans can derive from careful use of maps or satellite-based tracking systems, is the most powerful, as it allows you to go from anywhere to anywhere, without previous experience of either site. Although proposed several times for homing pigeons, no-one has ever come up with convincing evidence of such a sense in animals, so here we will restrict ourselves to, just as impressive, feats of *pilotage* and *vector navigation*.

■ Pilotage and landmarks

The digger wasp, as its name suggests, digs a hole in the ground into which it lays an egg. It provisions the hole with paralysed insect prey, so that its larva has food upon hatching. Niko Tinbergen noticed this behaviour and wondered how it found its way back to the burrow after each foraging trip. Each time the wasp emerged from its hole, he noticed that it hovered for a few seconds before flying off. Tinbergen devised a simple experiment to see if the wasp was pausing to memorise the landmarks around its nest. Whilst the wasp was in the hole, he placed a ring of stones around the entrance. When the wasp flew off, he then moved the circle a short distance from the real entrance. Lo and behold, the wasp flew to the circle of stones and hovered around searching for the non-existent entrance, before eventually finding its way. This, very simple but very revealing, experiment has been used, in various forms, to show that many species memorise landmarks in relocating familiar sites. For example, jays appear to pay particular attention to tall, nearby, objects as they hide acorns for the winter. This makes ecological sense, as flat objects might become obscured by snow.

■ Vector navigation

The vast majority of work on 'animal compasses' has been with homing pigeons, but it is worth noting what is known about longer-distance migrants which have to travel, perhaps thousands of miles, to their wintering grounds without any prior experience. Intriguing work on warblers (a family of songbird) suggests that the preferred migratory directions are innate and under strict genetic control (see p.110). Homing pigeons have to learn the location of their home loft, but there is good evidence that they can use a variety of natural compass information to return from unfamiliar sites. The most obvious natural compass is the sun. The sun rises in the East, sets in the West and, in the Northern hemisphere, is due south at midday; so, if you know the time of day, the sun can give you compass information. A wide variety of organisms have been shown to have internal clocks that direct daily patterns of behaviour, and pigeons are no exception. If you keep a pigeon on an artificial day-night cycle in an enclosed room, you can reset its internal clock. This happens to us when we travel, say across the Atlantic: at first we are 'jet lagged', as our biological clock makes us active or sleepy at the 'wrong' time of day, but after a few days we adjust to the new day-night cycle. Our internal clock has been shifted. If you release a homing pigeon that has been clock shifted by, say, six hours, it will fly off at 90° to the correct direction. If you released it at midday, according to its *biological clock* it would be 6 a.m., so the sun would be interpreted as being due East, when in fact it is really South! Such experiments show that pigeons use the position of the sun, in combination with their internal clock, to provide compass information. However, pigeons can also navigate under overcast skies, and many long distance migrants fly at night, so they must use clues other than the sun. Clock-shifting experiments with indigo buntings (a songbird which migrates at night), under an artificial planetarium sky, show that they learn and use the position of the pole star. Pigeons, which do not fly at night, seem to be able to use the Earth's magnetic field when the sun is obscured by clouds, as they become disorientated if a small bar magnet has been fastened to them. Experiments with captive warblers, where the aviary is surrounded by an artificial magnetic field, confirm that birds are sensitive to the Earth's magnetic field and can use it to orientate correctly for migration. Perhaps even more surprisingly, there is some evidence to suggest that pigeons learn the smells associated with different prevailing winds and can navigate by smell! What is clear is that birds have a variety of natural compasses available to them and use different mechanisms as appropriate.

■ Development of behaviour

At every stage from newborn to adult some behaviour is performed perfectly and helps the animal to survive whilst other behaviour is changing and improving so that later when it is fully functional it too will contribute to survival (Fig.9.15).

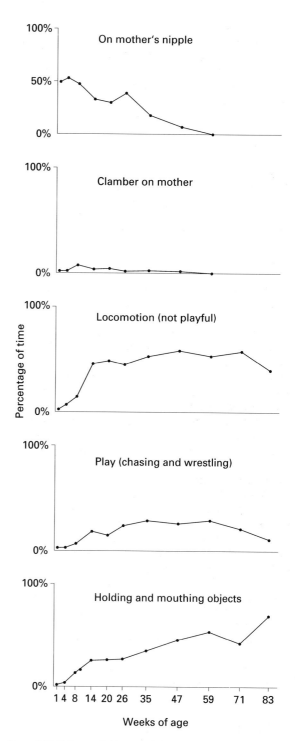

Figure 9.15 Patterns of change in the percentage of time spent by baboons performing five different behaviours. The data are from captive baboons in British safari parks

Behaviour is always the product of both genetic endowment and environmental influence. An animal probably inherits a predisposition to respond to stimuli in an appropriate way and then through learning becomes more efficient. Even after the behaviour is fully functional the animal is likely to continue improving its skill, efficiency and judgement with experience; for example mothers who have already brought up offspring tend to have more of their young survive than first-time mothers.

Strategies for survival change so that at different stages of life different behaviours are appropriate; newborn deer respond to predators by remaining absolutely still but later respond by running away, and most newborn mammals feed first on their mothers' milk, later on food brought to them by the mother and finally forage for themselves. Even whilst an infant mammal is relying on its mother there is a shift in the evolutionary goals (as opposed to motivational goals). Figure 9.16 shows how the relationship between rhesus monkey mothers and their infants change. From birth until approximately 14 weeks the mother actively keeps her infant close to her, then the mother tends to be the one who breaks contact while the infant attempts to stay close to her. We can interpret this change with the help of the selfish gene idea. For several weeks after the birth of her baby the mother's best strategy for ensuring the survival of her genes is to nurture the baby. Thus she is motivated to keep it close to her. After 14 weeks she is fertile again and can maximise the number of copies of her genes represented in the next generation by investing less time and energy in the first infant and more into having another. However, the first infant has selfish genes, too, and its best survival strategy is to get as much help as possible from its mother. So it seeks her attention at the time when she is turning her attention elsewhere. This is a possible *functional* explanation for the high levels of parent-offspring conflict around weaning (in mammals) or independence.

■ **Play**

At certain times of their life, particularly when young, many mammals behave in a conspicuous, energetic, repetitive manner which humans regard as playful. They chase and wrestle with each other, run and jump friskily on their own or manipulate objects. The movements are the same as those used in 'serious' contexts but are generally more relaxed. Actions tend not to have their usual outcomes and sequences are repeated again and again (e.g. bites do not injure, chaser becomes chased and fights have no winners). Playing animals frequently display a characteristic play face. In primates it is like an open-mouthed smile.

Play poses a problem. It can take up a large proportion of a young animal's time (sometimes twenty-five percent of waking time in infant baboons) and any behaviour costing so much in time, energy and risk of injury might be expected to confer benefits for gene survival which outweigh those costs. But what those benefits are is by no means obvious. It might provide an opportunity to keep fit; or practice for behaviour which only becomes functional in adulthood (such as sexual behaviour and fighting). It could be an extended opportunity to learn about the fighting skills of others, to develop allegiences or determine the dominance hierarchy. The somewhat eccentric nature of playful behaviour might sometimes lead to discoveries such as new ways to manipulate food.

■ **LEARNING**

'Human folk are as a matter of fact eager to find intelligence in animals. Dogs get lost hundreds

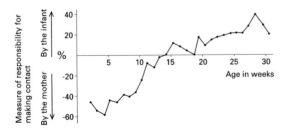

Figure 9.16 Changes in the roles of mother and infant rhesus monkeys in making contact. The measure of an infant's responsibility in making contact with its mother is the difference between the percentage of contacts made by the infant and the percentage of contacts broken by the infant. A negative value means that the infant is tending to break contact while the mother is responsible for making most of the contacts. A positive value means that most contacts are made by the infant.

of times and no one ever notices it or sends an account of it to a scientific magazine. But let one find his way from Brooklyn to Yonkers and the fact immediately becomes a circulating anecdote.' (Thorndike, 1898, in the journal *Psychological Reviews*.)

It was with this statement that Thorndike founded comparative psychology as a science, pouring scorn on the uncritical attribution of human emotions and mental abilities to animals. Take the weaver bird for example. It builds a nest by intricately weaving together grass in a complex pattern that would please a skilled human basket-maker. It would be easy to attribute this clever design to planning and intelligence, yet if you disturb the building process by altering one of the support loops for the structure, the bird will continue with the fault to create a misshapen disaster. Plainly the bird has no concept of what it is 'trying' to make, only a blind rule for what to build upon the previous foundation. The lesson? Apparently intelligent and complex behaviour can arise from very simple rules, strung together appropriately. Whilst the weaver bird's behaviour is instinctive, or innate, learned behaviours can likewise be chained together to produce very complex acts. It is this process which circus trainers rely on to create the illusion of human-like intelligence in their animals. But how do animals, including humans, learn things? Are there differences in how much, or what, different species can learn? Does learning imply conscious awareness? Such are the questions asked by comparative psychologists. They are important not only to students of the mind and behaviour, but central to debates on animal welfare and suffering.

■ What is learning?

When an animal's response to some environmental event changes as a result of experience, we can assume that learning has occurred. We have to remember that learning can take place without the animal's behaviour changing in obvious ways. For example, birds learn the sexual plumage characteristics of their species whilst they are young fledglings, yet do not make use of this information until mating, at least a year later. However, it is usually only changes in behaviour that tell us that learning has occurred. Spontaneous changes as a result of maturation of the nervous system are not usually classed as learning, so most learned

responses are reversible. It is this flexibility of response to stimuli that makes learning adaptive.

■ WHY LEARN?

Because humans are so dependent upon learning, we tend to assume that the ability to learn (and intelligence in general) is necessarily a good thing. However, learning has costs. It takes time, involves making mistakes, and the animal has to maintain a nervous system capable of allowing learning. Under some circumstances it is much better to have 'hard-wired' responses to the environment. For example, many avoidance and escape reactions of animals are hard-wired, or *innate* (see 'Nature Versus Nurture' on p.136), otherwise the animal would die before it had time to learn that predators are dangerous! Likewise, if the environment does not change, or changes in a predictable way, learning may not pay. Many taxes and kineses are innate. Birds do not have to learn which time of year is the best for breeding; their lives are too short, both for acquiring the information and for putting the information to good use. Instead, their gonads mature as a hard-wired response to changes in daylength, mediated by hormonal changes. The conclusion is that the capacity to learn is most advantageous in unpredictable environments, and the animals which depend most on learning are relatively long-lived.

■ TYPES OF LEARNING

When you first buy a new alarm clock, or put on an itchy shirt, you are at first very aware of the new sensory input. However, after a while, you cease to notice the annoying stimuli. This is called *habituation* and is not merely a result of fatigue of the sensory or nervous system, but an adaptive change in the response of the nervous system; in other words, a simple form of learning (Fig.9.17). Habituation describes the situation where the response to the stimulus gets less with repeated experience of the stimulus. It allows the animal to filter out repetitive, uninformative, information from the environment. The opposite, but qualitatively similar, sort of learning process would be an increased responsiveness to a repeated stimulus. We call this *sensitisation* (such as when one becomes increasingly aware of someone's squeaky shoes in a library).

'NATURE VERSUS NURTURE'

Early ethologists, such as Lorenz and Tinbergen, distinguished between *innate* and *learned* behaviour. They noted that some behaviours appear to develop spontaneously without apparent input from the environment or experience. Obvious examples are the call of the cuckoo and the tendency of young chicks to avoid yellow and black striped (wasp-coloured) objects. It is useful to distinguish such innate behaviour from learned behaviour, but much confusion and controversy has arisen from a confusion betwen *innate* and *genetic*. An innate behaviour is simply one that arises as part of the normal developmental process, and is little influenced by the precise conditions experienced during development. To say that such a behaviour is 'genetically determined' is perhaps confusing, as it is obvious that genes only code for proteins, not patterns of behaviour. It also implies that learned behaviours are not influenced by genes, and thus are not open to evolutionary pressures. Neither statement is true. There is nothing any more mysterious about a gene affecting behaviour, via its effects on nervous, sensory and muscular development, than a gene affecting eye colour, via its effects on pigment synthesis. When we say there is a gene *for* a behaviour, we simply mean that possession of the gene makes it more likely that the behaviour will develop. In this sense, even a behaviour that requires learning, such as chaffinch song, can be acted on by natural selection. If a mutation affecting development caused the sensitive period for learning song to begin after the fledglings had separated from parents, then there would be a risk of them learning the wrong species' song. Such a mutant chaffinch would not mate successfully, and in this way natural selection would favour genes that tune learning to the appropriate time period. Evolution, via genes, can thus shape when and what is learned.

Sensitisation allows the animal to become more attentive to potentially important new information from the environment.

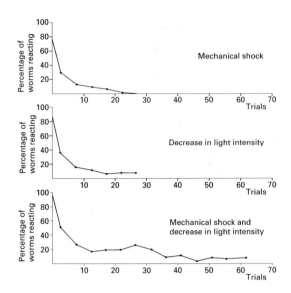

Figure 9.17 Habituation of the polychaete *Nereis* to mechanical shock, to a sudden decrease in light intensity, and to a combination of both stimuli presented simultaneously

The simple forms of learning described above involve a change in response to some environmental event (stimulus), simply as a result of repeated experience of that stimulus. Even the simplest animals are capable of habituation and sensitisation. However, these processes do not allow an animal to learn about its environment, nor to learn how to do new things. To allow this, the animal needs to be able to learn the *association* between two or more events. For this reason, habituation and sensitisation are often referred to as *non-associative learning*.

■ Associative learning

To be truly flexible in its responses to the environment, an animal needs to be able to learn two sorts of things. First, it has to learn which environmental events predict other events of biological importance (e.g. which noises signal the appearance of a predator, or which smells and tastes indicate edible food). That is, it has to learn which stimuli are associated with which other stimuli. Then it has to learn which of its own actions result in particular outcomes (e.g. how best to open a nut or capture an antelope). That is, it has to learn associations between stimuli and responses. If an animal is capable of making these two basic sorts of associations, then by chaining them together it can learn a vast range of new behaviour patterns. These two classes of problem (associating stimuli with stimuli, and associating stimuli with responses) are traditionally explained with reference to the two experimental systems by which they were first investigated (see below). Associations between one stimulus and another are formed via *classical conditioning*; associations between stimuli and responses occur via *instrumental conditioning*. In each case, the animal's experience causes alterations in the number or nature of synaptic connections between neurones (see *Biology Advanced Studies - Human Systems*). It is this change in 'wiring' that underlies any change in behaviour.

■ Pavlov's dogs - *classical conditioning*
Pavlov was a Russian physiologist investigating, amongst other things, the salivation response of dogs to food. This response to the smell and sight of food is innate, requiring no learning. Pavlov discovered that, although dogs certainly do not normally salivate on hearing a bell, by ringing a bell just prior to providing food over several occasions, the dogs would come to salivate as soon as they heard the bell, even without presentation of food. In psychological jargon, by pairing the bell with the *unconditional stimulus* (food), the bell had become a *conditional stimulus*, evoking a *conditional response*, salivation. These terms for the different stimuli are used because salivation in response to food is not conditional on any experience or learning, whereas salivation to a bell is totally conditional on it being associated with food.

In practice, it is clear that even animals with the simplest nervous systems are capable of simple associative learning (see Apylsia, p.80).

■ Thorndike's cat - *instrumental conditioning*
At the turn of the century, the American psychologist Thorndike started to investigate how animals learn new tasks. One experiment involved putting a cat into a 'puzzle box' and seeing how long it took to find the way out. This could involve pulling a string, pressing a lever, dislodging a bolt, or a variety of other means of escape. What he observed was that, on first being placed in the box, the cat's movements were undirected and apparently random. However sometimes, by chance, the cat managed to push or pull the object which caused the door to open. Each time the cat was replaced in the box, it became more and more likely to do the right thing and escape immediately. This is classic trial-and-error learning, with which we are all probably familiar. In Thorndike's theory, reward (here, escape) stamps in, or *reinforces*, the association between a stimulus (the appropriate lever, string, or bolt) and a response (pressing, pulling or pushing). Conversely, punishment (e.g. pain, illness, or any negative experience) reduces the probability of the behaviour that leads to it. Administering reward or punishment to change behaviour is of course how we train many domestic animals (and humans). What we are doing is using these *reinforcers* (positive or negative as appropriate) to change associations between particular stimuli and particular behavioural responses. In the lab, much research has involved how animals learn to operate levers or buttons to obtain food, so this form of learning is known as *operant* or *instrumental*.

■ Complex learning
The vast majority of animal learning can be explained in terms of the above types of associative and non-associative mechanisms (but see p.91 for *imprinting*). But we all have had the experience of wrestling with a problem and suddenly, out of the blue, the answer comes into our heads. We perhaps go through the possibilities in our heads, then suddenly a new connection is made. This is *insight* and lies at the heart of creative intelligence; it would appear to be different from simple trial-and-error learning. But is it uniquely human? Do other animals plan and scheme? (See 'Is human behaviour unique among the primates?' on p.100.) Such questions lie at the heart of understanding human consciousness, a deeply controversial issue that we cannot address adequately here. Since we now know that animals can communicate complex information (p.100), cooperate and act altruistically (p.118), have sophisticated social organisations (p.115), and make tools (p.100), can we remain certain that the human mind is qualitatively different from that of other animals?

 **APPENDIX**

MAKING AND USING KEYS

How does a biologist identify organisms from the vast range of different species? Only by experience of working either with a taxonomic group or in a particular type of habitat. But this is of little help to new workers with unfamiliar species - help is needed, either from other biologists or by checking with museum specimens, pictures or keys. There is an example opposite of a key. If the user follows the rules (and understands a number of technical terms) the correct identification is reached.

The example is a single access key because you must follow the correct sequence. It is also a dichotomous key because each stage divides the possible remaining species into two groups. Multiple access keys do not depend on a particular sequence of questions - the earliest ones used punched cards but now computer-based multiple access keys are being developed and used.

Constructing keys

All students of biology should be able to use keys and this often forms part of their fieldwork. Also, many examination boards expect students to be able to show that they can construct a simple key to separate a number of organisms, or parts of organisms. Insects, flowers, leaves or vertebrae are good subjects for such keys. Students' keys should be based on visible features only.

There are some general rules to follow when constructing a key. Apart from using only external, visible features, it is best to choose large, easily seen ones. The features should be permanent features of the adult organism and not ones which are found only in immature specimens or on one sex. Colour is not usually a good feature as it can vary, especially if specimens have to be kept or are preserved. It is also a good idea, in the early stages of a key, to avoid features which depend on another feature being present, for example the veins on the wings of an insect depend on the presence of wings. In this case, the 'wings present, wings absent' feature should come early in the key if it is going to be used, and then the difference in the veins could separate out two winged insects at a later stage.

KEY TO YELLOW BUTTERCUPS

1 Stem-lvs lanceolate .... Spearworts (p98)
   Stem-lvs lobed or round 2
2 Sepals 3, petals 7-12 -   *Ranunculus*
   lvs cordate .... *ficaria* (p96)
   Sepals 5, petals 5 (sometimes
   less in *R. auricomus*) 3
3 Achenes with spines or hooks 4
   Achenes smooth or warted only 5
4 Plant spreading - achenes
   with hooks on faces .... *R. parviflorus* (p96)
   Plant erect - achenes with
   spines, especially on edges ...... *R. arvensis* (p96)
5 Sepals reflexed 6
   Sepals not reflexed 7
6 Tuber at base of stem -
   achenes without warts .... *R. bulbosus* (p96)
   No tuber - achenes warter .... *R. sardous* (p96)

Size is a feature which needs careful handling in keys. 'Large' and 'small' are too vague to be used, but on the other hand precise measurements should also be avoided as organisms do not stay the same size all their lives. It is permissible to use a range of measurements, as in 'leaves 9-12 mm wide' or 'leaves 15-20 mm wide'. It is quite useful to use the size of one part of an organism compared with another part, as in 'tail more than half body length' or 'tail less than half body length', as proportions usually stay the same throughout life.

If you are constructing a key, a dichotomous single access key is the simplest to construct. The group of organisms to be used should be observed carefully and a list of suitable features drawn up. The best features to use are those which divide the organisms into two groups or sets with roughly equal numbers in each set. If you have eight organisms, you would look for a feature which might divide them into two groups of four, the four to be divided into two groups of two, and so on. This method is preferable to splitting off the individuals one by one, in which case more questions need to be asked, there is more chance of a mistake being made and the key becomes rather clumsy.

INDEX

adaptation 110, 111
Agaricus 29, 30, 35
aggression 124, 126
akaryotic 102
Alexander Fleming 36
algae 2, 4, 12, 19, 24, 26-8, 59, 77, 79
alternation of generations 21, 27, 33, 38, 42, 44, 46
altruistic behaviour 96, 118
Alyssum 53
Amoeba 15, 16, 17
amphibians 3, 87
Anabaena 10, 13, 47
Angiospermophyta 3, 38, 41, 44, 50, 51
animal behaviour 106
antheridia 22, 28, 44, 45, 46, 47
Anthocerotae 42
anti-viral enzymes 103
antibiotics 30, 36
Arachis hypogaea 54
Archaebacteria 10
archegonium 42, 44, 45, 46, 47, 50, 51
Arctic tern 132
Armadillidium 130
artificial selection 110
Ascomycota 29, 30, 32, 36, 37
ascospores 32
asexual reproduction 8, 15, 17, 18, 22, 23, 24, 25, 30, 31, 32, 42, 58, 59, 62
association 136, 137
autotrophic 4, 8, 10, 19
Avena 53
Azolla 46, 47
Azotobacter 10, 12, 13

β-carotene 19
baboons 117, 122
Bacillariophyta 28
bacteriophage 9, 102, 103, 104
bakers' or brewers' yeast 32
Bambusa 53
Basidiomycota 29, 30, 34, 35, 36
bats 2, 95-6
beer brewing 33
bi-coordinate 132
bilaterally symmetrical 57, 77, 80
binary fission 8, 17, 18, 20
biogas 11
biological clock 133
biosphere 10
Blechnum 47
bluebottle 130
Brassica 53
Bryophyta 38, 41, 42

calculating prey energy yield 78
Calliphora erythrocephala 130
Capsella 2, 50
capsid 103-5
capsomeres 103
carpel 51, 54, 55

causation 106
cheating 118
Cheiranthus 53
chemoautotrophic 12, 14
chemosynthetic 10
chemotaxis 129
chitin 8, 29, 32, 63, 67, 70
Chlamydomonas 24
Chlorococcum 24
chlorophyll 4, 12, 19, 24, 26
Chlorophyta 4, 15, 24-6, 40
chloroplasts 8, 12, 19, 24
Chorella 24-6
chromatophores 12
Chthamalus stellatus 78
cilia 8, 17, 18, 60
ciliated oral groove 18
cladistics 5, 6
Cladonia 30, 37
clamp connections 34, 35
classical conditioning 137
Clostridium 10, 14
coelom 60, 81
coenocytic 29
cohesion 121
colony 115
communication 107
comparative psychology 106, 135
competition 113
conceptacles 28
conditional response 137
cones (strobili) 41, 44, 46, 48, 49, 50, 51
conidiospores 30
Coniferophyta 38, 41, 48, 51
conjugation 8, 18, 30
consciousness 137
conspecifics 121
contractile vacuole 16
cooperation 118
cost-benefit 116
courtship behaviour 112
cross-breeding 110
Cruciferae 52, 53
Cyanophyta (Cyanobacteria) 2
Cycadophyta 38, 48
Cytisus scoparius 54

Darwin 2, 67, 106
defence 92
Dendrocoelum 130
dendrogram 6
Deuteromycota 30, 36
diatoms 27-8
Dicotyledones 50-3
digger wasp 132
dikaryotic mycelium 30
Diplococcus 10
diploid 17, 21, 27, 32, 33, 35, 38, 119
displacement behaviour 126
display 113
division of labour 117
DNA 5, 8, 9, 12, 17, 103, 104, 109
domestic breeds 107, 110
dominance hierarchies 120

dominant 120
double fertilisation 51
downy mildews 22
Driver Ant 118
Drosophila 110
dry rot fungus (*Serpula*) 35
Dryopteris 47, 48

Earth's magnetic field 133
ectoderm 57, 59
eels 132
elaters 43, 46
Elminius modestus 78
embryo 38, 50, 52
embryo sac 51
endocrine glands 129
endoderm 57, 59
endonucleases 103
Entamoeba hystolitica 17
Enteromorpha 24
Ephedra 49
ephemeral 52
epiphytes 28, 42
Equisetum 44, 46
Escherichia coli 10, 13, 102, 103, 104
ethologists 106
Eubacteria 10
Eucarya 4
Euglena 4, 19, 20
eukaryotic 8, 10, 12, 15, 29, 38
eusocial 119
evolution 106
exoskeleton 63, 67

Fagus 50
family 2
fertilisation 112
Filicinophyta 38, 41, 46
filter feeding 57, 73, 80
Firmicutes 10, 14
fitness 106, 111
flagella 8, 15, 57
flatworms 130
flower 41, 50-5
foliose 37
food chains 41
food vacuole 16, 18, 59
foraging 96, 111
fucoxanthin 26
Fucus 3, 26, 27, 28

gametophyte 27, 38, 41, 42, 43, 44, 45, 46, 47, 50, 51
gemmae 42
geotaxis 110, 129
Geum 55
giant kelps 26
Ginkgo biloba 48
Ginkgophyta 38, 48
glumes 51
Glycine max 54
glycogen 8
Gnetophyta 38, 48, 49
Gracilicutes 10, 12
Gram negative bacteria 9, 10, 13

Gram positive bacteria 9, 10, 14
Gramineae 51
grebe 113
green sulphur bacteria 12
grooming 122
gymnosperms 44

habituation 136
handicaps 113
haplodiploidy 119
haploid 18, 21, 27, 30-3, 35, 38, 49, 119
haustoria 23, 29
Hepaticae 42
herbaceous plants 47, 51, 52, 55
hermaphrodite 51, 55, 58, 61, 64, 66
herpes virus 103
heterocysts 13
heterosporous 44
heterotrophic 4, 8, 10, 15, 19, 22, 57
homing pigeons 132
homologous 3, 6
Homo sapiens 1, 3
homosporous 44, 47
Hordeum 53
hormones 129
hornworts 42
horsetails 44
human immuno-deficiency virus (HIV) 105
hunger 126
hyphae 22, 29-37
hypothalamus 129

imprinting 91
inclusive fitness 111
Indigo buntings 133
indusium 47
infection cycle 103
influenza virus 103-5
innate 110, 136
insight 137
internal clocks 133
isogamy 24
Iwanowski 102

jays 132
jet lag 133

keratin 89
keys 138
kin selection 118
kineses 117, 129
klinotaxis 129

l-integrase 104
laminarin 26
landmarks 132
Larix 49
larva 57, 64, 65, 70, 72, 73
Lathyrus odoratus 54
latitude 132
learning 80, 91, 135
Legionnaires' disease 17
legume 54

Leguminoseae   53
Lens esculenta   54
lichen   30, 37
Linnaeus   1, 2, 88
liverworts   42, 43
livestock   107
locust   69
longitude   132
lordosis   129
Lorenz   106
Lumbricus   2
Lunaria   53
Lupinus   39
Lycopodium   44
Lycopodophyta   38, 41, 44
lysis   103
lysogenic phase   104
lysozyme   12
lytic cycle   103, 104

macronuclei   17
malaria   21, 22
mammals   3
Margulis and Schwartz   5, 15, 29
mating preferences   91
maze   110
mechanism   106
Medicago sativa   54
megaphylls   46
megaspores   41
meiosis   18, 27, 31-5, 38, 49, 119
Mendosicutes   10, 12
menotaxis   129
mesoderm   59, 60
mesosomes   8, 12
metachronal rhythm   18
microphylls   44
microsporangia   49
microspores   41, 45, 50
microsporophylls   49
migration   107
mitosis   18, 32, 35
monarch butterfly   132
Monocotyledones   50, 51, 52
mosses   42, 43
motivation   111, 123, 126
Mucor   30, 31
multiple fission   22
murein   10
Musci   42
mycelium   23, 29-37
mycobiont   37
Mycophycophyta   30, 37
mycoplasmas   10
mycorrhizae   29, 30, 35, 49

Nasturtium   53
navigation   123, 129, 132
nematocysts   58, 77
neural basis of behaviour   128
neurones   69, 128
Neurospora   30, 34
Nitrobacter   14
Nitrococcus   14
nitrogen fixation   13, 53
Nitrosomonas   14
non-associative learning   136
Nostoc   37

oestrogen   129

Omnibacteria   13
oogonia   22, 28
ookinete   22
Oomycota   15, 22
oospheres   28, 42, 51
oospores   22
optimal foraging   78
orientation   123, 129
Oryza   53
osmoregulation   16, 18, 24
ovary   53, 54, 55, 129
ovules   49, 53
ovuliferous scales   49

Papilionaceae   52, 53
Paramecium   15, 18, 19
parasite   20, 22, 29, 60, 61, 62, 63,
     65, 71, 73, 74, 75
parent-offspring conflict   134
Parmelia   37
Pavlov   80, 137
pecking order   120
Penicillium   30, 36, 37
pentadactyl limb   3
peptidoglycan   8, 9, 10
peristome teeth   43
Phaeophyta   4, 15, 26
phagocytosis   14, 16
Phaseolus sp.   54
phenetics   5, 6
pheromones   112, 129
photoautotrophs   15
photosynthesis   4, 10, 12, 19, 25,
     26, 28, 38, 59
phototaxis   20, 129
phycobiont   37
phycoerythrin   28
Phytophthora infestans   22-3
phytoplankton   24
Picea   49
pigeon   110, 132
Pilobolus kleinii   32
pilotage   132
Pinus   49
Pisum sativum   54
Planaria   130
plasmids   12
Plasmodium   21
play   122, 134
Pleurococcus   24
pole star   133
polio virus   103
pollen   41, 49, 54
Porcellio scaber   130
Primula   2
prokaryotic   4, 8, 12
prophage (provirus)   104
prothallus   41, 47
Protista (Protoctista)   4, 15
protonema   43
provirus   104
pseudopodia   16
Psilophyta   38
PSTV (potato spindle tuber
     viroid)   105
Pteridium   47
Puccinia graminis   30, 36
purple sulphur bacteria   12
Pythium sp.   24

Quercus   50

radial symmetry   57
Ranunculus   1
Raphanus   53
receptors   128
red algae   28
reinforcers   137
relatedness   119
reproductive behaviour   84
reproductive success   111, 112
reptiles   3, 88-90
retroviruses   105
reverse transcriptase   105
rheotaxis   129
Rhizobium   13, 53
rhizoids   41, 42, 43, 47
rhizome   46
Rhizopoda   15, 16
Rhizopus   30, 31
Rhodophyta   4, 28
ribosomes   10, 29
ritualisation   113
RNA   4, 5, 10, 103, 104, 105
Rosaceae   52, 55
rusts   35, 36

Saccharomyces   30, 32, 33, 34
Saccharum   53
salmon   132
Salmonella   14
Salvinia   46
saprotrophic   22, 29, 30
Sargassum   26
sclerotin   67, 73
search image   125
Secale   53
secondary host   20, 36
secondary sexual characters   113
seed   41, 44, 49, 50, 51, 54, 56
Selaginella   44, 45
selective attention   123
selfish gene   109
selfish herd   117
Semibalanus balanoides   78
Senecio   50
sensitisation   136
sensory neurone   80
septum   8, 22, 29, 31, 34, 36
Sequoiadendron   49
sessile   57, 73
sex determination   119
sexual displays   107
sexual reproduction   8, 15, 17, 18,
     19, 21, 22, 23, 24, 27, 30, 31, 32,
     36, 38
sexual selection   113
shrubs   41
sign stimuli   123
slime moulds   4, 15
smuts   35
social behaviour   114, 116
social insects   118
solitary   114
Sordaria   30
sori   41, 47
Spartina   53
species   1, 2
Sphagnum   42

Sphenophyta   38, 41, 44
sporangia   23, 27, 30, 31, 41, 44, 47
sporangiophores   22, 23, 30
sporophylls   44
sporophyte   27, 38, 41-7, 50
Stanley   102
sterigmata   35
stimulus chains   125
Streptococcus   14, 36
stress   121
subordinate   120
symbionts   29, 59

target organs   129
taxes   117, 129
Taxus   49
Tenericutes   10
territory   84
thallus   28, 42, 43
thigmotaxis   129
Thiobacillus   14
thylakoids   12
Tinbergen   106
tobacco mosaic virus (TMV)   102
tracheophytes   38, 40
transduction   9
transformation   8, 9
Trebouxia   37
tree ferns   46
trial-and-error learning   137
Trifolium spp.   54
Triticum   53
tropotaxis   129
Trypanosoma   20, 21
tsetse fly, *Glossina* sp.   20
turn alternation   130

Ulva   24
unconditional stimulus   137
undulipodia   15, 17, 24, 29, 41, 42,
     49

vector navigation   132
vigilance   117
viroids   105
viruses   5, 102-5
Volvox   24
von Frisch   106
Vorticella   15

warblers   132
water moulds   15, 22
weaning   134
welfare   107
white rusts   22
Whittaker, R.H.   4
wine-making   34
Wistaria spp.   54
withdrawal response   80
woodlouse   73, 117, 130, 131

Xanthoria   30, 37

yeasts   29, 32, 33, 34

Zea mais   53
zig-zag dance   84
zoospores   22, 23, 24, 27
zygomorphic   54
Zygomycota   29, 30, 31